INCOHERENT EMPIRE

INCOHERENT EMPIRE

MICHAEL MANN

VERSO

London · New York

First published by Verso 2003
© Michael Mann 2003
All rights reserved

The moral rights of the author have been asserted

1 3 5 7 9 10 8 6 4 2

Verso
UK: 6 Meard Street, London W1F 0EG
USA: 180 Varick Street, New York, NY 10014–4606
www.versobooks.com

Verso is the imprint of New Left Books

ISBN 1–85984–582–7

British Library Cataloguing in Publication Data
A catalogue record for this book is available from the British Library

Library of Congress Cataloging-in-Publication Data
A catalog record for this book is available from the Library of Congress

Typeset in Bembo by YHT Ltd, London
Printed in the USA by R.R. Donnelley & Sons

CONTENTS

PREFACE

For 20 years I have worked as a historical sociologist on the nature of power in human societies. I have written mostly on very "macro" subjects—on religions, economies, wars and states, throughout history and across the world. I have recently focused on the twin horrors of fascism and ethnic cleansing in the twentieth century. Though I have in the past written short pieces of contemporary political relevance, I have been mainly a scholar embedded inside the groves of academe.

But I have been stirred by current events and my own dual British/American citizenship into writing this book about world politics today, at breakneck speed. My two governments are currently threatening the peace and order of the world by pursuing extraordinarily foolhardy militaristic policies. Since I am a scholar and not an activist, this book does not denounce them with high moral rhetoric. Instead, I analyze and pick apart their "new imperialism," armed with my general comparative knowledge of power and empires, militaries and clerics, and fanatics of all stripes. I hope to convince them—or at least you, the citizens and voters of various countries—that the United States has greatly exaggerated its powers, that it could found only a militaristic Empire, not a benevolent one, and that it will destroy very many lives, including American and British ones, before finally undermining the basis of its own power. Of course, the two countries are on a very different scale. Since Bush is the imperial leader, Blair only the camp follower, I discuss here the American bid for Empire, with Britain only playing its walk-on part. For the sake of the world, it must be stopped.

I should like to thank the research assistance of Nicole Busse, Maria Dziembowski and Jamal Ali, who also provided invaluable translations from the Arabic, and I thank John Hall, Nicky Hart and Ralph Schroeder for their support, advice and criticism. However, my greatest thanks must go to all those whistle-blowers, "leakers," and independent-minded experts and journalists whose testimony I have been able to use to challenge the new imperialists.

INTRODUCTION:
THE NEW IMPERIALISM

Two presidential declarations, a decade apart:

> We can see a new world coming into view. A world in which there is the real prospect of a new world order ... in which the principles of justice and fair play ... protect the weak against the strong. A world where the United Nations, freed from cold war stalemate, is poised to fulfill the historic vision of its founders. A world in which freedom and respect for humanity will find a home among nations. ... Even the new world order cannot guarantee an era of perpetual peace. But enduring peace must be our mission.

> We will not hesitate to act alone, if necessary, to exercise our right of self-defense by acting preemptively ... our best defense is a good offense. ...We must adapt the concept of imminent threat to the capabilities and objectives of today's adversaries. ... To forestall or prevent hostile acts by our adversaries, the United States will, if necessary, act preemptively.

Father and son spoke, in March 1991 and September 2002. The father, President George Herbert Bush, spoke as the Soviet Union collapsed and immediately after his victory in the First Gulf War. The son, President George Walker Bush, spoke through his "National Security Strategy of the United States of America," issued as the US was embroiled in two wars (in Afghanistan and against terrorism) while covertly preparing a third (against Iraq).

Bush the Elder offered a vision of "enduring peace," to be achieved by US leadership, but together with allies and through the United Nations. The speech did not mention any future military action by the US. This was an optimistic and apparently multilateral vision of world order. Bush the Younger was much more pessimistic. He called for "perpetual vigilance" against terrorists and wielders of weapons of mass destruction. Faced with "hostile acts," he said the US would act militarily, preemptively and on its own. Allies, he suggested, are only ad hoc and temporary. The United Nations is mentioned only in the same breath as the WTO and NATO. This is a unilateralist and militarist vision of how to overcome world disorder. It is the new imperialism. The world should know that the present United States government embraces the new imperialism. Do not think that US policy toward Kyoto, land-mines, Star Wars, Iraq, Iran or the Southern Philippines are ad hoc or unconnected. They are all part of the grand strategy for a global American Empire, first envisioned as theory, then after 9-11 becoming reality.

The vision is embraced by the majority of the top officials running US foreign policy. Most of them have a long track record as hawkish neo-conservatives. While Defense Secretary in 1989, Vice-President Dick Cheney had argued that since Gorbachev's Soviet reforms were only cosmetic, the US should not deal with the Soviets but keep up the cold-war and arms-race pressure. Through the 1990s he opposed withdrawing any nuclear weapons from Europe and South Korea, and asked for studies of new theater nuclear weapons to be used against Iraq and North Korea. Throughout the 1990s Cheney and Donald Rumsfeld, now the Defense Secretary, urged overthrowing Saddam Hussein by force. In 1998, together with about 20 others, all now holding senior posts under Bush the Younger, they called for "a determined program to change the regime in Baghdad." The same year Rumsfeld said that since "rogue states" would be able to deploy nuclear weapons "with little or no warning" in "about five years' time," "preemptive strikes" should be made against them. In 2000 he said the US should also weaponize space in order to prevent a "space Pearl Harbor."

In 1992 Rumsfeld's deputy at Defense, Paul Wolfowitz, together with other members of the present administration, authored a "Defense Planning Guidance" draft which was leaked to the *New York Times*. It advised "deterring potential competitors from even aspiring to a larger regional or global role." Remarkably, these included not only Russia and China but also "the advanced industrial nations," that is allies. As a Lebanese journalist was later to notice, Rumsfeld's attempts to split Europe, with his talk of "old" and "new" Europe, was not a passing phrase or slip of the tongue. It derived straight from this document.[1] The document also advocated "military steps" for preventing others developing weapons of mass destruction or blocking access to vital raw materials. It was completely silent on action through the UN and suggested all alliances were only temporary and military. Such an inflammatory document was hastily repudiated by President Bush the Elder, who released a far blander one. Yet it was clearly influencing American strategic planning.

The top officials were extreme on other issues too. Douglas Feith, now Undersecretary of Defense for Policy, worked to stop the ratification of the Chemical Weapons Convention, negotiated by Bush the Elder. Together with Richard Perle, now Chairman of the Defense Policy Board, he urged Israeli Prime Minister Netanyahu to "make a clean break" with the Oslo Peace Accords and reassert Israel's claim to the West Bank and Gaza by force. Feith wrote "the price in blood would be high, but it would be a necessary form of detoxification—the only way out of Oslo's web."

J.D. Crouch, now Assistant Secretary of Defense for International Security, advocated a first strike on North Korea's nuclear plants and missiles. John Bolton is the current Undersecretary for Arms Control and International Affairs, and so an important mole hawk, in the State Department. Hostile to the UN, in 1999 he attacked what he called "Kofi Annan's power grab," by which he meant Annan's request that UN forces should take the primary role in peacekeeping operations. Bolton declared, "If the United States allows that claim to go unchallenged, its discretion in using force to advance its national interests is likely to be inhibited in the future." He pronounced, "There is no such thing as the United Nations" and declared that if the top 16 stories fell off the UN building in New York, the world would be no worse off. At least he had a sense of humor.

In September 2000 Wolfowitz, Bolton and at least five others now holding senior positions in the White House or Department of Defense co-authored "Rebuilding America's Defenses," a report for the conservative think-tank, the Project for the New American Century. They urged reneging on the anti-ballistic missile treaty, developing theater nuclear warheads to attack underground bunkers, targeting weapons against Iran, Iraq and North Korea, and a 24 percent increase in military spending. They added that the world required American not UN leadership. All this has now come to pass.

We see the long-maturing militarist and unilateralist bent of these hawks. Only the more cautious Secretary of State, Colin Powell, and his deputy Richard Armitage seem to deviate much. "It's nice to say we can do it unilaterally," Powell told President Bush the Younger, "except you can't." Unfortunately for Powell, though his boss had shown no prior knowledge of foreign policy, he proved an instinctive imperialist. In his first two years in office, Powell was brought to heel. Complaining that European leaders wanted lots of consultations, Bush said, "You hold a coalition together by strong leadership and that's what we intend to provide." He revels in his reputation abroad as "the toxic Texan" and declared, "I will seize the opportunity to achieve big goals," adding, "we're never going to get people all in agreement about the use of force. ... But action—confident action that will yield positive results—provides kind of a slipstream into which reluctant nations and leaders can get behind." This was a man who wanted to act first, and consult with foreigners not at all.[2] He was raring for action. Like the others, he was actually a "chicken-hawk," a hawk who had never actually seen military action or its terrible consequences. Like the others, he would become a desk-killer, giving orders resulting in the deaths of thousands from the security of his office.

The actions of his administration were immediately clear. The post of US Ambassador to the UN was downgraded from Cabinet rank and filled with John Negroponte, a man whose diplomatic record as ambassador in Honduras had included repeated condoning of human rights violations by US client regimes in Central America. The US withdrew from a series of international treaties, refusing to renew or sign up to the Kyoto Protocol on global warming, the Anti-Ballistic Missile Treaty, the Biological Weapons Convention and the International Criminal Court; and it diluted a UN agreement to limit the small-arms trade. It will not sign the treaty banning land-mines (US forces took mines to Iraq). It denounced some of these agreements on the grounds that they lacked real teeth, but it opposed strengthening them since this would involve inspection of its own weapons systems, which was unacceptable "for reasons of national security." Almost all of this was developing well before 9-11, with almost no mention of terrorism.

They already possessed the will, and action had begun. But the new imperialism was very removed from the lives of ordinary Americans, who had shown almost zero interest in foreign policy. Before 2001 the half-hour "world news" programs of the main American television networks typically contained only one foreign news item, compared to ten domestic ones. Few Americans would be interested in Empire. Insofar as the withdrawals from the Kyoto or biological weapons treaties attracted attention, most comments were critical. This was not how the most informed Americans wanted their country to be represented in the world outside.

The events of 9-11 changed all that. Quite understandably, the terrible events of that day produced shock, anger and a cry for vengeance, emotions with which much of the world sympathized. The new imperialists were able to seize on this to induce Americans into global adventures for which they would have otherwise lacked interest. According to Wolfowitz, a meeting immediately after 9-11 discussed at length whether to attack Afghanistan or Iraq first. The Afghan chicken-hawks narrowly won. But in his State of the Union address in January 2002 President Bush widened the combat zone. Already engaged in a war on Afghanistan, he made two further declarations of war. One was "the war against terrorism."[3] He said evidence from Afghanistan revealed that

> thousands of dangerous killers, schooled in the methods of murder, often supported by outlaw regimes, are now spread throughout the world like ticking time bombs, set to go off without warning ... tens of thousands of trained terrorists are still at large. These enemies view the entire world as the battlefield, and we must pursue them wherever they are.

Who were these enemies? He did not mention Osama bin Laden or al-Qaeda. Instead, he declared, "a terrorist underworld, including groups like Hamas, Hezbollah, Islamic Jihad and Jaish-e-Muhammad, operates in remote jungles and deserts, and hides in the centers of large cities." To counter such a threat, he continued, American troops were being deployed in the Philippines, Somalia and Bosnia.

This reveals a very disparate collection of enemies—and an uncertain grasp of geography. First came three Palestinian and Lebanese militias fighting against Israel, not the US, and not involved in Afghanistan—plus a Kashmiri militia fighting against India, not the US. None of these fight in "deserts or jungles." The US troops he mentioned were despatched to quite different destinations, in Europe, Africa and South-East Asia. These terrorists were globally distributed, but their connection to the US remained utterly unclear.

As if one global struggle were not enough, Bush the Younger added another. "Our second goal is to prevent regimes that sponsor terror from threatening America or our friends and allies with weapons of mass destruction." National Security Advisor Condoleezza Rice explained that this meant "rogue states ... seeking chemical and biological weapons, improving long-range missiles and pursuing nuclear weapons capability." Bush mentioned by name North Korea, Iran and Iraq, adding, "States like these and their terrorist allies constitute an axis of evil, arming to threaten the peace of the world." He was declaring two new world wars at once, while still embroiled in Afghanistan.[4] Such is the ambition of the new imperialism in action, mobilizing Americans under the claim that imminent danger threatens the homeland.

The Quadrennial Defense Review, issued two weeks after 9-11, made no mention of US peacekeeping, humanitarian or sanctions-enforcing missions. Bush said the military budget must grow 15 percent between 2002 and 2003, with a further 8 percent increase projected by 2007. Spending would be increased on almost all programs, from Star Wars to counter-terrorism through a raft of traditional big-muscle programs. The Review declared that all wars would be prosecuted by "decisive defeat of adversaries," "regime change" and "occupying foreign territory until US strategic objectives are met." There was no ambition for permanent rule abroad. But it seemed that a "temporary territorial Empire" was being contemplated, a radical departure from the "informal Empire" which the US had run since 1945. The ambition of the new imperialists was astonishing in a country and a world which had seemed to reject territorial imperialism some while back.

The Nuclear Posture Review leaked in March 2002 escalated these military aspirations even further. It targeted Russia for first-strike (i.e. preemptive) rather than second-strike nuclear weapons, despite the fact that the US was now much stronger than Russia in conventional weapons. It increased to five the number of "rogue states," Iran, Iraq, North Korea, Libya and Syria, and said for the first time that they were potential targets for a nuclear strike. It called for the development of new low-yield and variable-yield theater nuclear warheads. Since these would require testing, more international treaties would have to be abandoned. In 2002 Bush the Younger repeatedly endorsed "pre-emptive strikes" and "regime change" even if the US "might have to do it alone." This was serious gearing-up for wars and occupations of territory around the world, to be fought by the US alone if necessary.

We cannot attribute all this escalation only to Bush the Younger and his chicken-hawks. For decades the US had used its enormous military machine quite freely across the world. Then, as the USSR collapsed, its newfound military preponderance led to interventions in Panama, the Gulf War, Somalia, Haiti, Bosnia and Kosovo. In contrast Europe turned inward to its own unification, reducing its defense budgets. UN interventions also declined. By 2002 only 24,000 UN troops were deployed around the world, far less than NATO forces in Yugoslavia alone. UN peacekeeping forces now came from the armies of developing countries, while NATO peacekeeping detachments were dominated by the US.[5]

The year 1993 had been a watershed. It was a Democratic administration that was then edging forward. President Clinton, in a speech at the Citadel military academy, avoided the customary "last resort" reference to the use of force, saying instead that force might be preferred if other options seemed "less practicable." His Defense Secretary Les Aspin talked of possible preemptive military action. The Pentagon's "revolution in military affairs," leading into the development of "smart" weapons, began with a famous memo to William Perry, Aspin's successor, that year. Samuel Huntington wrote at the time that "a world without US primacy will be a world with more violence and disorder and less democracy and economic growth."[6] Near the end of his administration, Clinton signaled unhappiness over Kyoto and the International Criminal Court, did not sign the Land-Mines Treaty, and bombed Iraq, Afghanistan and the Sudan. It was in 1998, under Clinton, that French Foreign Minister Hubert Vedrine coined the term *hyperpuissance*, "hyper-power," to vividly capture the sense of a hyperactive and anti-social superpower. The drift which culminated in the new imperialism was underway. It might be seen as the logical consequence of the untrammeled power which the American foreign policy establishment felt it enjoyed after the collapse of the Soviet Union.

But the Democrats would not have reached it unaided, and nor would Republican Party elders brought up on more pragmatic policies. Neither envisaged unilateral, uninvited and essentially unprovoked invasions of foreign countries—except of tiny countries viewed as being in the American "backyard," like Grenada and Panama. Major interventions during the 1990s had differed. In the 1991 Gulf War Saddam had violated international law by invading Kuwait and the US had assembled a UN-backed coalition which included his Arab neighbors. In Bosnia and Kosovo ethnic civil wars were raging and intervention was begged for by the groups suffering most and aided by the UN and NATO. True, the interventions were not even-handed, and bombing unaccompanied by troops who could control events on the ground worsened this (that was my view at the time). But in these cases American militarism was more or less normal for the post-1945 period. Behind them lay a mainly pragmatic and defensive notion of military power. If we were threatened, we could respond, with overwhelming force if necessary. But there was no sense of using militarism offensively to remake the world into a better place. An embryo version of this did emerge under Clinton—the notion of using US military power for "purely humanitarian reasons," to save the people of backward countries from their own rulers or each other. These might be seen as "civilizing missions," characteristic of the mindset of some past imperial powers.

But to get to the new imperialism, three further triggers were required. The first was pure accident. Thanks to the "hanging chads" of Florida and the bias of the American electoral system toward rural, smaller conservative states, Bush was elected despite winning slightly fewer votes than his Democratic opponent, Al Gore. Such was the low turnout, Bush the Younger received support from under a quarter of those Americans eligible to vote. Since very few Americans decide how to vote on foreign policy issues, the advent of the new imperialism was not due to any upsurge in aggression among the American people. Instead, it was due to world-historical bad luck.

The second trigger was the staffing of a US administration by neo-conservative Christian chicken-hawks with a mysterious affinity to the Israeli political right. They were raring for military action in support of "good" against "evil," not just in the name of humanitarianism but influenced by a Judeo-Christian fundamentalism and by visceral hatred of Clinton, whom they accused of cowardice in the face of the enemy. I do not pretend to fully fathom this coup within the Republican Party, and over their presidential candidate who had shown little knowledge or interest in foreign policy. It had complex domestic as well as foreign-policy origins. Domestic as well as foreign issues became more orientated to moral goals, and so less amenable to pragmatic compromise. The problem in foreign policy was compounded by the formidable power of the American military. Here, unlike domestic policy, the neo-conservatives sensed that they did not *need* to compromise. They could ignore the views of the rest of the world and achieve good through conquest. When I began to read their writings and speeches I recognized immediately the mindset, for the notion of achieving morally desirable goals through violence—if necessary, over piles of dead bodies—was familiar to me from all the imperialists, fascists and ethnic cleansers it has been my misfortune to study in recent years. I fear politicians when they come bearing morality!

Their dominance inside the new administration may also have had a near-accidental trigger. The inexperienced Bush invited Dick Cheney, the highly experienced but neo-conservative hawk, to supervise the "transition team" which initially staffed his administration. Cheney put his chicken-hawk cronies into most of the key positions in Defense, and a few in State. But their project remained incomplete, since neither the armed forces nor most of the top men in the State Department shared their ethos.

The third trigger changed that. It came suddenly, on 9-11-2001. Osama bin Laden gave them that day the popular mobilizing power and the targets. "Terrorists" everywhere were suddenly the main enemy, and poor countries (and rich Israel) had to be saved from the menace of "fundamentalist" Muslims and "rogue" states. The extension of these two adjectives, "fundamentalist" and "rogue," brought strange bed-fellows into their line of fire. Bin Laden, Saddam and Kim Jong Il really had almost nothing in common. For the next two years bin Laden and Bush were to dance their provocative *pas de deux* together, each radicalizing and mobilizing the forces of the other.

Inside the American military/strategic community—though not yet in the High Command—it also seemed that the US now had the military wizardry to achieve victory followed by moral good without risking the lives of American soldiers or civilians. Since we now could do these things, they reasoned, why not give it a try? That was the military temptation underlying the shift toward the new imperialism. The new imperialists in charge of the Department of Defense now had the mobilizing power and the budgetary resources to lure the more cautious armed forces into their plans. The notion of civilian control of the military became meaningless, since civilians were the leading militarists. We will see that the so-called new imperialism actually became something much simpler and much nastier—the new militarism.

But the new imperialists see their goals as entirely benign. These have been spelled out most fully by neo-conservative journalists and scholars close to the White House. They tend to avoid terms like "militarism" and "imperialism," but they do like the resonance of the noun "Empire" and its adjective "imperial." These terms suddenly seem full of noble, civilizing, even humanitarian sentiments. The Empire will bring peace, freedom and democracy to the world! They will save oppressed peoples from their own "rogue" leaders! Some hark back to the days of the British Empire. This is why I have styled the two Presidents Bush the Elder and Bush the Younger, recalling the titles of the two Pitts, father and son, the British Prime Ministers who led their country at the height of its imperial greatness. But for most Americans the British analogy raises uncomfortable images of redcoats and taxes.

Anyway, they say, the US today has a lot more power than the Brits ever did, and their power didn't last long (a potentially disquieting thought). Better skip the centuries to the noblest imperialists of them all, and to the couplet

pax romana,
pax americana.

"The fact is," said Charles Krauthammer, "no country has been as dominant culturally, economically, technologically and militarily in the history of the world since the late Roman Empire." The collapse of the Soviet Union, he said, left a "unipolar moment," an unchallengeable America ruling the world. Robert Kaplan wrote "Rome's victory in the Second Punic War, like America's in World War II, made it a universal power." He suggested America follow the Roman example, and develop "warrior politics," with eyes wide open.[7]

For Robert Kagan the new imperialism was realism.[8] Since the US actually *has* imperial powers, we might as well use them for good. He contrasted the recent American experience of reality with that of the Europeans. They had recently achieved European integration peacefully and multilaterally, by negotiations and without militarism. Europe "is moving beyond power into a self-contained world of laws and rules and transnational negotiation and cooperation ... the realization of Kant's 'Perpetual Peace.'" The United States, meanwhile, "remains mired in history, exercising power in the anarchic Hobbesian world." Only martial virtues can deal with this. It is no surprise that Europe is averse to military power. "It is what weaker powers have wanted from time immemorial." Since European military budgets are small and declining, Iraq, Iran and North Korea are simply not their problem. They *cannot* respond with vigor. Piety is their specialism. Actually, it is hypocrisy, since peace in Europe depends ultimately on US military might.

Krauthammer revealed even more resentment of Europeans:

> Our sophisticated European cousins are aghast. The French led the way. . . . They deem it a breach of good manners to call evil by its name. They prefer accommodating to it. They have lots of practice, famously accommodating Nazi Germany in 1940. We are in a war for self-defense. It is also a war for Western civilization. If the Europeans refuse to see themselves as part of this struggle, fine. . . . We will let them hold our coats, but not tie our hands.[9]

All these authors stressed that the US could bring peace to a world which remained obdurately Hobbesian. Kagan said that the "benevolent hegemony exercised by the US is good for a vast portion of the world's population." It is humanitarian.

The historian Paul Kennedy went way beyond Rome, as revealed by the title of his article, "The Greatest Superpower Ever."[10] Dinesh D'Souza concurred: "Since the end of the cold war, the US has exercised an unparalleled and largely unrivaled influence throughout the world—economically, politically, culturally, and militarily." He agreed that the US was more benevolent than all previous Empires. Observing that his own homeland of India used to be held down with 100,000 British troops, he made the enormous claim "the US empire [is] the most magnanimous imperial power ever. . . . If this be the workings of empire, let us have more of it."

Philip Bobbitt is the author of a massive book on the modern history of states. He emphasizes both their militarist origins and their recent drive toward peace and legitimacy. This is a grand teleological tome, history as destiny, culminating in a global benevolent American Empire—a terrible "Long War" between sovereign states ending with an American-guaranteed peace. His "constitutional theory" rates democracy and human rights above state sovereignty (which, he says, was responsible for the Long War). If a state is not democratic and does not protect human rights, then its "cloak of sovereignty" should no longer protect it from military intervention. He instances Iraq as just such a case. The United States, being immensely powerful, democratic *and* committed to human rights, is the only power which combines the might and the right to attack Iraq and others. For the same reason, he says the US has the right to take preemptive action against weapons of mass destruction, and to have immunity from international law for its own military forces.[11] Since over half the states in the world are neither genuinely democratic nor respectful of human rights, Bobbitt's so-called constitutional theory would seemingly place much of the world at risk of American invasion. This is a theory doing imperial service.

Even most liberals and leftists agree that American power is enormous, though they often disapprove. Joseph Nye, Assistant Secretary of State under Clinton, says, "not since Rome has one nation loomed so large above the others." But he adds that since others consent to American domination *because* it embodies benign values (which are also their own), the US must not abandon these values. He concludes that the US must resist the growing imperial temptations.[12]

A broader point lies behind such arguments. An Empire of pure benevolence might seem impossible. But an Empire to which the ruled routinely consent is not unusual. This is what we call "hegemony," a word which indicates that the imperial power establishes "the rules of the game" by which others routinely play. Others may come to approve of the rules as well, so that hegemony is also partly legitimate. But the basis of hegemony is more of a matter-of-fact acceptance of things "as the way they are." Then people's own everyday actions help reproduce the dominance without much thought. For example, the US dollar is the world's reserve currency, stable, secure, so foreigners routinely invest in the US economy, subsidizing American consumers and indirectly paying for the US military, without their even being much aware of this. Foreigners see this mainly as the way the global economy works, and so it is also the way they can make profits. In practical terms they consent, though they may occasionally grumble. Of course, the catch is that to be hegemonic, the US has to play by the rules it has established. If unilateral militarism abandons the rules, it risks losing hegemony. That is the worry of the liberals.

Leftists have long denounced American imperialism—the word itself is theirs. By fusing two giants together—the United States and capitalism—they have often blamed most of the world's ills on a single Leviathan, the capitalist-imperialist US. Leftists often credit the United States with simply enormous powers, and the conspiracy theorists among them see it as extraordinarily well organized. They agree with the hawks that this is imperialism, they just see it as a bad thing. Even much more sophisticated post-Marxists, like Perry Anderson, partake of this view. He sees no significant challenge to US power and hegemony anywhere. Other powers grumble, but they acquiesce. Even the consent of victims can be bought out by American capitalist development, he says.[13] Left, liberals and conservatives all agree: this is the Age of American Empire.

I disagree. But I do not argue here on high moral grounds, full of rhetorical denunciations of US policy. Nor do I claim that all we have to do is abandon imperial tendencies, embrace peace, and turn to nice caring multilateralists and peaceniks, embodied by the UN. Leaving everything to the UN might be a recipe for the deployment of high moral sentiments, endless political squabbles, and little action. Even so, this would be better than endless war. But better still would be more realism about the limitations of *both* sets of options—multilateral and unilateral, negotiations and force, carrots and sticks. Then perhaps we can work our way toward some more productive blending of their better qualities.

This book attacks the supposedly "realist" heart of the new imperialism. I draw up a comprehensive inventory of the more limited powers that are actually available to the US. As in my previous work, I distinguish four main types of power: military, political, economic and ideological.[14] Chapters 1–4 will detail these four types of power resource possessed by the US. I am not alone in arguing that the new imperialists exaggerate American powers. Like "world-systems theorists," the French demographer and essayist Emmanuel Todd suggests American decline has already set in and will not be reversed by the new imperialists. He says all its powers are weakening. Its military has a soft underbelly—reluctance to take casualties; its economic "tribute-taking" is increasingly fragile; its own democracy is weakening while global democracy is strengthening global resistance against the US; and the US is recoiling from American values which have had a universal appeal. While the US is weakening in all four ways, its potential rivals Europe and Russia—and later China—are beginning a resurgence.[15] I agree with some but not all of Todd's arguments. I do not see the demise of the new imperialists as coming from the rise of another power or from general imperial over-stretch, but from extremely uneven power resources. These lead not to general collapse but to imperial incoherence and foreign policy failure. Hopefully, this will be followed by voluntary abandonment of the imperial project by Americans, and this would preserve most of the US hegemony.

My argument can be illustrated with a rather ghastly metaphor. The American Empire will turn out to be a military giant, a Back-seat economic driver, a political schizophrenic and an ideological phantom. The result is a disturbed, misshapen monster stumbling clumsily across the world. It means well. It intends to spread order and benevolence, but instead it creates more disorder and violence. I further argue that the US has more uneven imperial powers than any of its historic predecessors, and I make comparisons with the Roman and with recent European Empires, from the massive British to the tiny Belgian Empire. Within their conquered terrains they were all far more powerful than the United States can be.

But the new imperialists do not want to rule permanently over foreign lands. They want only an indirect and informal Empire, though one that threatens, coerces and even sometimes invades foreign states, improves them and then leaves. Nor do they threaten the whole world. The prosperous North of the world contains neither disorder, nor military rivals, nor collective resistance. All that the US requires is that the Northern states stick to their own affairs and not interfere in American imperial projects elsewhere. It expects they will be too divided to do this anyway, and believes it can divide and rule among them. This was the purpose of Donald Rumsfeld's division between the "old" and the "new" Europe when European opposition did surface in late 2002.

Much of the South of the world remains off limits for different reasons. Some regions are racked by poverty, disease, oppressive but failing states, ethnic and religious conflicts and civil and neighborhood wars. The US does hope that its informal economic imperialism can contribute to "draining the swamp" of poverty amidst which many of these problems fester. I discuss this in Chapter 2. But rarely does the US sally forth with guns blazing across these difficult zones of the South. It almost totally ignores sub-Saharan Africa. In Latin America it presently confines itself to screwing down Cuba and projecting limited force into Colombia, though a sally into Venezuela has been recently contemplated. South Asia is left largely alone for a different reason, since India and Indonesia are too big and independent for the US to mess with them. Most of the world is left largely alone.

That leaves two main areas of serious concern for the US. The first involves the communist and post-communist countries of the world. But Russia and China are much too big and powerful to be messed with. The US surrounds them warily with bases, but does not intervene in them. It has been burned once in Vietnam, and Cuba is trivial. North Korea remains the only "serious" communist enemy ripe for action, and so North-East Asia gets close attention from the new imperialists. But the second "problem area" is the really big one. This is the Middle East, a region which is potentially expandable into the entire Muslim world stretching in a great belt from Nigeria in West Africa to Indonesia in South-East Asia. This is thought to require considerable American attention because it contains oil, Israel (America's closest but most unruly ally) and major internal instabilities. Islam is the most powerfully mobilizing of the world's religions, and its pan-Islamic reach tends to undercut the legitimacy of oppressive states (though it is also capable of oppression itself). As a long opponent of Western imperialism, it also resists American intrusions quite strongly. Israel also destabilizes its Arab neighbors. By exploiting all these issues, the cold-war superpowers added much more instability. Thus most states in the region maintain unusually large military forces and several of them actively seek nuclear, biological and chemical weapons. This is a conflicted, highly armed region.

So the two main thrusts of the new imperialism are into the Muslim Middle East and North-East Asia. My Chapters 5–8 examine the Empire in action in these regions, focusing on the ongoing wars against Afghanistan, terrorism and "rogue states" wielding "weapons of mass destruction"—which for the moment means mainly Iraq, but also North Korea. But the new imperialists have only just begun. Their ambition will not rest content with conquering Iraq and refusing to talk to North Korea. There is more to come, especially in the Middle East.

It might seem a little bizarre that new imperialists test their mettle not on major powers, but on an international terrorist movement consisting of less than a thousand people, and on small, poor, unpopular states of the South with few economic resources and armed forces which could not stand up in open terrain for a week against American military might. Emmanuel Todd pokes French fun at the prospect of the mighty Empire puffing up its chest with victories over such puny enemies. But this misses the point. The new imperialists say that the end only justifies the means where wars will be short and relatively easy, with few casualties. They do not advocate the much greater devastation that would follow from taking on China, even though China may be as "rogue-like" as Iraq. The problem is rather that the ends cannot be achieved even through short, easy wars, and while the wars are being waged, the really serious problems of the world drift by.

I here assess progress so far, and the prospects for opposition against the imperial project. We shall see that the new imperialists overestimate American power by focusing only on military power. They forget that US economic power is somewhat fragile, they neglect political power altogether (especially in their incompetent planning of the Iraq attack), and their actions completely contradict the sources of American ideological power.

Thus they consistently generate what Chalmers Johnson calls "blowback," resistance coming as the unintended consequence of their own actions.[16] Blowback may be from the victims and their sympathizers. That is why I devote much attention to detailing the experiences and opinions of Arabs, who are at present at the receiving end of the Empire. But blowback may also come from America's discontented allies. We shall see that the new imperialism creates more, not fewer, terrorists, that it creates more determined "rogue states," and that it weakens American leadership in the world. But the enemies of the United States are wrong to see it as the Great Satan or the Evil Empire. It is not that well organized. This is an incoherent Empire whose overconfident, hyperactive militarism will soon destroy it. In response to their limitations, the new imperialists are grasping ever more firmly on to the one power they do possess in abundance—offensive military devastation. My conclusion will be that in reality the new American imperialism is becoming the new American militarism. But that is not sufficient for Empire. Those who live by the sword . . .

NOTES

1. Raghda Dirgham, "Iraq Is a Tryout for the Doctrine of Anything Goes," *Al-Hayat*, available in Arabic at *www.alhayet.com*.
2. All these reports are available on the world-wide web through their titles. See also "Pentagon White Paper," *New York Times*, March 8, 1992; Frances Fitzgerald, "George Bush and the World," *New York Review of Books*, September 26, 2002; Jay Bookman, "Real Goal in Iraq," *Atlantic-Journal Constitution*, October 1, 2002; and *www.foreignpolicy-infocus.org*. The quotes from Powell and Bush are from Bob Woodward *Bush at War*, New York: Simon and Schuster, 2002, pp. 281–2, 333, 341.
3. Though one person's terrorist is another's freedom fighter, terrorists do what the name suggests: they seek to strike terror into the hearts of their enemies by killings that blur distinctions between soldiers and civilians. Terrorists are conventionally defined as non-state actors, but they are matched by "state terrorists"—states doing the same thing.
4. For the full speech, see *New York Times*, January 30, 2002.
5. Former UN Secretary-General Boutros Boutros-Ghali, writing in *Al-Ahram Weekly*, January 2–8, 2003, issue no. 619.
6. "Why International Primacy Matters," *International Security*, vol. 17, p. 83.
7. Krauthammer, "The Unipolar Moment," *Foreign Affairs*, 1990–91; Kaplan, *Warrior Politics: Why Leadership Demands a Pagan Ethos*, New York: Random House, 2001.
8. In his essays "The Benevolent Empire," *Foreign Policy*, summer 1998, and "Power and Weakness. Why Europe and the US See the World Differently," *Policy Review*, June–July 2002.
9. "The Axis of Petulance," *Washington Post*, March 1, 2002. Note that the US also accommodated to Nazism until Hitler actually declared war on it. And to those who say that but for the Americans

the French would be speaking German, I reply that but for the French the Americans would still be speaking English with a British accent. In 1763 the British defeated the French and Indian enemies of the American colonists. Their gratitude lasted less than two decades. Then they revolted. Gratitude does not extend through the generations.

10. In *New Perspectives Quarterly*, winter 2002.

11. *The Shield of Achilles*, New York: Knopf, 2001, pp. 678ff.

12. *The Paradox of American Power*, New York: Oxford University Press, 2002.

13. "Force and Consent," *New Left Review*, New Series, no. 17, September–October 2002.

14. I have previously deployed this fourfold model in my history of the development of human societies, of which two volumes have appeared so far: *The Sources of Social Power, vol. I: A History of Power From the Beginning to 1760 AD*, and *vol. II: The Rise of Classes and Nation States, 1760–1914*. Both Cambridge University Press, 1986 and 1993. Volume III, *Globalizations*, is now underway.

15. Emmanuel Todd, *Après L'Empire*, Paris: Gallimard, 2002. For a world-systems theorist, see Immanuel Wallerstein, *Geopolitics and Geoculture: Essays on the Changing World System*, Cambridge: Cambridge University Press, 1991, and Giovanni Arrighi and Beverly Silver, *Chaos and Governance in the Modern World*, Minneapolis: University of Minnesota Press, 1998.

16. *Blowback: the Costs and Consequences of American Empire*, New York: Henry Holt, 2000. Johnson initially restricts his term to the intended consequences of secret, CIA-style US policies, but later uses it in the broader sense used here.

ONE

THE MILITARY GIANT

American military power has no rival. Japan and Europe do not pursue military power, the Soviet enemy collapsed, and both Russia and China want entry into our capitalist world. Almost all the world's military budgets are declining, except the American. By 2001 it comprised 36 percent of the entire world's—six times the size of the number-two power, Russia, and seven times the size of the next three, France, the UK and Japan. The US budget for 2003 takes it to over 40 percent of the world's total. It exceeds the spending of the next 24 states combined, and is 25 times greater than the combined spending of all seven "rogue states" identified by the US as its enemies. The gap also grows steadily wider.[1] Remember, in military terms Europe is a worm. Even worse—it does not exist. The US is the only military superpower.

US military power may be gigantic, but can it create Empire? Empires require four military resources: secure defense or deterrence against attack, offensive strike-power, the ability to conquer territories and peoples, and the ability to pacify them afterwards. How appropriate are American forces for these tasks?

THE AMERICAN ARSENAL

1. Nuclear weapons

Since 1945 nuclear weapons have been used to deter attack. The US is clearly the number-one nuclear power, though it currently only has the same number of nuclear warheads as Russia, about 9,000. Under the

START III Treaty of 2002, Bush and Putin agreed to reduce their operational warheads down to about 2,000–2,500 by 2007, though more warheads can be stored for potential later use. The US but probably not Russia will store them, so it will soon have far more nuclear weapons than anyone else. Nonetheless, Russia will maintain its downsized arsenal at a level of effectiveness capable of obliterating the US if necessary. America has to respect such power. It has no imperial military power over Russia.

Nor really over the next three powers. France has 340 warheads, China 250, and Britain 185. Should the improbable thought ever occur to them, these three also have enough destructive power to deter us from using our weapons against them (should that improbable thought ever occur to us). Then four states have mostly shorter-range nuclear missiles. Israel is believed to have 100–200 warheads, India and Pakistan each 30–50, and North Korea has one or two, but seems to be acquiring more. Several other countries could acquire basic warheads and delivery systems in a decade or so if they wanted to, while advanced countries like Japan and Germany could presumably acquire them in months.

Its nuclear arsenal makes the US invulnerable to attack from any rational enemy who is dependent on fixed assets—that is, any state not controlled by a madman or someone made reckless by the prospect of imminent death and destruction. This is a higher level of defense than any state has ever possessed throughout history. The rest of the world should worry more about defense than Americans do, especially since Bush's embrace of the US Star Wars anti-ballistic missile defense system program and his threats of nuclear preemptive strikes. This is a very secure base for an imperial motherland. But nuclear weapons cannot be used as part of a rational offensive, except a purely punitive one, nor can they pacify usable territory. They are irrelevant for Empire, unless we want a radioactive one.

2. Conventional force mass

Empires require conventional, not nuclear forces. In numbers US forces are big but not overwhelming. They total 1.45 million men and women under arms, down from 2.2 million in the 1980s. This is less than China's 2.5 million, while India, North Korea and Russia have just over one million each. The US has only 5 percent of the world's soldiers. This is obviously insufficient to patrol the whole world.

Lack of numbers might also detract from lesser imperial roles. Add up the forces necessary for military interventions, a global network of bases, and heightened security for the homeland and US embassies, pipelines, etc. abroad, and US forces are almost fully engaged. How many "wars" can it pursue at once? When General Ralston, US Commander of Europe, was asked by lawmakers whether he had the resources to invade Iraq while maintaining commitments in Europe, the Balkans and elsewhere, he replied, "We do not have forces to do the missions you have outlined."[2] He seems to have exaggerated, but current policy is that the US could fight one and a half wars at once, one being an active engagement, the other a holding operation. But the latter would have to involve very few new troops. But the major problem of numbers would come after the war in pacification, especially if enduring occupation is involved. For, as we shall see, this requires more soldiers than war itself. The problem of numbers worsens if wars are won through technological superiority in fire-power. The European Empires increasingly faced this problem, as their handguns and artillery gave them increasing superiority over the peoples they conquered. In Africa 3,000–5,000 men would be typically enough to secure a large colony. A force of 1,000 could win a small one. This force could generate a concentrated fire-power to destory any native levy. But holding the colony down required dispersion of forces, in garrisons and patrols across the land. This required larger numbers. They had a solution, as we shall see.

The Americans are in the same position of fire-power superiority, and so face the same problem of pacification. So far they have no solution. There may be constraints on Empire unless Americans are willing to pay higher taxes for bigger forces—and bigger body-bags. So far Americans have lacked enthusiasm.

3. Global deployment

The crucial American military superiority is not nuclear weapons or weight of numbers but global deployment and fire-power. Only the US has global reach. It has refueling facilities, staging-posts and forward troop bases spread across the world. The Pentagon says there are US military facilities in 132 countries. Only about half are proper bases, but nowhere lies outside the American striking-range. This is the first military force deployable over the entire world.

Al-Udeid air base is in a desert location in Qatar. There is no human habitation near by. It is heavily protected by high wire, steel fences and guard towers. It needs to be, since some locals try to kill its soldiers. In outward physical appearance it is not unlike the forts and garrisons of past imperial states. But there are big differences.

There is firstly a legal weakness, since US bases must respect the sovereignty of the local ruler.[3] The Emir of Qatar must approve of all US troop movements in or out. US warplanes stationed on Saudi territory cannot launch attacks abroad except in self-defense. The Saudis gave permission for a US command and control center to direct the air war in Afghanistan and the patrols over Iraq during the 1990s, but in 2003 did not allow any attacks on Iraq to be launched from their territory. Turkey turned down a bribe of somewhere between $16 billion and $32 billion in 2003 when refusing to allow US troops or planes to use its bases for the war in Iraq. Both countries also withdrew permission for US cruise missiles to be launched from ships over their air space into Iraq when errant missiles hit their territory by mistake. Some longer-term allies were more helpful. Germany gave base rights even though it opposed the invasion of Iraq. And some of Iraq's neighbors gave limited and covert help.

The smaller and more dependent the country, the greater the cooperation. Sovereignty can sometimes be bought. Qatar would do almost whatever the US wanted, and Kuwait made very few conditions. The ideal location for a base would be an uninhabited island. The British base on Diego Garcia, a 17-square-mile atoll in the middle of the Indian Ocean is just perfect. It is useful for refueling long-range bombers and other long-range staging activities in Eurasia and Africa. It is uninhabited because the British deported all the inhabitants to Mauritius in the 1970s! The British Empire always used islets and enclave territories as naval staging-posts, like Gibraltar, Port Mahon, Malta, St Helena. This has been a standard technique of Empires.

But nineteenth-century client rulers were much less troublesome than today's. They could not refuse or bargain with the British or French, or even the Belgian imperialists. The Europeans overthrew them if they tried. The European Empires ruled among and over the locals. US military personnel mostly live in isolated bases well away from the local population. All the base personnel are Americans—not just the soldiers, but also the clerks, the maintenance men, the nurses. The Pentagon's website for prospective soldiers says: "Military installations are really like small, secure towns. The same things happen in both places—family life, social life, shopping, dining, child care, school, worship, medical care, sports, hobbies, recreation, and so on." When US soldiers go out to conduct exercises, these are usually in secure areas, cordoned off from the local population. Only in Afghanistan and Iraq do US soldiers sally out of the bases on local patrols or "shows of force." The bases are not "garrisons" pacifying the country. US troops may intimidate local dissidents by their presence, but they do not project their power into the country. Since they do not defend the local ruler, they cannot coerce him.

The main US base in Saudi is a secure area inside the Saudi Prince Sultan air base in a remote desert location. It is home to over 4,000 military personnel, all Americans. They live in air-conditioned accommodation units with recreational facilities and a cinema showing the latest Hollywood movies. The US base was developed in the wake of two terrorist attacks on more exposed facilities in 1995–96, in which 26 Americans were killed. Faced with deep local hostility, all the Gulf States seek to make the American presence invisible. The Kuwaiti killers of a US marine in October 2002 were given a martyr's burial. The imam declared to general applause: "They were better than us because they stood up against infidels bent on usurping our rights."[4] The American presence perversely makes the local regime *less* not more secure domestically. What kind of Empire is this? The network of US bases has grave imperial limitations.

4. Fire-power

The biggest American military asset is fire-power. No one can rival the strike-power of American airplanes, missiles, ships, tanks and other capital-intensive, technology-laden toys. It has a virtual monopoly of "smart" (self-guided, once launched) and "brilliant" (completely robotic) weapons. American fire-power was enhanced during the 1990s by the so-called "revolution in military affairs," the RMA. The term was coined in 1993 by Pentagon guru Andrew Marshall to refer to "a major change in the nature of warfare brought about by the innovative application of new technologies which, combined with dramatic changes in military doctrine and operational and organizational concepts, fundamentally alters the character and conduct of military operations." It combined long-range precision radar-guided missiles and bombs with "information warfare" deploying satellites in space, airborne cameras, handheld global positioning systems and robot sensors. One of RMA's main weapons carries neither guns nor bombs. The Global Hawk is a US reconnaissance jet aircraft that provides military commanders with near real-time imagery of ground targets. It is used in conjunction with ground station and handheld GPS equipment. This hawk does not swoop down on its prey; it hovers at 60,000 feet and tells others where to swoop.

Appropriately organized, RMA forces can inflict enormous damage on the enemy, with very low US casualties. Even the individual US infantryman can devastate. His improved M-16/M4 rifle can now deliver 90 rounds a minute, disintegrating human beings 2,000 feet away—even without the attachable grenade-launcher.

Today many believe Marshall's predictions were correct. The weapons were first used in the Gulf War of 1991 and enjoyed moderate success. In the Kosovo and Serbian campaign of 1999 US forces were able to devastate Serb fixed power grids and communications infrastructures, though they failed to inflict much damage on mobile Serb forces. But there were almost no US casualties. This was just the beginning. Since then, new "smart" weapons have been coming onstream, greeted enthusiastically by the US media. In 2002 star treatment was given to robotic Predator planes, self-steering tank-buggies, and land-mines which detect an oncoming vehicle and jump into its path—a disconcerting thought to all drivers! The Army spokesman told the press proudly: "Robotics can . . . keep soldiers out of harm's way, do the laborious and boring tasks and keep going long after a soldier is exhausted. And they have no fear."[5] An army without fear, a first in human history! In 2003 there were leaks about "directed energy weapons," lasers, microwaves and electromagnetic pulses that destroy electrical and electronic circuits and fry the human skin without necessarily causing death. This is not yet reality. But the Afghan war of 2001–2002 and the Iraq invasion of 2003 showed the offensive utility of the system.[6]

RMA does give big advantages to US forces. Only American boys have such toys. The US monopolizes space-based military assets, with its E-8 JStars airborne control center giving accurate radar portraits of the battlefield from 42,000 feet. In *War and Peace* Tolstoy unforgettably evoked the battlefields of the Napoleonic Wars. Once the cannon started firing, smoke engulfed the battlefield and no one could see what was happening. Napoleon and Kutuzov were peering bleerily into the fog of war, desperately sending out scores of staff officers to find out what was going on in the next field. No more. US generals look down with satellite eyes which penetrate the fog, the clouds and the dark. They can then rain down missiles from heaven! At all levels—planes, ships, artillery, tanks and the individual soldier—most enemies can be destroyed at long-range before they can even get within their own firing-range. Not all potential enemies. We presume that well-organized militaries command sufficient air defense systems to deter American attack. But the new imperialists are careful to attack only poor states with lesser militaries.

It was hoped that the precision of "smart" bombs would also bring low civilian casualties. Marshall himself claimed "only the bad guys get hurt." American wars would now be fought from long range, involving small, fast "in and out" expeditionary forces, minimizing US and civilian casualties alike. The claim is exaggerated. A "smart bomb" is likely to produce fewer civilian casualties. But if the US drops many of them, some will go off target, the targeting will sometimes be wrong, and the enemy will respond with "civilian-shielding" tactics. Then the civilian casualty rate may not drop much. The casualty-free Empire is a delusion, as we shall see.

HOW USEFUL IS THE ARSENAL FOR EMPIRE?

Nonetheless, we have to be impressed (or depressed) by all this. As the new imperialists say, no comparable military power had previously existed. This is true of relative military expenditures, capacity to deter attackers, global offensive reach, and level of offensive fire-power delivered with minimum risk to oneself. The combination gives a massive intimidatory presence to the United States vis-à-vis any state which dares to stand up to it. Military defiance would be a very high-risk strategy.

The lack of rivals is truly unique in the history of the world, as the new imperialists say. The US utterly dwarfs Britain's nineteenth-century military leadership. True, its Royal Navy was deliberately kept bigger than the next two largest navies combined, and in reality it sometimes exceeded the next four. This meant that Britain was also defensively invulnerable (since it is an island and there were no airplanes). It also possessed unrivaled striking power across the seas and along the coast-lines of the world. But British Army strength only ranked fifth in the world, behind Germany, France, Russia and Austria-Hungary. So Britain could not coerce or conquer its own continent, and it had well-armed rivals spread across the Northern hemisphere.

Even British naval supremacy did not last long. Exactly one hundred years after Trafalgar Britain launched the first of its new Dreadnought class of battleships (appropriately named after one of Nelson's ships). The Dreadnoughts had more powerful engines, longer-range 12-inch guns, and tougher steel-plated hulls than any ship afloat. Dreadnoughts could outpace and destroy any other ship. Unfortunately, though the British led, any industrialized country could follow. They all began to build Dreadnoughts. The arms race soon made irrelevant British numerical superiority in ships, since foreign Dreadnoughts could sink all its lesser ships. British naval superiority lasted another decade, through World War I, but not thereafter. Today even smart and brilliant weapons might eventually be cloned and satellites pirated. But America's present global reach, fire-power and the lack of rivals do give it battlefield dominance.

The main military problems come later, in consolidating victory on the ground and especially in pacifying the country afterwards. How did earlier Empires manage such tasks? I leave their political and ideological polices until later chapters. But their military policies differed according to whether they initially entered with the support of native allies. If the British or Belgians—or the Romans—entered a region accompanied by native allies, then after battlefield victory, the fleeing enemy would usually be finished off by the allies, whose local clients would then help pacify the country. If the imperialists entered without allies, then they really needed far bigger forces for pacification—much bigger than the original invasion force. In fact, they usually economized and substituted ferocious "exemplary repression," massacring the rebels they caught, as an example to others. In either situation, with the local authority deposed and food supplies disrupted, looting would occur, local scores would be settled, and general mayhem could break out. The early days of Empire could be extremely nasty. It is unlikely American troops or the American electorate could stomach such ferocious orders. Thus the Americans would have to invade either with local allies or with much bigger forces than needed for battlefield victory. They ignored this advice in Iraq, to their cost.

Later, when perhaps the allies or the first native levies mutinied, or the British sought more direct rule, mayhem might ensue again. But by then the British were usually better prepared. By this point most of the imperial army consisted of native levies. The officers would be Europeans, but not the non-commissioned officers or the ordinary soldiers. In India the regimental bands were mostly Eurasians, the children of marriages between a British soldier father and an Indian mother. By the early 1800s over 80 percent of the 291,000 imperial troops in India were

Indians. Actual war-fighting never involved more than 25,000 men at a time. It was the garrisons required for pacification that consumed the manpower. The first big mutiny came in 1857, provoked by British insensitivity to the soldiers' religious dietary needs. The mutinous Indian soldiers killed at least 200 Europeans before a much more brutal revenge was exacted on them and their wives and children. The British now took over direct rule of the country. Most Indian artillery regiments were disbanded, and every Indian brigade had one British unit assigned to monitor it Yet two-thirds of the imperial army always remained Indian. The British could never have ruled India without being assisted by Indian soldiers and civilians who benefited from British rule but were not regarded locally as traitors—until Indian nationalism began to spread in the twentieth century. Then the British were finished.[7]

In the less valuable African colonies, conquest and rule depended even more on local friends. Some African rulers could invariably be found to fight as allies against their local rivals. The British strengthened the authority of loyal chiefs and tribal and village councils, and essentially ruled through them. So not all that many soldiers, and very few British soldiers, were needed. A ratio of one imperial soldier per 1,000 natives was considered high. In 1912 in Northern Rhodesia, now the country of Zambia, the British deployed one battalion, comprising 750 Africans and 26 British officers, to enforce taxes and trade and suppress discontent over the whole colony. The Belgians used over 18,000 troops for their much harsher rule in the much larger Congo, but no less than 98 percent of them were Africans. In Africa only the Germans used substantial numbers of Europeans—about 40 percent of their force—and they were the least successful and most repressive colonizers, committing genocide in South West Africa in 1908.[8] Again, far more soldiers were stationed in dispersed garrisons than in field armies. In fact, the largest battlefield deployments of native troops actually occurred abroad. At times of imperial need, colonial troops were assigned overseas, where they fought loyally for the European power. Indian troops were routinely deployed in Africa, and over 130,000 Indian troops fought in Belgium and France in World War I. The French used even more colonial troops in World War I. Over 150,000 African troops fought for Britain in Asia in World War II. It seems extraordinary today—what concern of theirs were these European wars? But these were real Empires, ruled through the natives themselves.

Imperial garrisons were not in remote enclaves but in or just outside main cities or marketplaces. At first they might be fortified with high walls and limited access, but as the colony was stabilized, more open barracks emerged, sometimes surrounded by only picket fences. In India the British officers' clubs were typically on the edge of the encampment, commanding the nicest location and view. The officers were relaxed about their personal safety, sipping their whiskey and soda and gin and tonic in full view of the natives. The garrisons were not fortified against all natives, for they comprised most of their inhabitants—NCOs and soldiers, servants, stable-hands, drivers and sometimes their families. All over the Empires, the soldiers would routinely leave the barracks on patrols and "shows of force" throughout the colony. As required, they would sally forth to disperse and sometimes shoot demonstrators and rioters. After rebellions they would be fiercely repressive, but for most of the time this was ritual—a show of force, escalating carefully to beatings with batons, a volley over the heads, and then a volley into the crowd. Hopefully, the natives would run away before this point was reached, but the imperial authorities were perfectly prepared for the worst, not as routine, but as persisting episodes.

The US did this in the Philippines in the early twentieth century, and the islands were quite peaceful by the time they were lost to the Japanese in World War II. There has been no subsequent American experience of routine colonial pacification. US bases are not much help, for they overleap the host country altogether, projecting offensive air and carrier strike-power somewhere else—not imperial pacification, but offensive intimidation from afar. The US army contains no "natives" at all, and not even any foreign mercenaries (like the French Foreign Legion or the British Gurkhas). It is not suited to imperial roles. American soldiers have no expertise in crowd control or in dispersing mobs. If they used their M-16s against the locals, their fire-power would cause a level of casualties quite inappropriate to routine pacification. This might seem ridiculous. Of course, American troops are not there to shoot the locals! Americans would be appalled by the brutalities which British and Belgian imperial forces inflicted when encountering resistance. But that is how real Empires were ruled. We shall see later the distinctive American weakness in these roles in Afghanistan, where there were local allies, and in Iraq, where there are not (apart from Kurds in the far north).

The lack of an imperial American culture makes for further weaknesses. American kids are not brought up to be as racist, as stoic in combat, as self-denying in crisis, or as obedient to authority, as British kids once were. Roman kids lacked the racism, which made for an ultimately less repressive Empire, but this made them able to make the natives into Romans. All Western culture became more pacific in the second half of the twentieth century, but American culture is especially individualistic, egalitarian and hedonistic. This is not supportive of military discipline, and it weakens the stomach for a long fight, especially one involving casualties.[9] The US has long fought wars with a high regard for its own soldiers' lives and comforts. In World Wars I and II the US was already substituting fire-power for frontal assaults, and its losses were proportionately lower than any other combatant country. Vietnam threatened that strategy, and demoralization was the outcome.

So the US became determined not to repeat the Vietnam experience. What became known as the "Powell doctrine" declared that military interventions must be made with overwhelming force and minimal US casualties. That governed the First Gulf War, Panama, Kosovo and Afghanistan. Caution reached its zenith after the Lebanon in 1984 and Somalia in 1994. US forces immediately withdrew from both when, respectively, 241 and 19 US soldiers were unexpectedly killed. Americans were publicly derided as cowards by Osama bin Laden. Yet the new imperialists believe that the immensity and precision of their fire-power now means that US soldiers do not *need* to be especially brave nor its citizens at all self-denying. This is a paradoxical form of militarism, accompanied by an ostensibly pacific culture which holds American lives truly sacred, not to be expended in war or Empire-building.

But can Empire be conquered and especially pacified without expending American lives, essentially by offense from a distance? Recent experience up to 2003 was that this did not lead unaided to the capitulation of any enemy. The 1991 Gulf War was not pushed this far. In Bosnia in 1992 and in Kosovo in 1999, US bombing was coordinated with Croatian and Albanian ground offensives. In Afghanistan in 2001– 2002 the US depended almost entirely on Northern Alliance ground forces. These three allies, not the US, actually took the territory which made the enemy yield.[10] Of course, this meant that the US could not control its allies on the ground. In Bosnia and Kosovo, the few NATO forces on the ground could not resist their allies' ethnic cleansings, yet these subverted the whole ostensible purpose of the war, which was to stop ethnic cleansing. The same was to happen on a lesser scale in Afghanistan, as we shall see in Chapter 5. In Iraq the US expected to get local allies once the war started, but except for some Kurdish forces in the north, this didn't happen—and the Kurds had their own agenda. Elsewhere in Iraq, US forces were compelled to fight harder than many expected, incurring more casualties and inflicting more on civilians. However, they did not pull back. They took casualties and conquered. The underbelly was not that soft. The main problems would come later, with pacification afterwards.

As I noted, reliance on allies often characterized historical imperial campaigns in their early stages. The allied native rulers could achieve their own purposes by using the British, just like the KLA or the Afghan warlords use the Americans. But from there on, the British steadily tightened the controls on them. This failed to happen in either Yugoslavia or Afghanistan. In Afghanistan almost 8,000 American troops boss a rag-tag collection of warlord militias, even sometimes going out on patrols with them. But these are not "native levies" actually under US control. The militias are structurally quite separate from the Americans, under their own Afghan commanders, and it is the warlords who rule each local area and dominate the nascent Afghan army. Since the US does not want direct territorial control, it cannot control occupied territories like the Europeans used to. As we shall see, its practices in Afghanistan and Iraq are too rudimentary to be considered imperial.

NEW THREATS: WEAPONS OF THE WEAK

But US defenses are also unexpectedly weakening as a second revolution in military affairs begins to take effect. This involves the proliferation of "weapons of mass destruction" wielded by "rogue states," small arms wielded by paramilitaries, and small arms plus bombs wielded by terrorists. Thus this revolution runs contrary to the first one by strengthening the weaker against the strong. These are weapons of the weak, being employed across the world against the strong—including the US.

1. Rogue states with weapons of mass destruction

The term "weapons of mass destruction" conventionally refers to nuclear, biological and chemical weapons. However, it is a very biased term. It is rarely invoked against the present members of the nuclear club who obviously possess far more "weapons of mass destruction" than do the Southern countries now seeking them, like North Korea. Nor does the term include "conventional" weapons, though these still remain far more destructive than chemical or biological ones—especially when wielded by the US. The US is the greatest possessor of WMDs, and it is also the greatest proliferator of highly destructive weapons, through its massive arms sales abroad. Nor does the term seem to include the uranium-depleted "conventional" weapons wielded by the US (and Britain) which have harmful long-term chemical effects on the soldiers wielding them (as well as on the populations in areas in which they are used). Nor does it include low-tech chemical warfare using napalm or Roundup Ultra, currently being dropped by the US on the Colombian countryside. In March 2001 four Colombian provincial governors went to Washington to beg the administration to stop a chemical bombing program which harms humans, livestock and legal crops as well as coca plants. They failed and the bombing of their homeland has accelerated. So the very term "weapons of mass destruction" is not a neutral term. It used to denounce our enemies when they try to acquire them too.

But let us stay with the conventional view of WMDs. The deadliest by far are nuclear. At first, these were only wielded by the most powerful states. The US, the USSR, Britain and France were all highly developed countries, and China had vast resources. Israel, though small, has an impressive high-tech sector. But then nuclear weapons began to spread to more backward countries. India is large and poor, Pakistan only mid-sized and poor. North Korea is rich only in soldiers. Iran, Iraq, Syria, Libya (coming close to nuclear weapons) are poor, smallish countries.

Nuclear proliferation is no longer spreading across the advanced countries. Japan, Germany, Italy, Spain, Canada, Australia could easily acquire them but presently show no interest (though Japan might change its mind). The basic reason for this is that they do not feel threatened by anyone. They are all friends. Friendship is clearly the best anti-proliferation policy. But in more threatening environments in the South of the world nuclear weapons are at present proliferating since they produce a big deterrence pay-off at relatively low cost. Above all, they seem to protect a state against American imperialism. The US will think twice about attacking a country with established nuclear weapons, they reason.

These are not offensive weapons. Anyone who fired off their warheads against the US would invite total obliteration, so they cannot possibly threaten the US. Nor can they be used against neighboring states for most of the reasons that usually start wars—territorial disputes or protection of one's own co-ethnics abroad—for radioactivity would also effect one's own side. But any country fearing a much stronger neighbor or the US has a strong incentive to acquire them in self-defense. George Fernandes is the long-serving Indian Defense Minister. This is his account of his own decision to acquire nuclear weapons for his country

> I went through a deep anguish—an atom bomb was morally unacceptable. I had campaigned against it in Britain, spoken against it at various universities and fora. But I said that if today the five nations which have nuclear weapons tell us how to behave and what weapons we should have, then I should say that we keep all our options open . . . by all options I mean every option. I did not say that we make the bomb but that was implied.[11]

Indian nationalist politicians acquired nuclear weapons because they reasoned this would stop the Great Powers, especially the US, from pushing them around. Now they welcome the new American doctrine of preemption. Under the headline "The idea of preemption is as valid for India as it is for America," *India Today* (international edition) on October 14, 2002, editorialized "the only way to ensure national security is preemption." It quoted approvingly Indian Finance Minister Jaswant Singh's declaration "preemption cannot be the monopoly of one nation," especially with "the dictator over the border," meaning President Musharraf of Pakistan. He also endorses the same logic, pointing to the Hindu nationalists over the border.

When one country acquires nuclear weapons, its regional rivals feel more threatened and tend to seek them also, especially if weaker in conventional forces. Having acquired them, the conventionally weaker side then declares that it may launch a nuclear first strike if threatened by attack from its rival. This is what the Western Allies announced in Europe against the USSR, which had greater ground forces stationed there. It is what Israel has declared in the Middle East, and it is what Pakistan has declared against India. It is the logic of nuclear deterrence: if you have weaker conventional weapons, you threaten nuclear war. It is the deterrence North Korea seeks against the US/South Korean alliance; and it is what Iran, Iraq, Libya and Syria would like to have against either Israel or the US or each other. They are all unlikely to use their weapons against the supposed enemy, for that would be to invite terrible retaliation. But the lure of these weapons is that they can suddenly ratchet up the mainly defensive military powers of poorer countries, against each other and against the US. That is why proliferation is so difficult to stop.

Chemical and biological weapons embody the same logic, but squared, since they are even cheaper and easier to smuggle. Like nuclear weapons, they did not start in the South. Chemical weapons were used in World War I by the Great Powers. Then they also developed biological weapons. But both types of weapon were felt to be illegitimate, since they are not easy to control and they discriminate poorly between combatants and non-combatants. Germany, Japan and Italy were forced to stop their programs after their defeat in World War II. France and Canada also discontinued their programs then. Britain says it followed in the late 1950s, and the US says it stopped its biological program in 1969 and its chemical program in 1985. All these powers signed up to treaties banning these weapons. So did the Soviet Union and then Russia, but they secretively maintained stockpiles and continued some research programs. Maybe others do, too, and they could all quickly reactivate biological and chemical weapons if they wished.

These weapons are not yet nearly as deadly as the dual bomb-blast/radiation effects of nuclear bombs, and maybe they never will be. But smaller and poorer countries can acquire them much more easily than nuclear weapons, since they are derivatives from the ordinary pharmaceutical and chemical industries. If they became a lot more accurate and controllable, they might be used for offensive warfare, though right now they serve more as a counter-strike option, analogous to nuclear weapons though less devastating. So the temptation to acquire them is considerable. Iran, Iraq, North Korea and Syria have almost certainly have one or both types of weapon in small quantities. China, Cuba, Egypt, Ethiopia, India, Israel, Libya, Myanmar and Taiwan probably had one or both. Algeria, Sudan and Vietnam may possibly have them. Estimates of countries that probably have them range between 16 and 25.[12] These weapons enable Southern countries to jump up the military hierarchy. Once acquired, they are deterrents against anyone else attacking them, including much stronger powers. In the 1980s Iraq used them in its war against Iran because Iran was stronger in conventional forces. They are weapons of weaker states, but they are predominantly deterrent, rather than offensive weapons.

Proliferation is more of a future than a present threat, since they still remain inaccurate, difficult to handle and require accurate ballistic missiles for delivery. At present, only short-range and inaccurate missiles are circulating—though North Korean Nodong missiles may be of better quality. But greater specters now haunt us, of agents or terrorists smuggling in a "suitcase bomb"—nuclear, chemical or biological—

bypassing the need for a ballistic missile. We are probably a decade away from this prospect, but the world is beginning to shiver. It might deal with the threat of proliferation in four ways.

1. *International amity.* Encourage everyone to be friends. This is obviously the best policy. Then they will not want WMDs. Many states have decided not to acquire nuclear weapons and a few have renounced ongoing nuclear programs, mainly because they have not felt threatened by other states. This has been true of Brazil, Argentina, South Africa, Ukraine, Belarus and Kazakstan.[13] If international friendship spread through the whole world, no one would need WMDs. The only problem is how do we get from here to there. If the main incentive to acquire WMDs is fear of other states, an effective anti-proliferation policy might be to reduce and not increase their sense of being threatened. States seemingly acquiring WMDs might be soothed rather than alienated—which is the opposite of the American "rogue states" policy. But perhaps this is utopian.

2. *Deterrence.* Do nothing. Assume, as in the past with nuclear weapons, that "deterrence works." This is to bet that human beings are generally rational, and that leaders of states always are—since they got there by endless calculation of political probabilities and advantages. In the past the US and the USSR did not launch nuclear strikes against each other because they rationally feared devastating retaliation from the other. India and Pakistan have been learning the rules of deterrence more recently. They rattle their sabers, even launch a few frontier troops against each other, but then they get on the telephone hot-line and back off. In the last days of 2002 President Musharraf of Pakistan let it be known that he might have used nuclear weapons earlier in the year had the confrontation with India escalated into an Indian invasion of his country. The leak was a deterrent warning to India for next time. And India recognized it as such. Saddam Hussein wanted to remain the ruler of a viable country. He had no rational motive to use WMDs against the US or its allies, though he might rationally give the impression he would use them if the US threatened to attack him with overwhelming force. So would North Korea. That is also what we used to tell the Soviets, since we believed they could overwhelm our conventional forces stationed in Europe. These are the rules of the nuclear deterrence game. Maybe all the world's states can learn them.

Kenneth Waltz is the major Realist theorist of international relations. He says the more nuclear states the better.[14] He claims nuclear weapons have helped keep the peace. Even if war did break out among nuclear powers, it would likely be settled quickly, for the higher the stakes and the closer to victory one side got, the more surely it would invite nuclear retaliation and the loss of everything. States act with more care if the expected costs of war are high (as in the Cuban Missile crisis). States with a nuclear deterrent do not need to aggress to acquire a defense in depth in the form of more territory. The deterrent provides defense instead. Nuclear weapons are not useful in civil wars nor (I would add) in local ethnic/religious wars. Highly urbanized states (like Israel, Egypt, Syria or Iraq) are vulnerable to very small nuclear arsenals—a few missiles can do them enormous damage. But even the greatest powers can be deterred by fairly small arsenals. Nuclear states with feeble conventional weapons are more intimidating opponents, since in war they will be quicker to resort to the use of nuclear weapons. Even untested arsenals constitute a deterrent. Nuclear weapons make further arms races less likely, for even out-of-date nuclear weapons can be devastating. None of these risks can be precisely calculated. But that is the point, says Waltz. It is what nuclear weapons *can* do which deters others.

All this might seem to require too much rationality from human beings. What if a madman or a zealot seized a state? Waltz replies "find me one." Hitler, he notes, probed rationally for possible responses before attacking. He was surprised and dismayed by the British and French declarations of war over Poland. After the Rhineland, Austria and Czechoslovakia he had not expected that. He would have been stopped by credible threats—especially nuclear weapons. But conversely, Waltz adds, no one will press war against a nuclear power right on to unconditional surrender, because that is when a desperate fanatic like Hitler might use his nuclear weapons. Thus wars are either less likely or less intense.

Perhaps this is too rationalistic and unitary a view of states (a common criticism of Realism). What about unstable, divided states? Aren't they more dangerous? Waltz says this is when rivals will be especially careful not to be provocative. "No country will goad a nuclear adversary that finds itself in sad straits." He finally quotes Bernard Brodie: "war has to find a political objective that is commensurate with its cost" and concludes that no objective is commensurate with nuclear devastation. Brodie had asked "How do governments behave in the presence of awesome danger?" His reply: "very carefully."

Scott Sagan has sought to rebut these arguments.[15] He notes that effective deterrence really resides in the possession of a second-strike capability to retaliate after being hit by a first strike. Yet small nuclear states normally lack that capability and so cannot really deter bigger powers. Of course, the big state would have to be absolutely certain of that before attacking. It also follows that preemptive strikes might become more likely, which would make us fear the bigger nuclear powers—especially the US—more than small states of the South. Sagan also doubts whether states and their officials are always rational. In crises disaster can result from misinformation and accidents. On the basis of extensive psychological tests the US military transfers 5 percent of its staff away from nuclear weapons. It only takes one of them to do something terrible. Sagan argues that this is more likely in poorer states which lack psychological programs and sophisticated warning systems needed for accurate information. They might mistake an attack by conventional bombs as a nuclear attack.

This seems a little ethnocentric. Sagan warns us against a Pakistan under jihadi leadership, but I fear the Bush/Cheney/Rumsfeld pre-emptive troika quite as much! But if there are 40 WMD states by the end of the century, Sagan is surely right to say that the risk of an accident would grow. More risk might come from a terrorist suitcase bomb, stolen or bought from a careless or corrupt state. At the very least, the world needs better security for the safe protection of its WMDs. Moreover, deterrence might produce a very low risk of a mistake, but only one mistake might have devastating consequences for the world. So let us see what additional protections might be available from more active policies.

3. *Unilateralism.* The imperial option is that the US acting alone enforces the destruction of WMDs. The US shows no desire to denuclearize existing nuclear powers, but it could pressure would-be acquirers. This might involve just carrots—simply buy them out—or a combined carrot-and-stick alternation of economic incentives and sanctions, rewarding good behavior, punishing bad. Alternatively, preemptive military action might be launched—the policy of the new imperialists.

Paying for the demolition of surplus ex-Soviet weapons is the main example of an all-carrot policy. The US Cooperative Threat Reduction (CTR) Program is generally called Nunn-Lugar after the two senators who sponsored it. It helps destroy surplus ex-Soviet weapons. By

July 2002, CTR had paid for the destruction of 5,970 nuclear warheads, 1,269 ballistic and long-range nuclear cruise missiles, 829 missile-launchers, 97 long-range bombers and 24 ballistic missile submarines—about a quarter of the surplus ex-Soviet arsenal. Thousands of former Soviet weapons scientists have also been supported by US funds in non-weapons-related research. Other US programs also helped Ukraine, Belarus and Kazakhstan go non-nuclear. Bush the Younger was initially hostile. He blocked Nunn-Lugar, pressured by conservative Republicans saying that every dollar spent in the clean-up freed up Russia to spend its roubles on new military programs. In January 2003 the administration finally did authorize the programs for three years, though on a modest scale, about one-third of the $3billion Nunn and Lugar had wanted. Lugar said it would be mainly spent on destroying two million chemical weapons, artillery shells and SCUD missile warheads at a storage facility in Shchuchye in the Urals. He said these were in "excellent working condition and many are small and easily transportable. They would be deadly in the hands of terrorists, religious sects or para-military units." He noted that they could kill the world's population 20 times over—"a direct proliferation threat to the American people," he concluded, in something of an understatement.[16] Since these arsenals dwarf those which all the rogue states combined might amass, they are much more important to non-proliferation than any policy against the so-called "Axis of Evil." Yet the Bush administration was spending $100 billion invading Iraq and only $1 billion on disposing of ex-Soviet weapons.

A policy based entirely on carrots might be thought to reward bad behavior, though the carrots would likely cost a lot less than invasion. The US bribes Egypt $2 billion a year not to attack Israel, so why could it not try to buy out Saddam's weapons? But Americans have chosen a different anti-proliferation policy, wielding the stick, to threaten, "contain" and sanction states suspected of acquiring weapons (and, more erratically, corporations supplying them).

Not without bias, however. The US favors its allies. It has ignored Israel's nuclear and suspected chemical weapons for 40 years. Against neutral India it did belatedly cut off further supply of some nuclear materials, but by then India could produce them itself. It deprived Pakistan of military aid only when it was not an ally. Now it pours in aid and it ignored intelligence reports of the exchange of Pakistani nuclear technology for North Korean ballistic missiles, which continued until at least July 2002.[17] The US did pressure its allies Taiwan and South Korea away from nuclear-weapons research, but has never made an issue of their suspected chemical weapons—or of Egypt's suspected chemical weapons or its missile links with North Korea.[18]

In December 2002 the Bush administration made an embarrassing climb-down after Spanish marines boarded a North Korean ship off the Arabian coast. The Spaniards had found missiles hidden in its hold. When the Yemeni government, a US ally, said it had purchased the missiles, and so they belonged to it, the US meekly handed them over. It would not have handed them over to Iran. It is even OK for the "evil" North Koreans to make profits out of missiles as long as their customers are American allies!

The US naturally has no intention of disarming itself. It will not submit to inspections of its own arsenals. Nor does it favor any general controls of conventional weapons, since its own arms sales constitute the greatest proliferation of devastating weapons. It did not sign the Comprehensive (Nuclear) Test Ban Treaty, which provoked India not to sign either. Though Presidents Bush the Elder and Clinton pressed for anti-proliferation treaties, their bureaucracies—especially the Pentagon—blocked them. So did leading congressional Republicans. The US has not signed conventions, unsigned them later, or been a grudging member in technical violation of their norms.[19]

Assistant Secretary of State for Disarmament, John Bolton, recently sabotaged the Fifth Annual Review Conference of the Biological Weapons Convention by rejecting its agreed Protocol and offering new proposals only hours before the end of the conference. He said the Protocol's proposals "merely defer to slow moving multilateral mechanisms that are oblivious to what is happening in the real world. … By giving proliferators the BWC stamp of approval, the Protocol would have given them a 'safe harbor,' while lulling us into a false sense of security." Yet the Protocol text did strengthen the existing Convention, whereas Bolton's statement explicitly rejected any language which would strengthen multilateral action, establish legally binding measures, or invoke the authority of other international treaties.[20] The US was in reality declaring an alternative policy of unilateralism, which it would enforce only on its enemies. Hollow laughter from around the world greeted this so-called anti-proliferation policy.

Greater nuclear threat would also result if members of the present nuclear club deployed its weapons more actively. Nuclear weapons have been traditionally thought legitimate only in cases of retaliation against a prior nuclear attack or against "an immediate threat to national survival" (like a large-scale Soviet invasion of Western Europe). Otherwise a normative "firewall" was erected between nuclear and all other weapons. But under Bush the Younger the US is breaching this firewall in two ways. First, it is deploying the Star Wars anti-missile defense system. If this actually works, then the US could then also use its nuclear weapons offensively, since the system could destroy missiles sent in retaliation. The world remembers that the US has actually used them offensively, twice. This threat has already forced Russia and China to actively consider such defenses as well. Second, the 2001 Defense Posture Review stated that "nuclear weapons could be employed against targets able to withstand nonnuclear attacks (for example, deep underground bunkers or bioweapon facilities)." This suggests that the US might use nuclear weapons simply if its other weapons fail to eradicate targets like deep bunkers. The US Strategic Command (STRATCOM) was in January 2003 given authority to consider the full range of weapons, including nuclear ones, when confronted by enemy forces in Iraq. Some believe that the choice of which weapons to use was delegated to the military.[21] The US itself constitutes the biggest present threat of nuclear proliferation.

So US anti-proliferation policy is primarily aimed against poorer, unfriendly countries, then against poorer, friendly ones, then against other rich countries, leaving the US completely unscathed. This does not inspire confidence around the world. Why should other states disarm if it only increases American military preponderance? If considered unfriendly by the US, they have a greater incentive to acquire and develop WMDs as a deterrent against the US. That is the enormous flaw in present US unilateralism. Of course, American unilateralism might be accepted if the US was seen as being truly benevolent by other states across the world. But it is not. Indeed, it is actively demanding regime change.

4. *Multilateralism.* Offer the carrot and stick jointly through the greater powers collectively or through the UN as a whole. Present nuclear policy preserves the existing nuclear club. The Nuclear Non-Proliferation Treaty allows the US, Britain, France, Russia and China to keep them, while others are barred. A blind eye is also turned toward Israel, India and Pakistan. The Missile Technology Control Regime allows the advanced countries to possess unlimited ballistic missiles, but obliges them to ban sales of missile technology to others. Two senior Indian security experts expressed understandable resentment, saying,

"underlying the proposition that advanced industrial nations have a right to develop sophisticated weapons, while the developing nations do not, appears to be the old attitude of 'white man's burden'."[22] Resentment bred defiance in the Indian case. The UN route can offer more legitimacy for sanctions and more burden-sharing for economic incentives, while compliance is enforced by UN weapons inspection. If it fails, the UN might pass a resolution authorizing military intervention. The US would have to lead this, but following this route might bring the approval of much of the world.

The chemical and biological conventions, the nuclear non-proliferation treaty (NNPT), and the Comprehensive Test Ban Treaty (CTBT) have been signed by most of the world's states. They affirm common norms, reinforced by inspections and penalties for transgression. They are effective in stopping proliferation among countries who do not feel greatly threatened. Six countries actually abandoned nuclear weapons or programs during the 1990s: Ukraine, Belarus, Kazakhstan, South Africa, Brazil and Argentina. The nuclear pact holds the best, then the chemical, then the biological. There is no pact for ballistic missiles, which is an active area of proliferation. But the treaties have little effect on non-signers, especially determined, secretive violators. Concealing nuclear exports is not easy, but chemical and biological components can be concealed amid "dual-use" industrial exports. So enforcement focuses on key technological "choke-points," components which are essential to the production of weapons but which are easily targetable by inspectors. All this slows but does not completely stop proliferation.[23]

Nor is the UN Security Council an ideal enforcement body, since it often stalls amid wrangles between the permanent members. Even when united, the Security Council's actions slow down but do not stop violators hell-bent on acquiring WMDs. Iraq, North Korea and Israel try to evade; and the US itself ignores all multilateral programs. The world might also want the US to disarm, but who can enforce that? Inspection works quite well for nuclear and ballistic weapons, less well for chemical and biological weapons, which are easier to conceal. In 1995 UNSCOM was within weeks of giving Iraq a clean bill of health when unexpected defections of Iraqi leaders provided evidence of severe chemical violations. Even then, the UNSCOM inspectors did not find everything, though they greatly reduced Iraq's weapons stocks.

For intelligence and military pressure the UN relies heavily on the US. A joint UN/US program of sanctions and military pressure produced some results in the case of Libya, which did hand over for trial the two suspects in the Lockerbie bombing. It required years of patient diplomacy, designed to obtain specific ends with the promise of definite benefits if Libya did compromise—a carrot-and-stick program. In general, however, the US and the UN have not often seen eye to eye and each has subverted the supposed common policy, as we shall see in the case of Iraq.[24]

Without all this combined US/UN activity, more states would possess WMDs. But successes have been offset by the cumulative spread of weaponry. Offsetting the six renouncers of nuclear weapons are three recent acquirers, India, Pakistan and North Korea. Each new member of the WMD club becomes a possible further proliferater. If, say, North Korea, Iraq and Iran all now developed and exported WMD technology, the floodgates might open. Other countries might feel forced to arm against them or with their help. The world would then be bristling with WMDs. More anti-proliferation teeth might be necessary, but only the US can provide them, yet the US bites selectively, encouraging threatened states to acquire WMDs.

So all four alternatives have problems. I explore them further with respect to North Korea and Iraq in Chapters 7 and 8.

2. Guerrillas

Guerrillas present the second threat to American militarism. They operate with much less technology and organization. The symbol here is the name of a Russian peasant tank sergeant in World War II, frustrated that he and his comrades were worse armed than the German enemy. Mikhail Kalashnikov perfected his *Automat Kalashnikov* in 1947, hence its acronym, the AK-47. His self-loading, automatic assault rifle is the most widely available weapon in the world. There are an estimated one hundred million of them in circulation. Its durability and simplicity—it has just nine moving parts—makes it easy to produce and clone. It can be handled by child soldiers and became a symbol of national liberation movements around the world. Its image appears on Mozambique's national flag and it features on six national coats of arms. It is also very cheap, selling on the Eurasian black market from $200 to $1,000. The less accurate ones then get recycled to Africa, where they sell for only $15, about the cost of a large sack of corn. For his invention Kalashnikov got medals galore, but not a kopek. Now in his eighties, he says:

"I'm proud of my invention, but I'm sad that it is used by terrorists. I would prefer to have invented a machine that people could use and that would help farmers with their work—for example a lawnmower."

His is not the only such weapon. Slightly higher-tech are hand- or shoulder-held surface-to-air and anti-tank weapons like the Russian SA-7 (Strela-2M) missiles being widely smuggled around the world. Though mostly old and unreliable, they cost only a few hundred dollars and have downed American Black Hawk helicopters in Somalia, Russian Mi-26 helicopters in Chechnya, and they narrowly missed the passenger plane bringing back Israeli tourists from Kenya in November 2002. Better-quality ones downed US helicopters in Iraq in 2003. American Stinger missiles are apparently more reliable, but rarer and more expensive, at over $1,000 each.

The collapse of the Soviet bloc produced an enormous global supply of hand- and shoulder-held weapons, now challenging the more advanced weaponry of states and terrorizing unarmed civilians. Ironically, this hero of the Soviet Union's invention challenges the power of Russia, since a single Chechen fighter cradling a $250 anti-tank rocket-propelled grenade-launcher can pop up out of a hiding-place behind a $1 million Russian tank and destroy it—if the Russian infantrymen supposedly guarding the tank do not wish to expose themselves to Chechen AK-47s. In August 2002, a Strela surface-to-air missile killed 114 Russian troops being carried by an Mi-26 helicopter. In September a bomb placed in a Russian police station killed dozens of security policemen. Bands of fighters like these Chechens have easy access to one of the best organized and most transnational of global industries. In 2001 over 600 companies in 95 states were manufacturing small arms. Many were conniving for profit in evading the end-user licensing laws which supposedly govern arms.[25]

Aided by arms manufacturers and smugglers, this revolution has the opposite effect to the first RMA, leveling the playing-field between combatants of very different technological capacity. The weaker states of the South are the most vulnerable. Somalia, the Congo, Liberia and the Ivory Coast are laid waste by low-tech civil wars. Even powerful states like Russia, India, the Philippines and Indonesia have not been able to pacify some of their peripheral areas—Chechnya, Kashmir, the Southern Philippines or Aceh. They, plus states with segregated ethnic populations, like Israel, face guerrillas able to merge into a local disaffected population. Israel finds that its American F-16s and M-16s cannot finish off Palestinian gangs armed only with AK-47s and home-made bombs. That is the military reason why the number of low-intensity wars around the world has increased, and why the world has become more Hobbesian.

None of these paramilitaries should threaten the US, since it has not ruled in foreign lands. But an attempted territorial Empire changes that immediately, and so might an invasion of a foreign country. Since few states can stand up to US offensive fire-power in the field, resistance would have to come from guerrilla tactics, with forces dispersed into forests or cities, where they could live among the people, harrying rather than frontally assaulting US forces. RMA aerial surveillance and bombing techniques may mean that even rural guerrillas can no longer hide very effectively, though cities could resist—as we see in Iraq. Though the US could respond with wholesale bombing of cities, even the new imperialists recognize that too many civilian casualties would make Empire impossible. The term "guerrilla," little warrior, was invented by weak Spanish opponents of the great Napoleonic Empire. They helped make it very short-lived.

3. Terrorists

Terrorists overlap with paramilitaries, and they also use the weapons just discussed. But their arsenal became complete on October 23, 1983. On that day two Hezbollah militants drove a truck filled with explosives into the multinational peacekeeping force headquarters in Beirut, Lebanon. When they detonated it, 241 American servicemen were killed. In a separate attack 58 French paratroopers were killed. Since the bombers had accepted that they too would die, they became the first suicide-bombers of modern times. The attack was provoked by Western troop incursions into the Lebanon, which were increasingly targeting guerrillas operating from refugee camps. Hezbollah was more of a Lebanese nationalist than an Islamist movement. In fact, the clerics among its leaders tended to oppose the new tactic, saying Islam could not justify suicide. But the tactic was so effective that it began to spread across much of the Muslim world. Bombers often attack military targets, especially isolated police or army outposts, or patrols straying into territories they control. But where armies are strong and vigilant, guerrillas have difficulty killing soldiers. They tend then to turn to easier civilian targets.

Despite current stereotypes, suicide bombing has not been monopolized by Muslims, still less by "fundamentalist" Muslims. The militants of the secular Tamil Tiger "national liberation" movement in Sri Lanka were already carrying cyanide pills to be swallowed in case of capture. In 1987, influenced by Hezbollah, they began strapping bombs to their chests. So far almost 200 suicide attacks have been launched by the Tigers, about the same as the total of all Middle Eastern incidents. Suicide bombing is potentially the ultimate weapon of the weak. It has recently spread into conventional warfare in Iraq.

Terrorists have received assistance from sympathetic states. The US State Department identified seven such "rogue states" in 2001. Elsewhere, some state officials covertly support comrades engaged in national liberation struggles in neighboring countries. Agents of the Pakistani security service, the ISI, have aided Kashmiri and Afghan terrorists for over a decade. But terrorists increasingly act without much state assistance. Arms smugglers continue to provide the weapons, while the most effective weapon is their own morale. The Hamas leader Sheikh Ahmed Yassin says, "The Palestinian people do not have Apaches or F-16s or tanks or missiles. The only thing they can have is themselves to die as martyrs." Dr Ramadan Shalah, Secretary-General of Palestinian Islamic Jihad, says of Israel: "our enemy possesses the most sophisticated weapons in the world and its army is trained to a very high standard. . . . We have nothing . . . except the weapon of martyrdom. It is easy and costs us only our lives . . . human bombs cannot be defeated, not even by nuclear bombs."[26]

Britain and Spain had long faced terrorists, but nothing had prepared the US for casualties in its homeland. Even the cataclysm of World War II had killed only seven civilians in the entire continental United States. All seven died in a single bizarre bombing. A church picnic party in Oregon chanced upon a package fallen in the bushes. It had been attached to a home-made hot-air balloon, laden with explosives on Japanese beaches and then astonishingly driven by trade winds all the way to the US. The device blew up in the picnickers' faces when they tried to open it. During the next two wars, in Korea and Vietnam, there were no homeland casualties at all. But on 9-11-2001, inside one hour, almost 3,000 persons were killed on American soil, an extreme example of weapons of the weak. The strong are become fearful.

The tactic may spread. Many Colombians are angry at the US for using their country as a battleground in American's own drug problem. FARC and ELN rebels, with legitimate rural grievances over the theft of their land rights, are being machine-gunned and chemically sprayed from US helicopters and planes. A staggering 81 percent of all attacks against US citizens or interests in 2001 occurred in Colombia. Up to now these Marxist-influenced guerrillas have targeted American property (oil pipelines) not Americans.[27] Leftist revolutionaries have not taken naturally to suicide bombing, since they are materialists. But this luck may not hold. Some may carry their war onto US soil and attack Americans.

Terrorist weapons are easily overcome on the set-piece battlefield. They work much better where lightly networked guerrillas challenge failing states, and even better where guerrillas seek merely to expose the inability of a state to provide order. They terrorize the enemy population and expose its state as having feet of clay. These movements remain fluid and factionalized. From the IRA were spawned the Provisionals and the Real IRA. They are confronted by several loyalist paramilitaries, currently killing each other. Palestine now has the PLO, the Popular Front for the Liberation of Palestine, the Al-Aqsa Martyrs Brigade, Hamas and the Palestinian Islamic Jihad. Colombia has the rival FARC, the ELN and numerous rightist paramilitaries. New groups of fighters split off to form their own factions. They are difficult to suppress when they can "live among the people." They need finances, but not much. AK-47s, semtech, fuses, trigger systems and mobile phones are cheap. Bomb-making techniques are widely diffused, mythically through the Internet, in reality through printed manuals and instruction from veteran terrorists like the IRA and Hezbollah. Major plots cost major dollars. 9-11 may have cost between $200,000 and $500,000 to accomplish, though this was not much to bin Laden and wealthy sympathizers.[28] Irish Americans used to fund the IRA; Saudis and others fund the Palestinian paramilitaries.

There is one further degenerate spin-off. These paramilitaries work best of all in failed states, where Kalashnikov-wielding youths can terrorize the local unarmed population and their leaders can finance them by extorting from the unarmed people or by seizing easily transportable high-value goods like diamonds or cobalt. Many such paramilitaries operate in Africa. These are the truly desperate places of the world, its "black holes," sucking whole populations into violence, terror, extortion, famine and death. The weakest of all are those without weapons.

States in the South of the world are the most threatened. But even US defenses are not impregnable. The military giant is vulnerable to small rats scuttling undetected around its feet, armed with "weapons of the weak." Perhaps the giant cannot keep order in its own homeland, let alone its Empire. Terrorists form not armies, but loose networks. Such an amorphous enemy may induce paranoia. Terrorists seem to be everywhere and nowhere. As Bush the Younger says, in his inimitable way, "When I was coming up, with what was a dangerous world, we knew exactly who they were. It was us versus them, and it was clear who them were. Today we're not so sure who the they are, but we know they're there."

How does he fight such an invisible enemy? Not with advanced weapons systems—not with nuclear weapons, tanks or smart bombs. Terrorist networks present difficulties not previously faced even by security agencies. Communist parties have central committees; foreign embassies have fixed locations and personnel. Since this is low-tech militarism, the vital resource is manpower—not ours (we have plenty), but theirs. The key issue is less today's committed militants, for terrorists/freedom fighters are resigned to heavy losses. It is rather how to stop future sympathizers from signing on as their replacements. The crucial struggle is over the hearts and minds of the civilian population from whom terrorists are drawn. Why do some of them attack us? Is there a way we might change their minds? Why should 19 young men from Saudi Arabia and the Yemen, half a world away, attack us so brutally? As Syrian President Bashar al-Assad said, "It would be better to eradicate the causes rather than waste time condemning them." Causes primarily concern not military, but economic, political and ideological resources.

The US is obviously a military giant—rather a dangerous one. Its powers of offensive devastation may lure Americans into believing we can use them to make the world a better place. But can this flow from the barrel of a gun? Can pacification flow from these guns, this base network, this force size and these sacred military lives, when deployed against guerrilla and terrorist opponents? We shall see.

NOTES

1. Data from Stockholm Peace Research Institute, and Center for Defense Information websites, plus Carl Conetta's "The Pentagon's New Budget, New Strategy, and New War," Project on Defense

Alternatives, Briefing Report no. 12, June 2002.

2. *New York Times*, April 19, 2002.

3. There are exceptions. In its South Korean and its Guantanamo Bay, Cuba, bases the US possesses extra-territorial powers and is essentially free from significant local controls.

4. *New York Times*, October 12, 2002.

5. *New York Times*, April 16, 2002.

6. Andrew W. Marshall, "Some Thoughts on Military Revolutions," Memorandum for the Record, OSD Office of Net Assessment, July 27, 1993. See also the *New York Times* Magazine, March 10, 2002.

7. M. Hasan, *John Company to the Republic*, New Delhi: Roli Books, 2001, pp. 107–8, 120; P.S. Gupta and A. Deshpande, eds, *The British Raj and its Armed Forces, 1857–1939,* Oxford: Oxford University Press, 2002, pp. x, xx, 8; T. A. Heathcote, *The Military in British India*, Manchester: Manchester University Press, 1995, pp. 117, 127; T. Royle, *The Last Days of the Raj*, London: Michael Joseph, 1989, p. 34.

8. L.H. Gann and P. Duignan, *Colonialism in Africa 1870–1960,* Cambridge: Cambridge University Press, 1977, vol. II, pp. 5–8, 316.

9. One of the new imperialists, Stephen Kurtz, concedes this weakness: "Finishing the Job: the Clash at the End of History," *http://www.nationalreview.com/kurtz.*

10. The Serbian case does not entirely fit. Milosevic yielded mainly from fear that the bombing might intensify and that Russia was withdrawing its support. He did not anticipate that yielding would cause his own overthrow (which required local political forces on the ground).

11. January 16, 2002, interview, *http://www.amitavghosh.com.*

12. Data from The Monterey Institute of International Studies. See *http://cns.miis.edu/research/cbw/possess.htm*; CIA, "Unclassified Report to Congress on the Acquisition of Technology Relating to Weapons of Mass Destruction and Advanced Conventional Munitions, 1 January through 30 June, 2001," *http://fas.org/irp/threat/bian_jan_2002.htm*; and Joseph Cirincione et al., *Deadly Arsenals*, Washington, DC: Carnegie Institute of Peace, 2002.

13. Though motives were usually mixed. For example, Belarus and Kazakstan also felt they could not safely maintain and guard their weapons; while the last white South African President, de Klerk, also became nervous about Africans getting possession of nuclear weapons.

14. "The Spread of Nuclear Weapons: More May Be Better," *Adelphi Papers*, no. 171, London: International Institute for Strategic Studies, 1981.

15. Their debate can be found in Kenneth Waltz and Scott Sagan, *The Spread of Nuclear Weapons: A Debate*, New York: Norton, 1995.

16. See *www.bellona.no/en/international/russia/nuke-weapons/nonproliferation; www.disarmament.org/nunnlugar.pdf; www.psr.org/s11/ctrfull.html*; and *Los Angeles Times*, December 2, 2002.

17. *New York Times*, November 24, 2002.

18. Michael Klare called US anti-proliferation policy an "ambivalent crusade": *Rogue States and Nuclear Outlaws*, New York: Hill & Wang, 1995, ch. 6.

19. See David Cooper's detailed analysis of US policy in *Competing Western Strategies Against the Proliferation of Weapons of Mass Destruction*, Westport, CT: Praeger, 2002, especially ch. 3; cf also Jan Lodal, *The Price of Dominance*, New York: Council on Foreign Relations, 2001.

20. Bolton's text is available at *usinfo.state.gov/topical/pol/arms/stories/01111902.htm*. See the critique by Graham Pearson et al., "Strengthening the Biological Weapons Convention," Review Conference Paper no. 4. "The US Statement at the Fifth Review Conference: Compounding the Error in Rejecting the Composite Protocol." Available at *www.bradford.ac.uk/acad/sbtwc/*.

21. William Arkin, "The Nuclear Option in Iraq," *Los Angeles Times*, January 22, 2003.

22. Quoted by Michael Klare, *Rogue States and Nuclear Outlaws*, pp. 175–6. All non-proliferation programs have inbuilt biases. If all WMDs in the world were abolished, the US would dominate even more, through its unchallengeable conventional weapons. The only genuinely "fair" policy would be total abolition of all weapons, which is totally impracticable. Realism requires some degree of inequality.

23. For a review of multilateral efforts to contain WMDs, see David Cooper, *Competing Western Strategies*, chs 1 and 2.

24. For how the US repeatedly blocks multilateralism, see Phyllis Bennis, *Calling the Shots. How Washington Dominates Today's UN*, New York: Interlink Publishing, 1996.

25. Amnesty International, 2001.

26. Much of this paragraph and the quote derives from Ehud Springer, "Rational Fanatics," *Foreign Policy*, September/October 2000.

27. "Patterns of Global Terrorism, 2001," US State Department, May 21, 2002.

28. Rensselaer Lee and Raphael Perl, "Terrorism, the Future, and US Foreign Policy," *Library of Congress, Congressional Research Service*, August 6, 2002.

TWO

THE ECONOMIC BACK-SEAT DRIVER

Economic strength at home and abroad is the foundation of America's hard and soft power. Earlier enemies learned that America is the arsenal of democracy; today's enemies will learn that America is the economic engine for freedom, opportunity and development.

So declared US Trade Representative Robert Zoellick, nine days after 9-11. But is it true?

The American economy is indeed formidable. World War II left it with half the world's production capacity and its reserve currency. The US was able to appoint the director-generals of the World Bank and was given the only bloc vote in the IMF big enough to veto any policy initiative. American multinational corporations marched over the world.

But then the European and Japanese economies revived, and other East Asian economies developed. The US economy remains the main engine of global growth, though nowadays this owes more to the massive consumption of its citizens than to leadership in productive industries. There is a slight leadership in high-tech communications and bio-technology, but not in manufacturing technology as a whole. In its overall volume of production and trade the US is only one of three roughly equal economic blocs, level with the European Union, some-what ahead of Japan/East Asia. Nor can the US act unilaterally in bodies like the WTO, the G8, and other global organizations of economic coordination.

The decline of communism strengthened rival regional blocs more than it did the US. Russia's economic links with Europe are stronger than with the US. In 2002 37 percent of Russian trade was with the European Union, compared to only 5 percent with the US. In fact, the

US ranked below two individual EU countries, Germany and the Netherlands. The US has 16 percent of foreign investment in Russia, slightly below Germany's and well below the combined EU total. China's main partners are Chinese expatriate business in the rest of Asia, and then Japan, with the US and the EU level in third place. The former communist powers have tighter links with their neighbors than with the US. So any hegemony in production and trade would be more accurately called "Northern." It is the three Northern blocs which collectively dominate the world economy, providing over 80 percent of world production, trade and finance, and over 95 percent of its R&D. On the basis of its own productive engine, the US could afford perhaps twice the military effort of Britain and France combined, but less than the combined EU. The US presently spends much more than that.

It is finance which keeps the US in a league of its own. Though the US came off the gold standard in 1973, the dollar remains the world's reserve currency, while the value of Wall Street trading is almost two-thirds that of the whole world's stock markets. Peter Gowan appropriately calls the international monetary system the "Dollar/Wall Street Regime." Since values are ultimately denominated in dollars, much of other nations' reserves and savings are held in dollars, for this is the safest currency. This security means it offers only low interest rates. The world invests through Wall Street in the US economy, allowing American consumers to amass large debts and American governments to finance their massive trade and budget deficits. This means that the poorer countries subsidize the American economy far more than they ever receive in US development aid. The US is the biggest debtor nation, a sign not of weakness but of strength, giving it a unique degree of financial freedom. Finance, seemingly so transnational as it races around the world, actually carries an American passport.[1] Foreign investors provide most of the cash behind military strike-power. What could be more convenient for Americans?

But it would not last if the rest of world got so unhappy with the US that its investors withdrew their savings. And they are largely held in securities, bonds and equities which can be easily liquidated. Japanese holders of American government bonds are crucial; so are the OPEC oil producers who denominate their sales in dollars. Foreign investors would only move out of the dollar and the US if they lost confidence in the US economy or US ability to guarantee global economic and geopolitical stability. But as Robert Brenner has shown, neither the US nor the global economy has been in very good health recently. For decades there has been an excess of global manufacturing capacity and production, reducing real profit levels. During the 1990s this was masked by financial dealings which generated the hi-tech stock-market bubble. When that bubble burst, crisis resulted. This was strongest in the US, which was also rocked by revelations that some of its major corporations, like Enron and WorldCom, had routinely falsified their book values, assisted by major accountancy firms like Arthur Anderson. US corporations no longer seemed quite as predictable investments. US equity values are falling, and this also had a knock-on effect on US bond markets. This is a structural problem, not just a problem of a few criminals, since it results from the dominance of finance over productive capitalism in the US.[2] Indeed, the first signs of loss of confidence came as equity flows into the US sharply declined from 2000 onward. The dollar weakened against the euro by about 20 percent, tax revenues declined, and fiscal deficits grew.

This is a problem for the entire global economy. As Brenner notes, solutions would have to be multilateral, involving coordination among the US, Europe and Japan. Obviously, American unilateral militarism cannot help this, especially if it is costly. Add a major war and American overstretch might begin. In the first 15 months of the Bush administration $150 billion went on new military spending, over and above the inherited annual budget of $329 billion. Later wars against terrorism and in Afghanistan cost about $2.5 billion per month. The 1991 Gulf War cost $80 billion in today's dollars, but the allies picked up 80 percent of the tab.[3]

The US and Britain have to pick up the tab for the 2003 invasion of Iraq. Official estimates of its cost began at around $50 billion, then rose closer to $100 billion. Lawrence Lindsey, then chief economic advisor to the President, said it might cost up to $200 billion. He was fired, but he was probably right if we include the aftermath as well as the invasion itself. Iraq might be a second Vietnam in its impact on the American economy. The economic engine was not designed for this. Markets run on confidence and the US does not control them, for this is capitalism. This is the first sense in which the US is only a Back-seat driver. The US should be careful not to exhaust the confidence of foreign investors and oil producers.

But for the moment the engine runs well enough to power three imperial economic policies. First, the US can withhold economic resources, using sanctions to discipline actual and potential enemies. Second, it can provide economic benefits through aid or preferential loans or tariffs or armaments. These might buy general global goodwill or be targeted on strategic countries. They are not mere "gifts," since Americans benefit from the normal requirement that aid recipients spend the money on US goods and services. In fact, the US is quite stingy with its aid, and this is a problem for any imperial ambitions. Third, the US pursues a policy of encouraging the world toward more open trade under the ideology which the rest of the world calls "neo-liberalism." Note that the Clinton administration pushed this at least as strongly as the Bush administration. In fact, the neo-conservatives deviate slightly from neo-liberalism in pressing for bilateral rather than general trade agreements. But despite economic power being primarily a pragmatic realm of human activity, their neo-liberalism is not merely a technical economic theory. It is also a view of freedom, and of good against evil.

US ECONOMIC SANCTIONS

Sanctions will not detain us long. Unilateral economic sanctions only work when imposed on close hemispheric neighbors who cannot easily substitute distant Europe and Japan as trading partners. Cuba has been ruined by the US boycott. Though Cuba has not yielded, this has presumably deterred other Caribbean or Central American countries from following its example and defying the US. The ruthless treatment of Nicaragua, whose leftist government was largely brought down by US sanctions, reinforced the message. These were ruthless acts of economic imperialism, driving communist-leaning countries into the ground. Almost no other country approved the American conduct, but they accepted US domination in its "backyard." Here the US is imperiously, but not benevolently, effective.

But elsewhere in the world effective boycotts require international organization. Sanctions against South Africa, Serbia, Iraq and others were quite effective because of fairly general compliance with UN resolutions. Unilateral US sanctions would not work, since rival nations would free-ride and grab the business. Multilateralism is what makes sanctions successful. The US can lead other nations, but it cannot dispense with their support for sanctions.

AID AND DEVELOPMENT PROGRAMS

Opinion polls reveal that the average American thinks the US spends above 15 percent of its total budget on foreign aid. That would be extraordinarily generous.[4] But Americans are wrong. The aid program is miserly and until 2003 it was steadily declining. Then the Bush administration surprised most people by announcing steady rises over the next few years. By 2005 the total foreign aid bill would be $18 billion, over 50 percent more than in 2001. Even so, this would be in real terms only half what was spent in the 1960s, and even the 2005 figure would be under 0.2 percent of total GDP.

Thirty years ago the UN asked wealthier countries to contribute 0.7 percent of their GDP to aid—hardly a crippling figure. Only four countries (all in Europe) met the target. The US ranks last of all the 22 wealthiest countries, and it will still rank last in 2005. The Netherlands, Norway, Sweden and Denmark give almost ten times more per head of population.[5] US aid is only about half its annual arms sales abroad, while the 2003 military budget plus the State Department's security appropriations total a staggering $390 billion, 30 times the size of the aid budget for that year. Imperial priorities are clear—guns over butter. But guns are also hiding in the butter. Just over a quarter of the aid budget actually goes to military assistance and training programs, and a further quarter goes to "security aid," which means providing US weapons. So in reality all the US aid figures given above must be halved![6]

Some have talked of a new "Marshall Plan" to jump-start development in poorer countries. The original Marshall Plan had absorbed 2 percent of US GDP over the four years 1948 to 1951. This was possible because the government did not really have to raise more revenue. It effectively transferred a small part of the enormous revenues obtained to prosecute World War II into the Marshall Plan. To repeat this now would require increasing present aid spending sixfold by finding new revenue. That isn't going to happen. The US political system is unlikely to invest large-scale in Empire. Yet Bush's 2003 increase will more than double the $4 billion actually going to poverty reduction, adding $5 billion by 2005. The poor must be grateful for small mercies.

Examining who gets the aid brings another surprise. It does not go to the poorest countries. A third goes to one of the 20 richest countries in the world—Israel. A fifth goes to Egypt, which is effectively being paid not to attack Israel. Tiny Jordan, also paid not to attack Israel, rivals massive India and Russia as the next largest recipient. So over half the total aid program goes to prop up the small state of Israel, which contains one-thousandth of the world's population! The average Israeli gets over $500 annually from US tax-payers. In fact strategic rather than developmental needs dominate most aid. Other sizeable sums go to ex-Soviet countries who form a strategic buffer zone around Russia, and to other allies in the Middle Eastern danger zone, and to countries aiding the US in its various current wars. Finally, 10 percent of economic aid does go the poorest region in the world, sub-Saharan Africa, which is something to cheer about. The "Millennium Challenge Account," added by Bush to the aid program in 2002, should amplify the cheering, for it is designed to hand aid to the poorer countries. That might increase the handout to the average African from about 3 cents to 10 cents a year. I wonder what she will spend it on.

Israel is also uniquely favored by getting its aid in cash, with no accounting required. Israel can do what it likes with the money. Uniquely, it does not have to purchase US goods, and it can use the money to build nuclear missiles, synagogues, or whatever. We trust Israel. All other countries have to buy US goods and account in detail for their budgets. Since the Clinton presidency others are also vetted for their human rights violations. Each year US embassy personnel write a human rights report for the country. In theory if it is negative, aid is withheld, though there is fudging in the case of strategic friends.

For many years Israel has also been the largest recipient of military aid. It leads the 2003 appropriations with $2.2 billion. Egypt comes second, with $1.3 billion, though some of it is now on hold for human rights violations. Jordan comes next, with almost $200 million, and then Colombia with $100 million. All but Israel have to purchase US arms exclusively—Israel having to spend only 75 percent of the aid on US arms. Also uniquely, Israel can go straight to American arms suppliers. None of its purchases are first vetted by the US Department of Defense. It is as if Israel was part of the United States![7]

So as a force for global development, US aid is puny. In this respect, talk of a benevolent Empire is mostly cant. The benevolence is much more strategic. The US props up Israel, and bribes others to show moderation toward Israel. It helps ex-Soviet states because it wants buffer states against Russia. Colombia gets most of the aid to Latin America, and Peru is number two, because the war on drugs has spread there. Countries aiding current wars get new tranches of economic or military aid—like Pakistan, the Yemen, Djibouti, Indonesia, Qatar, Oman, Georgia, the Philippines and the central Asian "stans." But the

US does very little for the rest of Africa or Latin America, which are of less strategic significance. There is nothing particularly malevolent about this. Empires reward strategic allies, not the world at large. But this differs from the more disinterested benevolence shown by a Netherlands or a Sweden.

Even this meager aid has been criticized, especially by conservatives who charged that the aid got syphoned off into corruption by oppressive and often evil regimes. The administration responded rather creatively to this argument (which does have some force) in its Millennium Challenge Account, announced March 2002. This would increase US aid through a series of bilateral contracts. Governments receiving aid would have to be "accountable" and adopt three principles of rule:

> *Good governance.* Root out corruption, uphold human rights, and adhere to the rule of law.
> *Health and education of the people.* Investment in education, healthcare and immunization provide for healthy and educated citizens.
> *Sound economic policies fostering enterprise and entrepreneurship.* "More open markets, sustainable budget policies, and strong support for individual entrepreneurship to unleash the enterprise and creativity for lasting growth and prosperity." This is the neo-liberal principle, here concealing (as it so often does) US economic interests, for governments must sign up to US intellectual "property laws," i.e. US patent rights.[8]

Poor countries would compete for the aid funds. They would be awarded points and the highest scoring would get the cash—like a college scholarship fund, officials explained. Since under a dozen countries would get an award, the average one would be about $100 million a year (about double the previous average). Not to be sniffed at, but not exactly Israel. On the very same day these details were released, Israel asked the administration for an extra $12 billion. The US agreed to $9 billion in loan guarantees and $1 billion in military aid, defining these payments as being extra costs imposed not by the intifada but by the war on Iraq.[9]

Unfortunately, about a third of Southern countries would not qualify for the Account since they do not meet "principles of good govern-ance." They comprise a "Deep South," effectively excluded from the global economy. Their foreign investment and international trade decline; their citizens get poorer. Sub-Saharan Africa has almost dropped out of the formal international economy (apart from its three oil-exporting zones) and Middle Eastern and some South American economies still regress. In some of them, dictators, colonels and warlords devise an economy which is profitable only for men with guns—Kalashnikov capitalism. The people get poorer, lose their human rights, and fall to disease and famine.

How can they escape this fate and become "accountable"? In most cases their repression is a response to real social conditions, often ethnic or religious conflict, almost always a lack of more routine infrastructural controls over the country. The state, whether good or bad, does not in practice control all the army and police, still less the provincial elites. It may seek to buy their compliance, but then corruption spreads as they use their autonomy to increase their cut. Corruption and violence is how these states maintain such limited order as they can muster. President Aristide of Haiti (recently denied US aid) probably *cannot* end the abuses quickly or without help. Nor can somewhere around 50 rulers around the world. The Challenge Account might be amended by devising some accountable staging of aid tranches linked to *reductions* in corruption and repression. Otherwise most of the poorest countries will not qualify. This might seem too pragmatic, too accepting of "evil" for the neo-conservatives.

To qualify for US aid, poor countries might try one of four strategies. Some can qualify for the Millennium Challenge Account, though probably not the very poorest ones. Second, they might become an Israel. Unfortunately, there is only one Israel. The third strategy is to declare hostility to America's enemies, currently by voting for its UN resolutions. This is useful, but not sufficient, though being a swing Security Council vote might help. Much better if you also border on an enemy or offer strategic places and bases from which the enemy can be attacked. Pakistan, Uzbekhistan and Djibouti would not satisfy the Millennium Challenge accountants, being corrupt and repressive. But they do satisfy the Pentagon, a more powerful branch of American government. They should remember to bargain hard before they let the Americans in.

President Karimov of Uzbekistan is as repressive as Saddam Hussein, and he is also smart. He delayed the US war on Afghanistan a month until he got promises of substantial assistance, help with the IMF, and no human rights strings attached. Only then did he open up his air bases and his Friendship Bridge into Afghanistan. He got $160 million in aid in 2002. President Ismail Omar Guelleh of Djibouti was not so smart.

He let the Americans in before binding promises were made. He got only \$4 million, of which \$3 million was for increased airport security.[10] The fourth strategy is the highest-risk one: get US enemies onto your own territory and then declare war on them! This worked in Afghanistan and Colombia, though the costs outweigh the benefits, which in any case might not last long. US aid has not helped many countries achieve development. It has helped some small friendly countries, though they tend to be repressive as well as poor, and the aid is mostly for narrowly military purposes. There has so far been no discernible policy of investing in imperial development.

FREE TRADE

Aid programs cannot bring sustained development, unless on the scale of a Marshall Plan or aid to Israel. But aid is much less important than trade. Africa contributes only 2 percent of world trade, and that proportion has been declining. But even this puny proportion is over ten times more important for the continent's economies than all the aid it receives. Recent US administrations have declared that free markets are the keystone of their development policy. Zoellick said in the speech quoted earlier, "the United States is committed to global leadership of openness." The US says it believes that growth flows from freeing up markets, and that market-friendly policies and cutting back the role of government must be the primary role of government. This is called "neo-liberalism" or "the Washington Consensus," and is considered one of the main thrusts of a benevolent US imperialism.

Freer international trade would benefit the main exports of poor countries, which are agricultural and low-tech industrial goods, for low labor costs give them comparative advantages over rich countries. They would jump at the chance of free trade in agriculture with the US, as they would with all the rich countries of the North. These spend more than six times as much in protecting their farmers than on their entire foreign aid programs.[11] But free trade in higher-tech industries would tend to hurt Southern countries, for these are rarely competitive enough to survive open competition from the North. But despite these consequences, if the aim is simply to counter starvation now, free trade might be an answer.

The US has been gradually opening up. The first US zero tariff agreement was (predictably) with Israel, in 1985. Partial free trade with

Canada began in 1989, and in 1994 Mexico joined the US and Canada in the North American Free Trade Agreement (NAFTA), which is moving toward zero tariffs on all goods. Jordan (still not attacking Israel) got a partial free trade agreement in 2000 which ingeniously tied free trade to goods produced jointly by Jordan and Israel, thus encouraging conciliation between them. The US is pushing for a more general Free Trade Area for the Americas, to begin in 2005.[12] In May 2003 the US announced an intention of moving toward free trade with the whole Middle East.

Free trade is partly pushed because of its ideological resonance in the US. American politicians constantly equate free markets and free trade with democratic freedoms themselves. President Bush declared in his 2002 State of the Union speech: "In every region free markets and free trade and free societies are proving their power to lift lives ... we will prove that the forces of terror cannot stop the momentum of freedom." The President implies that opposition to free markets and free trade would be support for "the forces of terror." This is good against evil. It is also absurd, as we shall see.

NEO-LIBERALISM AS AMERICAN INTERESTS

Does the US live up to its own ideology? It has indeed led the movement toward more open global markets. Its average level of tariffs is only 4 percent, low by historic standards. But self-interest is the cause. Most US industries are highly competitive and will broadly benefit from open trade. The same was true of Britain in the nineteenth century, which championed completely free trade. US banks, flush with funds, have been especially keen to lend abroad through open capital markets. In these respects, free trade might benefit the US (as it did the British Empire).

Yet the most protected US sectors are those in which poorer countries specialize. Agriculture is the most protected. US farmers get direct subsidies and cheap insurance if they export. Unlike other rich countries, the US does not give cash to foreign countries experiencing food shortages. This would enable them to buy food and so encourage their own farmers. But the US exports its food surpluses to them "to develop commercial outlets" for US commodities—at the expense of local farmers whose produce cannot compete with the subsidized US exports. This is not "aid," but ruthless price gouging. Of course, all the wealthy countries protect themselves more against poor countries than against each other.[13] They protect agriculture and lower-end industrial technologies like textiles, clothing, shoes, and increasingly (as poorer countries move into these areas) steel and autos. This adversely affects poorer countries. Compare US imports from France, a wealthy country, with those from Bangladesh, one of the poorest. French imports have a dollar value 13 times as big as Bangladesh's. But Bangladesh pays more import tariffs in the US than France does! The $331 million it pays in import tariffs dwarfs the $84 million the US provides it in aid.[14] This is redistribution toward the rich. The US is not actually very benevolent to poor countries, though here it behaves no differently from other wealthy countries. Their development programs are also often full of cant.

President Bush also undercut his own free trade ideology in March 2002 when in response to important domestic lobbies he slapped tariffs of up to 30 percent on steel imports, and increased farm subsidies by 80 percent. He exempted 80 poor countries from the steel tariff—those with no steel industries! Russia, China, Korea, Brazil and others protested and retaliated. Mexico's President Fox said he was disturbed by the agricultural subsidies. From January 2003 all agricultural tariffs between the US and Mexico were to be removed, yet US farmers would continue to be subsidized, while Mexico cannot afford such subsidies. This is American protectionism by non-tariff means. Brazil's President Cardoso (the world's highest-placed sociologist) focused his attack on American hypocrisy, railing against "discretionary anti-dumping and agricultural subsidies used in scandalous proportions to impede free competition." Luiz Inacio "Lula" da Silva was now electioneering to succeed Cardoso by denouncing the "annexation of Latin America by the United States." Free trade, he declared, was imperialism.[15] He got elected.

Honey is not a major player in the American economy, but it is in Argentina, the world's largest producer. Abroad, Argentina is often disparaged as being uncompetitive, too concerned with protecting inefficient local producers. "They don't have any export industry to speak of at all," US Treasury Secretary O'Neill rudely said. "And they like it that way." But Argentina's beekeepers had proved him wrong. Argentina rapidly went from almost nothing to being the world's leading exporter, almost half of it to the US. So American honey producers complained the honey was being "dumped," sold at below cost price. The US Department of Commerce investigated and gave the

Argentine beekeepers 30 days to answer a 150-page questionnaire in English. Few beekeepers responded. How many American beekeepers would have responded to a Spanish questionnaire arriving from Buenos Aires? The result? The US slapped on tariffs of up to 66 percent, causing $50 million in annual sales losses for Argentina. The dumping complaint baffled Argentine beekeepers, small producers of limited means and education, ignorant of the ways of accountants and lawyers. Their low prices came from cheap labor costs and efficient processing plants run by a nonprofit coop (set up with a $500,000 loan from the Inter-American Development Bank). Their case is supported by US importers who say Argentine honey is of high quality, cleaner as well as cheaper than US rivals.

Juan José Baudino, a 40-year-old son of a windmill repairman, began with 20 hives and a $2,000 loan. By 2002 he owned nearly 1,000 hives, and estimated his family income at $12,500 a year. "When I began, I had nothing at all," he says. "I'm not rich by any means, but to go from nothing to where I am now in just 16 years is quite a feat in Argentina, and I owe it all to honey." The manager of the local processing plant added, "as small producers, we couldn't possibly remain in business if we were selling below the cost of production."

"What's really going on is that they don't want to buy from us," said José Ignacio de Mendiguren, Argentina's Minister of Production.

> Argentina is a large and very competitive exporter in the agricultural sector, but we're matched against agricultural economies in the United States and Europe that not only close their borders to us, but subsidize the same products that we make. ... This always happens. It happened with lemons too. Whatever Argentina is capable of exporting, we know that the United States will administer its own trade in such a way as to be able to protect its own producers at our expense.

The president of the American Honey Producers Association responded stonily, "They were unable to prove that they weren't dumping. ... Everybody has an equal opportunity to defend themselves, and if they don't want to do that, they have to accept the consequences." But this is not actually equality before the law, since some do better in the courts than others.[16] A dispute over cat-fish is now souring relations between the US and Vietnam.

In November 2002, the Bush administration announced it would seek to eliminate all normal tariffs on manufactured goods by 2015. Steel would be excluded, since its tariffs are "special" ones. The silence on agricultural tariffs and subsidies was deafening. Since it would not open up US markets to Southern agriculture, overall the policy would hurt poorer countries. Rahul Bajaj, head of an Indian industrial conglomerate, said of US free trade proposals, "There is no question of moving forward, if you move forward in a direction that suits you. They seem to be looking after their own interests ... without being concerned about other countries."[17] American policy is not free trade. It privileges American interests.

HIV/AIDS, malaria, tuberculosis and non-infectious diseases like diabetes and asthma are now sweeping through the poorest countries. The UN says 40 million people are now living with HIV/AIDS, 30 million of them in sub-Saharan Africa. Stephen Lewis is the UN representative for AIDS issues in Africa. He said the war in Afghanistan had dried up funds to fight AIDS, and that the war with Iraq would do the same. A consortium of nations and NGOs was attempting to raise $7 billion to fight disease in 2003 and 2004. But he said, "the response to the fund has been abysmal." He then spoke with a passion which UN representatives usually avoid:

> I think the nadir was reached for me in the pediatric ward of the University Teaching Hospital in Lusaka. The infants were clustered, stick-thin, three and four to a bed, most so weakened by hunger and ravaged by AIDS. ... Every 15 minutes, another child died, awkwardly covered with a sheet, then removed by a nurse, while the ward was filled with the anguished weeping of mothers. A scene from hell. ... You will forgive me for the strong language ... the time for polite, even agitated entreaties is over. This pandemic cannot be allowed to continue, and those who watch it unfold with a kind of pathological equanimity must be held to account. There may yet come a day when we have peacetime tribunals to deal with this particular version of crimes against humanity.[18]

Maybe his passion had an effect, or maybe Bush the Younger believed that the resonant issue of AIDS would counter growing world perceptions that his administration wanted only to bomb poor countries. In his 2003 State of the Union speech he announced a big increase in US funds to combat AIDS in Africa and the Caribbean, from $1 billion to $3 billion a year over a five-year period. True, his subsequent budget appeared to only increase current spending by $550 million, and this was almost canceled out by his cutting $500 million from child-health programs, including vaccinations. But presumably the increase would be bigger in the following years.[19]

But this was more than canceled out by another Bush policy. By far the most blatant protectionism in the world economy has been produced by the intellectual property rights and patents law agreement pushed through the WTO by the rich countries. This especially protects the "drug companies" high prices for drugs that are essential to keep people in the poorest countries alive. Anti-AIDS drugs costing $10,000 a year for a patient can actually be produced in India and Brazil for $300, but under US pressure the WTO was declaring that these drugs infringed the patent laws. This was such an abuse of human rights that the principle of allowing developing countries access to cheap versions of drugs still protected by copyright had been agreed at WTO talks in 2001. But in December 2002 the US killed the deal. The Canadian representative, Sergio Marchi, declared "One hundred and forty-three countries stood on the same ground, we were hoping to make that unanimous." The US negotiator, Linnet Deily, said her country "could not meet the consensus on the issue." She meant that the US drug companies objected and the Bush administration would not overrule them.[20] This made a mockery of Bush's pious declarations about AIDS in his State of the Union speech and at the May/June 2003 G8 summit meeting. There is neither benevolence nor free trade in drugs.

FREE CAPITAL FLOWS AND STRUCTURAL ADJUSTMENT PROGRAMS

But the main American neo-liberal thrust has been in finance, made through the US-dominated IMF, World Bank and other international development banks. Former UN Secretary-General Boutros Boutros Ghali says that as US power increased at the end of the cold war, so the UN role in development began to flag: "Economic cooperation and economic development have moved from being the prerogative of the UN to being that of the World Bank, the IMF and the WTO." The UN Economic and Social Council, he says, was reduced to a body "through which countries receiving aid can do no more than express their hopes and dreams." The UN Development Program's budget was reduced by 50 percent.[21]

Foreign countries are sovereign states, free to reject the "Washington Consensus." But if they fall into debt, this becomes difficult. In the 1970s Northern banks had offered very low interest rates to Southern countries, so they borrowed very large sums to finance economic development. But in 1979 Paul Volcker suddenly raised US interest rates (for reasons unconnected to the South), which meant their interest payments shot up and they couldn't pay. A massive Southern debt crisis began and still exists.

When any business gets in debt to a bank, the bank seeks to restructure the payment of the debt and it seeks to vet the firm's business plans. This also happens at the global level. The US Treasury controls the IMF and World Bank. If they refuse a loan, then all the other international lending organizations also refuse. So the US Treasury becomes effectively the world's creditor bank and presses neo-liberal terms for debt repayment, called "structural adjustment programs." Their primary purpose is not economic development but to get the debts repaid. To achieve this, the US seeks to impose a neo-liberal program, including fiscal austerity (cut government spending and raise taxes), high interest rates, currency stabilization, privatization of government enterprises, and liberalization of trade, capital markets and labor markets, removing government controls. Let markets rule, is the policy. The programs have affected almost all developing countries. They have furthered their integration into the global economy, shrunk budget deficits, ended hyperinflation and enabled some debt repayment. But the side-effects have been damaging and overall growth has been negligible.

NEO-LIBERALISM AS CLASS INTERESTS

Neo-liberalism tends to favor the rich. Structural adjustment programs increase unemployment and widen the gap between rich and poor in poorer countries. Latin America is the most indebted region in the world, and so has experienced most neo-liberalism. Most economists agree that the programs adopted in the 1980s and 1990s widened inequality across most of the continent. Samuel Morley shows that the tax reforms were the worst offenders, since they reduced marginal rates of taxation to encourage investment, and they increased sales taxes to cut budget deficits. So the rich got lower marginal rates of taxation, while the poor had to spend a greater proportion of their income on taxes levied on basic consumer goods. Freer trade was also somewhat regressive, especially in agriculture and in its tendency to widen the differentials between skilled and unskilled labor. Other elements in the packages had smaller and more variable effects, according to each country's factor endowments. Capital account opening tended to increase investment, and so this actually narrowed inequality slightly, though it also led to foreigners owning more of the national resources. But overall, neo-liberalism did widen inequalities.[22]

The programs also contain a pro-capital, anti-labor bias. They attack labor union powers and welfare programs, and are silent on reforms which might strengthen workers' rights—safer workplaces, maximum hours, organizing freedoms, upholding labor contracts, regulating child labor, prohibiting non-free labor. The Millennium Challenge Account is completely silent on labor rights, as is the World Bank's adaptation of the Account's criteria for aid.[23] Neo-liberalism attacks labor and welfare institutions and does nothing to aid workers who lack these institutions. Yet all these figured in America's own economic development. Think how exploitative US capitalism would be, and how violent labor relations would now be, if no workers' protections existed—and the US has fewer labor protections than most rich countries.

Under US leadership capitalism has expanded across the world, carrying the promise of an enriched life, potentially integrating the world stably and peacefully. Yet capitalism also brings class conflict, which has been compromised through democracy, labor conciliation, and social insurance and welfare programs. These have given capitalism a human face and made it more peaceful and profitable by boosting stable mass consumer markets. American workers only had to struggle against local bosses and governments. Now Southern workers must also fight American neo-liberal imperialism.

Today across poorer countries, logging and mining corporations and agro-business seek to exploit land which at present belongs to poor peasants. They are often aided by governments desperate for foreign investment, who sometimes profit corruptly from dispossessing the peasants. New settlers are often brought in to assist the land thefts. Civil wars rage over such issues in peripheral areas of Colombia, Guatemala, India and Indonesia. Land reform would settle them, and the US might assist this. In the peculiar case of Colombia, this would succeed in separating the drug issue from more resonant popular grievances in the country, enabling the drugs war to be fought with more prospects of success. But even after the end of the cold war, US class biases remain evident. The US is not even-handed in dealing with the war between Colombian peasant guerrillas and landlord paramilitaries, or between peasant Maoist guerrillas and the pro-landlord monarchy of Nepal. In both cases it gives military aid to suppress the peasant insurgents. This is not benevolent and it creates enemies.

Industrial conflict involves sweatshops, child labor, unfree labor and police repression. Protest against this increasingly involves NGOs, many of them American. They were out in force in New York during the World Economic Forum meetings of February 2002. NGO and union activists introduced Sofia Sazo to the press on the sidewalk outside a Gap store. Sofia had been a garment worker at the Shin Wong factory in Guatemala, which is a subcontracting firm making blouses for Gap and Polo stores. She said:

> Gap stores in the United States are so elegant and so beautiful, but people do not know how much workers suffer to produce these expensive clothes. Supervisors would abuse workers. They'd throw material in our faces, and verbally harass us. Workers who tried to organize unions or "caused problems" for the plant were fired.

Sofia averaged 10 hours per day at her machine but on some days managers demanded she stay until 4 a.m. and then return by 7 a.m. Like many workers she kept a sleeping-bag in the factory. In order to keep up the pace, employees drugged themselves. "I too took pills to hold up under the hours," she said. Workers were searched on their way in and out the plant. "It was humiliating, they touched us all over."

Her total wage, after very long hours, was US $50 a week, a poverty wage even in Guatemala. "I became very upset at the way we were being treated at Shin Won," says Sofia. "The situation was the same at other nearby factories producing for the US market." This is how we get our Gap clothes so cheaply. But having spoken out, Sofia lives in fear of retaliation by the factory owners. She's not alone. Many workers refuse to talk to independent monitors or to anyone who inquires about their working conditions. Gap initially said that conditions at Shin Wong were not their business, but under consumer pressure introduced a code of conduct for subcontracting employers. But enforcement remains the problem.

Santiago Perez Meza had been pleased to land a job at Kukdong, a Puebla, Mexico, company making shoes for Nike. The plant promised social security, day care, a cafeteria and transportation to and from work. The transportation turned out to be dangerous, the meat in the cafeteria had worms, and workers had almost no rights to sick leave. "It was so hard to get sick leave, we felt like getting sick was a kind of divine punishment," he said. Most surprising to Perez and co-workers was the discovery that they already belonged to a union—a corrupt official union whose officers warned them to leave negotiations to them. Perez disagreed and helped organize a walkout. When the company settled and the workers returned, Perez and four others were summarily fired at the request of the official union. But the strike won notice among anti-sweatshop activists in the US, who protested to Nike. Plant managers were later ordered to end harassment, improve health and safety conditions, and recognize an independent union.[24]

Sweatshops are better than no shops, child labor is better than child mortality. To be exploited by capitalism is better than to be excluded from it. Textiles go to Guatemala or Bangladesh because labor costs are so low there. Raise them substantially higher and corporations go elsewhere, driven by competition to seek the cheapest suppliers whatever their labor practices. Only regulation can curb this tendency of free-market capitalism. Foreign governments are often reluctant to regulate, for they are desperate for business and often beholden to local oligarchies of the rich. The US rarely pressures them, despite signing on to OECD Guidelines for multinational enterprises in 1976. Two hundred and twenty labor union organizers were killed in Colombia during 2001—an astonishing number of murders, greater than any terrorist outrages in the world that year, except for 9-11. The US government deplored this in its Human Rights Report for Colombia but actually *increased* its aid to the Colombian military, which is implicated in the butchery. Workers enter the neo-liberal view of a free economy mainly as obstacles, and the US looks the other way if they are eliminated.

The Bush administration does pressure foreign governments on behalf of other interest groups. The initial contract between the US-owned power plant at Dabhol (the largest single US investment in India), and the Indian state of Maharastra had favored the company, thanks to bribes from the company to state officials. It continued bribing to overturn the recommendations of Indian reports on the deal. Human Rights Watch found evidence that the company paid local police to beat up villagers who were peacefully protesting the company's illegal acquisition of their land and water. The police were lent company helicopters to attack the demonstrators.

So the Indian government sought to renegotiate the contract. This brought heavy lobbying from the company and from the Bush administration supporting the company. During 2001 the company CEO met with Vice-President Cheney, whose national energy task force then modified its final report to include the statement that India should boost its oil and gas production. Why should this be a matter of vital national energy interest for the US? The Cheney Report was issued

after he or his staff had consulted at least six times with the company. Secretary of State Powell also lobbied India's Foreign Minister, Jaswant Singh, warning him that "failure to resolve the matter could have a serious deterrent effect on other investors." He repeated this to Sonia Gandhi, the President of the opposition Congress Party, and to Prime Minister Vajpayee himself. Undersecretaries of State and Economic Affairs also lobbied top Indian officials. Finally, Bush himself was prepped to raise the company's case at his meeting with Prime Minister Vajpayee on November 9. But the day before, the US company admitted it had illegally overstated its earnings by a whopping $600 million. The scandal quickly forced the company into bankruptcy. Its enormous Dabhol complex lies rusting, awaiting a cut-price takeover by a foreign company.

The company's name? Enron. Its CEO? Kenneth Lay. Suddenly, on November 9, the day of his meeting with Vajpayee, Bush fell silent on Dabhol, as did all top US officials. The lobbying was now left to the US ambassador who quietly warned an Indian business audience, "I hear a frequent buzz from the United States that the sanctity of the contract may now be in doubt here, a concern that can spell death for future investments."[25]

Contrast the treatment received by these two classes of persons. Energetic lobbying by the very highest levels of government on behalf of a giant corporation (a major Bush campaign contributor, engaged in criminal activities), but no lobbying on behalf of workers. This is a very traditional bias of US policy. During the cold-war period it was presented as defending the free-enterprise system from communism. Now, with communism gone, the workers stand alone as the enemy. Neo-liberalism is not just an economic theory. It is class warfare. The effect of its programs is to intensify class conflict.

NEO-LIBERAL GROWTH?

Neo-liberals admit that structural adjustment programs may lead in the short run to widening inequality and reductions in workers' rights. But, they say, in the long run class bias does not matter, for the economy will grow and its benefits will trickle down to everyone. This is "trickle-down economics." The comedian Bill Maher prefers the more graphic term "pissing-down economics"—the rich stand on the shoulders of the poor and piss down on them. But perhaps these are life-sustaining liquids.

Yet the theory has not brought sustenance to the poor of the world. Growth would be good for the poor, but there hasn't been much of it around. The 1980s and 1990s were dominated by neo-liberalism, following two decades of more Keynesian policies. But they saw a very sharp dip in economic growth for most of the poorest regions of the world. The poorer the country, the worse it did in these decades.[26] In trade policy, neo-liberals only demonstrated the obvious: that foreign trade is good for growth. But they failed to find any correlation between tariff levels and rates of growth. Trade is good, but free trade is no better than protected trade. It is better to join world markets if you can, but it is not better to participate by simply opening up your markets to foreign competition. And there is another correlation: the bigger the state, the lower the tariffs.[27] So both states and markets provide resources *and* hindrances to growth, depending on circumstances. Effective, equitable states are also better for growth than ineffective or class-biased ones.

Joseph Stiglitz is a Nobel Prize-winning economist, a former Chair of the US Council of Economic Advisors. From 1997 to 2000 he was chief economist at the World Bank. This insider became disenchanted with the Washington Consensus. He was appalled at the Bank's substantial responsibility, through opening up capital markets, for the Asian crisis of 1998, and especially at its response, which worsened the crisis and helped spread it around the world. In his book *Globalization and its Discontents*,[28] Stiglitz mounts a more general attack on neo-liberalism, arguing that most of its key policies have actually worsened crises. Imposing fiscal austerity on depressed economies makes things worse, for it damps demand further down. It may then lead to massive social disturbances which deepen the recession by scaring away investment and increasing government control costs. For example, in Indonesia in 1998 the government eliminated food subsidies at IMF behest, and was engulfed by food riots. IMF-dictated high interest rates also force bankruptcy on otherwise productive companies. Forcing free trade on them before they are competitive wipes out local industries. Increasing foreign capital flows should not be a priority since most developing countries have high savings rates, and foreign capital inflows tend to be short term and destabilizing. Privatization is fine in theory, but the state must be able to regulate privatization and restrain the quasi-monopoly corporations that result. Most developing countries lack such a state, and so privatization produces kleptocratic capitalism, as in Russia. This is a formidable catalogue of criticisms. Underlying them is one brute fact:

the period of neo-liberal domination has seen less growth than did the earlier Keynesian phase.

It seems obvious that there can be no "one model fits all" recipe for growth, whether it be neo-liberal, Keynesian or whatever. Countries must make the best use of what distinctive resources they have, and they are also at very different stages of development. On balance, they should nurture and protect potential growth resources which are not yet competitive, while opening up markets where they can compete. They should encourage foreign capital if they need it but be wary of volatile short-term flows. They should attack unproductive privileges in labor markets and government, while being careful to preserve social peace and justice. They should be wary of over-large states, but ensure that they can regulate and protect the health, education and welfare of their citizens. For social cohesion is good for growth and it lowers policing costs, while class conflict has the reverse effect.

Neo-liberal economic theory correctly perceives that as the economy globalizes and trade grows, economic efficiency requires some liberalization of markets. But to force liberalization on countries before their economies are ready produces disaster, as happened in the Asian crisis of 1998. The opening-up of Asian financial markets to short-term capital flows was the main cause of the Asian collapse. Growth requires less neo-liberalism, more sensitivity to each country's social and political needs and its portfolio of economic resources and comparative advantages.[29]

But the clincher is history. With the possible exception of Great Britain around 1800, no modern country has achieved substantial economic development through measures compatible with today's neo-liberalism. All of them subsidized their infant industries, subsidized exports and taxed imports, built up regulatory states, institutions of class compromise and welfare systems, *and then* they began to liberalize. This was true from the surge forward of the US and Germany at the end of the nineteenth century, through that of Japan and the "Little Tigers" of East Asia in the 1950s and 1960s, to the most recent surge of China and India. It is bizarre that neo-liberals should consider India, China, Vietnam and Uganda to be the exemplary recent success stories for neo-liberalism, since their growth began under highly protected statist economies—two of them are communist—and they are among the world's more egalitarian countries.[30] Alice Amsden notes that "statist" development techniques first applied in Japan and East Asia diffused to recent success stories like China, India, Indonesia, Malaysia, Taiwan,

Thailand, Brazil, Chile, Mexico and Turkey. They subsidized high-tech and export industries but subjected them to performance standards— export targets, local content requirements, investment in R&D, etc. So on balance government subsidies were profitable investments.[31]

Indeed, recent attacks on IMF and World Bank neo-liberalism have hit home. The IMF defensively renamed its "structural adjustment" programs "poverty reduction and growth" programs, though the change seems largely cosmetic as yet. And whereas in the past World Bank pronouncements ignored or condemned states, they now recognize effective states as promoting growth. Education and health programs also made it into the Millennium Challenge Account's list of criteria for aid, an encouraging sign. The high-water mark of neo-liberalism may be passing.[32]

NEO-LIBERALISM AND NATIONAL SOVEREIGNTY

Neo-liberal reforms also produce political turmoil and anti-Americanism. Not among the rich, who (in the short run) benefit from American policies. But the masses often see them as part of a global economic imperialism in which the rich exploit the masses and the US exploits the rest. Southern governments must respond to such sentiments. Since they are sovereign states in a world of sovereign nation states, they, not the US, implement their economic policies. They have their own political priorities. Politicians want re-election, oligarchies want to keep power, and even generals fear social unrest. They may want to combat inequality; they may be protecting their own core constituencies; or they may be simply corrupt. All these motivations result in a contradiction between the demands of the American-led international financial community and the needs of local political leaders. Thomas Friedman has written with fervent neo-liberalism that only the losers and the bloated bureaucrats oppose liberalization.[33] But most democratic governments *cannot* produce short-term economic misery for the sake of some dubious neo-liberal vision of the long term, for in the meantime they will lose the next election. The Pinochet military dictatorship in Chile came the closest to following all the neo-liberal prescriptions, for it did not have to win elections!

Even if they are in debt, the US cannot *force* reform on them. In the global economy, it is only a Back-seat driver, nagging the real driver, the sovereign state, sometimes administering sharp blows to his head. But the US does not steer the automobile and hitting the driver makes a crash more likely. What usually follows is compromise, which may not be the best way to steer an automobile. Latin American governments liberalize the more internationally visible banking and trade sectors, while dragging their heels on labor markets, and preserving social security provisions. Sometimes the compromise seems to work, as in Brazil, but sometimes it produces disaster.

Argentina started in 1989 with a compromise, liberalizing trade and privatizing state businesses, but not otherwise cutting government expenditures. State deficits remained high, and to placate the bankers' demands for fiscal soundness, the peso was pegged to the US dollar. Amid a global boom, Argentina hit a virtuous circle of foreign investment fostering growth which attracted further cash to fuel more growth. Argentina was hailed as a neo-liberal success story. By linking the peso to the dollar, Argentina had ceded financial sovereignty. It had adopted a currency whose exchange rate was set in the US, unrelated to its own economic conditions. When the global economic downturn came, the government had already deprived itself of fiscal tools useful in such crises. The Asian currency crisis began to cause serious problems in 1998. When the value of the Brazilian real plummeted next year, the pegged Argentine peso was unable to follow, as it should have done. Argentine exports were now much too expensive. A decline in world prices for farm products and a global economic slowdown made things worse. Lower exports meant less foreign currency to repay debts that were dollar-denominated. The government lacked the cash to balance budgets. No doubt corruption and inefficiency were also increasing public spending. The central government also has difficulty controlling the spending of provincial governments. Nonetheless, government expenditures were not increasing through the period of the crisis. Rising interest rates and the pegged currency were the factors mainly responsible for the crisis. Governments sought handouts from the international financial community, which asked for the usual neo-liberal conditions.

From late 2001 Eduardo Duhalde's government was buffeted between an IMF demand that it slash government spending in order to get a $15 billion IMF bailout, and massive street demonstrations attacking any cuts. Foreign Minister Carlos Ruckauf confessed, "We are on a knife edge—we know we have to reach an agreement with the monetary fund to save our country's accounts, but we cannot go against the interests of the people." He did not impose cuts, but continued to borrow internationally, now at very high interest rates. In December the IMF hit back, freezing $9.5 billion of promised funds. US Treasury

Secretary O'Neill backed the decision, saying, "they just didn't reform." The reception given in the Americas to his dismissive statements on Argentina showed that everyone assumed he was the power behind the IMF.

But the Argentinians resisted. They managed to regain financial sovereignty by devaluing the peso, ending its fixed peg to the dollar. The peso fell, making Argentine products cheaper. This helped restore foreign currency earnings, but hurt businesses that had invested in Argentina, as well as Argentinians who had borrowed under the earlier currency scheme but are paid in pesos. The IMF said it would establish a new loan program once "sound monetary policies" were followed. Duhalde did implement some IMF requirements, but stalled over the demand that public spending be cut by 60 percent by February of 2003. This would include massive layoffs, cuts in salary, social security and social aid programs. Duhalde said it would mean firing 400,000 employees, on top of an existing unemployment rate of 20 percent. Asked how the Argentinians could cut spending without forcing so many into poverty, an IMF official responded stonily, "It is not the concern of the IMF how it is done, but by when."

Instead the government began defaulting on some of its debts. Since they were now so big, Argentina had acquired power. If you owe the bank $1,000, it's your problem, but if you owe $140 billion (as Argentina did), it's the bank's. So in January 2003 the IMF granted a short-term loan of $3 billion just so that Argentina could pay back its previous loan rather than default. Some IMF members objected to this shift in the balance of power toward Argentina. But meanwhile the urban poverty rate rose to 44 percent and unemployment to 25 percent. The middle class became called *la clase tuvo*—the class that used to have. Stories abounded of people with worthless savings bartering goods and services, of men turning to crime and women to prostitution, and of the *cartoneros*—"scavengers"—scouring the city, stuffing cardboard, cans and salvaged food from trash-cans into handcarts. One man described the *cartoneros* as "ex-waiters, ex-factory workers, ex-maids, ex-something from the 1990s, who step into the twenty-first century with scavengers' shoes, worn-out Reboks."

There was even a little black comedy. Under the headline "Man Robs Argentine Bank of His Own Money" we learned that an Argentinian man used a grenade to rob a bank of his own money. Customers could only withdraw small amounts, since the government wished to avoid capital flight. Argentinians call the ban the *corralito*, the little corral, since it did not apply to the big foreign corporations. The man went into his bank in the town of Tandil and told staff he needed his money to pay for medicines. Rebuffed, he returned with a grenade and brandished it angrily at them. Terrified, they handed over his savings. He got away but not for long. He was arrested. Better steal other people's money since they might not know who you are.

Demonstrations against the government, the IMF, foreign banks and the US turned violent, and over a hundred people were killed. Anti-Americanism grew. They denounced the US farm subsidies and steel tariffs, which hit them hard. In Buenos Aires US banks fortified branches with steel barriers and hired security firms to protect employees from mobs. Argentina's two leading news magazines, *Noticias* and *Veintitres*, published sensational cover stories that Washington might be conspiring to worsen the crisis, topple another president and devalue the peso. Then, it was widely believed, US companies could move in and pick off farmlands on the fertile Pampas. US interests "have already taken most of what we have—and now, they are coming for our lands," said leading politician Elisa Carrio.

The government continued to resist IMF demands and in 2003 the economy began to improve a little. In May Nestor Kirchner, a leftist Peronist, won the Presidential election and promised a "neo-Keynesian" policy. He was part of a new center-left populism rising across Latin America. In Brazil, "Lula" easily won the presidential election by tapping into the frustrations of ordinary Brazilians, who view free trade and globalization as biased toward the US and other rich countries.[34] Left populists also came into power in Venezuela and Ecuador and surged in Bolivia. They spoke clearly—neo-liberalism is made in the US and it doesn't work. This indirect form of imperialism *cannot* overcome determined resistance, though resistance may sometimes produce a worse mess. So the US gets the worst of both worlds. Even where its indirect imperialism fails to instal neo-liberalism, it is denounced.

But who in Washington really cares about Argentina? It has no strategic significance. US policy differs where it has strategic interests. While Paul O'Neill was abusing Argentina, he was soothing Turkey, also hit by the Asian crisis, and pressured to adopt similar structural adjustment programs. It pegged its currency in 1998, and was forced to abandon this in 2001, leading to devaluation. But, acting under US pressure, the IMF readily granted Turkey $16 billion in credits. This was a front-line state in the war against terrorism. It looked set to get double that in 2003 to help the war against Iraq, when the Turkish parliament unexpectedly turned it down on principle. In 2002 Pakistan also suddenly got favored treatment from the World Bank. Even these banks, the advocates of market forces, are not averse to fiddling the books for American imperialism. This is a formidable though highly selective imperial power.

CONCLUSION: A GREATER DANGER?

The US productive engine remains formidable, the global financial system providing its fuel. But the US is only a Back-seat driver since it cannot directly control either foreign investors or foreign economies. It has very limited powers over the economies of the North or other big economies, like Russia, China and India. Elsewhere in the South structural adjustment programs and trade agreements pressure though they do not actually drive their economies. Occasionally, the driver jumps into the front seat. The African Growth and Opportunity Act of 2000 contained a clause requiring participating African countries not to oppose US foreign policy. This was used in late 2002 to get African support within the UN for an invasion of Iraq—though Mauritius had to dismiss its ambassador who still refused to sign on! The dollar also exacts indirect imperial tribute. In principle, the world is free to withdraw its subsidies to the US, but unless the US really alienates the world *and* over-stretches its economy, this is unlikely. For the moment, the US can finance substantial imperial activity. It does so carefully, spending billions on its strategic allies, however unworthy and oppressive they may be.

These are substantial imperial powers. Most states go along with American instructions most of the time. But they dug in and resisted over the invasion of Iraq. In February and March 2003 the US tried all its economic carrots and sticks to win a majority of the Security Council members to its side, but failed. Chile, Mexico, Pakistan, Guinea, Angola and Cameroon all seemed to refuse to vote for the invasion. Perhaps some did not trust the US to keep its promises either. Many promises of aid made to countries at the time of the 1991 UN vote over Iraq were not kept. Indeed, the first small tranche of aid promised 18 months ago to Pakistan (for support over Afghanistan) was only handed over in early March 2003 just as the US was trying to win all their votes. An administration which is trying to cut taxes while waging war will not be able to hand out much cash around the world. This back-seat driver will not pay for the gas. It is difficult to build an Empire without spending money.

Other Northern countries are complicit in the exploitation of the South. They give more aid and criticize the US at the margins. They are skeptical of neo-liberalism and run their own economies on more social democratic or corporatist lines. But their business classes are happy to hide behind the US and let it take the blowback. Yet the US must be wary of alienating the other wealthy and big countries, for their investments in the US ultimately subsidize its more direct imperial powers. The Back-seat driver would then see the automobile being steered in a direction it did not like.

This is all hypothetical, of course. But the idea that this is *benevolent* economic imperialism is not correct. Intentions may often be benevolent, and Americans may believe the rhetoric that neo-liberalism works—indeed that free trade and free capital flows are a part of freedom itself. But reality differs. The US aid program is negligible and subordinated to strategic military goals. Neo-liberalism does not bring development to the poorest parts of the world, and it is biased toward the interests of the US, the North and the world's wealthy classes. To describe this as benevolent would be self-delusion or hypocrisy. This is not good against evil. On balance it tilts the other way according to most views of morality.

It could be more benevolent. The Millennium Challenge Fund seems the most promising initiative introduced by the administration of Bush the Younger. It could potentially offer the basis for an ambitious, benevolent policy of world development. Increase it tenfold, add more social programs and labor codes into it, and also into IMF and World Bank structural adjustment programs. Then compromise more sympathetically toward poor countries on protection and free trade. This would bring more economic growth to the world, and so would indirectly benefit the US economy itself. But if the US continues as at present, it creates a greater potential danger. If it remains the protector of rich and oppressive states, landlords and corporations, if it subordinates its aid program to bribes for oppressive allies, then it will incur increasing global hostility.

The *only* delegate to get jeered, slow handclapped and heckled at the Johannesburg Earth Summit Conference in September 2002 was not some oppressive dictator, nor even some stony-hearted corporate CEO. It was Colin Powell, representing the United States of America. President Bush had not dared attend, but imagine what they would have done to Donald Rumsfeld! Since the poor lack power resources, the US might ride roughshod over them. But it should expect most of them to drag their heels on matters which benefit the US alone, like Security Council votes. And it should expect some of them to hit back, a few of them armed with the weapons of the weak in the name of the poor and the oppressed of the world. To a degree, the US would have deserved it. Poverty does not create terrorism, though oppression does. But poverty is the swamp in which oppression, ideologies of resistance, and mass support for terrorism breed.

NOTES

1. Peter Gowan, *The Global Gamble. Washington's Faustian Bid for World Dominance*, London: Verso, 1999.
2. Robert Brenner, *The Boom and the Bubble. The US in the World Economy*. London: Verso, 2002. Such American fragility is also emphasized by Emmanuel Todd in *Après l'Empire*, Paris: Gallimard, 2002, ch. 4.
3. Figures from *Arms Trade Resources Group*, *www.tompaine.com/feature.cfm/ID/6504/*.
4. See *www.worldviews.org/*; "Americans' Perceptions: World Affairs," *Gallup Poll*, February 15, 2002.
5. Center on Budget and Policy Priorities, Report on US Development and Humanitarian Aid, June 18, 2001 and March 20, 2002, *www.cbpp.org*.
6. These calculations are based on current year totals. Economic development aid is projected to increase over the next few years, but (given the new imperialism) military aid will as well.
7. My Israeli totals add together USAid, Department of Defense Funds, various separate funds (e.g. so-called refugee settlement funds), interest forgiven by the US, federal loan guarantee funds, the tax-deductible part of private donations to Israel, and loans which are never repaid. Some of the rockets launched at Palestinian settlements are only "loaned"! Sources were USAid Congressional Budget Justification Summary Tables, FY2003, *www. USAid.gov/pubs/cbj2003/fy03_tablexp.html*; *www.washington-report.org*; Stephen Zunes, "The Strategic Functions of U.S. Aid to Israel," *Middle East Policy*, vol. 4, October 1996; Shirl McArthur, "A Conservative

Total for US Aid to Israel: $91 billion—and Counting," *Washington Report on Middle East Affairs*, January/February, 2001.

8. USAid, Millennium Challenge Account, Factsheet Update, June 3, 2002.

9. *New York Times*, November 27, 2002 and March 27, 2003.

10. Bob Woodward, *Bush at War*, New York: Simon & Schuster, 2002, shows the administration repeatedly putting the invasion plans on hold while the Uzbeks were bargaining; contrast with "Djiboutians Still Await a Payoff for US Presence," *Los Angeles Times*, December 23, 2002.

11. George Soros, *On Globalization*, Oxford: Public Affairs, 2002, p. 33.

12. Note that the term "most favored nation," commonly used in matters of trade, refers not to unusually low tariffs but to normal tariffs. Only a few unfriendly countries are denied this status.

13. George Monbiot, "Africa's scar gets angrier," *Guardian*, June 3, 2003. Bernard Hoekman and Michel Kostecki, *The Political Economy of the World Trading System*, Oxford: Oxford University Press, second edition, 2001, table 1.4, p. 43.

14. IMF, *Finance and Development*, vol. 39, no. 3, September 2002.

15. *Los Angeles Times*, March 7, 2002; *New York Times*, March 14, 2002. Trade barriers also do harm within the countries that impose them. US protectionism in steel and agriculture hits American consumers with higher prices. They far outnumber steel and agricultural workers. Trade wars should also take place *within* countries.

16. Larry Rohter, "U.S. and Argentina Fight Over Honey," *New York Times*, March 5, 2002. There was later a compromise, but one which favored the US producers.

17. *BBC World Business Report*, November 26, 2002, *http://news. bbc.co.uk/2/hi/business/2513531.stm*.

18. Quoted by John Goldman, "Iraq War Would Quash Efforts to Fight AIDS, UN Africa Envoy Says," *The Los Angeles Times*, January 9, 2003.

19. *New York Times*, February 17, 2003.

20. See *news.bbc.co.uk/1/hi/health/2596751.stm*, December 21, 2002.

21. *Al-Ahram*, 2–8 January 2003, issue no. 619. Available at *www. ahram.org*.

22. See Samuel Morley, *The Income Distribution Problem in Latin America and the Caribbean*, Santiago, Chile: CEPAL/ECLAC, 2001; see also Albert Berry, ed., *Poverty, Economic Reform and Income Distribution in Latin America*, Boulder, CO: Lynne Rienner, 1998; and Francisco

Ferreira and Julie Litchfield, eds, *The New Economic Model in Latin America and its Impact on Income Distribution and Poverty*, New York: St Martin's Press, 1996. World Bank aggregate data suggest inequality widens most in the poorest countries. In middling-income countries like Colombia, Chile and the Czech Republic, a slightly progressive effect usually begins. See William Easterly, "The effect of IMF and World Bank Programs on poverty," World Bank, unpublished paper, February 2001; and Branko Milanovic, "Can We Discern the Effect of Globalization on Income Distribution?" World Bank Policy Research Working Paper 2876, April 2002.

23. D. Kaufmann and A. Kraay, "Governance Indicators, Aid Alloca-tion, and the Millennium Challenge Account," World Bank, December 2002.

24. See *www.globalexchange.org/economy/corporations/gap/*; Tom Robbins "Global Witness," *Village Voice*, February 5, 2002; *www.behindthe label.org/pdf/Sazo.pdf*.

25. Minority Staff Committee on Government Reform, US House of Representatives February 22, 2002 "Fact sheet: Background on Enron's Dabhol Power Project"; Human Rights Watch, *The Enron Corporation: Corporate Complicity in Human Rights Violations,* 1999; *www.corpwatch.org/issues/enron+dabhol*.

26. Mark Weisbert and Dean Baker, *The Score-Card on Globalization 1980–2000: Twenty Years of Diminished Progress*, Washington DC: Center for Economic and Policy Research, 2001.

27. Dani Rodrik, "Why Do More Open Economies Have Bigger Governments?" *National Bureau of Economic Research*, Working Paper 5537, 1996.

28. New York: Norton, 2002.

29. Contrast the neo-liberal position of David Dollar and Art Kraay, "Trade, Growth and Poverty," unpublished paper, World Bank Development Group, 2001, with their colleague Branko Milano-vic's "The Two Faces of Globalization: Against Globalization as We Know It," unpublished paper, World Bank, Research Department 2002; and Dani Rodrik's "Feasible Globalization," unpublished paper, Harvard University Department of Economics, 2002.

30. Dieter Senghaas, *The European Experience. A Historical Critique of Development Theory*, Dover, New Hampshire: Berg 1985; Linda Weiss and John Hobson, *States and Economic Development*, Oxford: Polity Press, 1995; and Ha-Joon Chang, *Kicking Away the Ladder*, London: Anthem Press, 2002.

31. Alice Amsden, *The Rise of the "Rest": Challenges to the West from Late-Industrializing Economies*, Oxford: Oxford University Press, 2001.

32. I should make clear that these agencies do fund many individual projects which help the poor, exploited labor and economic growth. Some World Bank staff also urge more active engagement with these issues.

33. In his *The Lexus and the Olive Tree*, New York: Farrar, Straus & Giroux, 2000.

34. The Council on Hemispheric Affairs, *www.coha.org/opeds/01-Argentina.htm*; *Washington Post*, May 19, 2002 and January 25, 2003; *Los Angeles Times*, November 19, 2002; *New York Times*, May 18, 2003.

THREE

THE POLITICAL SCHIZOPHRENIC

Out of the ashes of Empires came the Age of Nation States, complete with its own ideology, nationalism. There are now 190 self-styled nation states, that is states claiming sovereignty over their territories in the name of the nation or people. Not all states are effective sovereigns—witness Afghanistan, Colombia and Somalia. But in a world of nation states no one else can legally wield sovereignty in their territories. The Charter of the United Nations enshrines the principle of non-interference in the internal affairs of member states, and in reality the second half of the twentieth century saw fewer invasions than pre-viously. As we have seen, no single state can challenge the American Empire. But the Empire would also have to overcome a whole world of sovereign nation states. Challenge might come collectively through multilateral geopolitical resistance. But it might also come from within the individual nation states in which the US seeks to interfere. That duality is the source of its schizophrenia. Behind these political con-straints lie two connected ideological constraints, mounted by powerful nationalist and anti-imperialist ideologies across the world. I shall discuss the ideologies in the next chapter.

CHALLENGE 1: MULTILATERAL GEOPOLITICS

Multilateralism is premised upon the formal sovereign equality of states. Thousands of interstate treaties imply mutuality and equality between the signatories. The General Assembly of the United Nations embodies one nation, one vote. The UN and its many agencies—health, education, refugee, peacekeeping, development, etc.—have a large presence across the world. We owe to them essentials of life like the global postage system and airline safety regulations. Millions owe their lives to UN programs for refugees, famine relief and development. Other International Governmental Organizations (IGOs) help regulate everything from fisheries and the sea-bed to atomic energy and satellite frequencies. They often work in tandem with Non-Governmental Organizations (NGOs)—pressure groups which some say form a new "transnational civil society," mobilizing "global public opinion." Multilateralism is ever present in "soft" geopolitics concerning such issues as the environment, the economy and mundane criminal and civil law. It even intrudes a little into the "hard" geopolitics of war and peace. As we saw, the US has to seek permission of the local state to use its overseas bases; while multilateralism tempers just a little the practice of war through treaties, UN resolutions and regional alliances.

But in this multilateral world some are more equal than others. Great powers constrain the sovereignty of lesser ones. The United Nations Security Council still oddly embodies the power inequalities of the late 1940s, with five veto-bearing permanent members (the US, the USSR/ Russia, China, Britain and France), supplemented by ten rotating non-vetoing members drawn from the rest of the member states. In reality two superpowers, and then only one, dominated the inner workings of the Council. In practice the US has recently dominated UN resolutions, sanctions and military interventions. The US has essentially decided who should be the UN's Secretary-General—for example forcing Boutros Boutros-Ghali's resignation and replacement by the more anodyne Kofi Annan. If there is a crisis situation or a "rogue state" flouting international norms, the US has usually determined whether and how action will be taken. The US has used its veto more than all the other Security Council powers combined. If the US will not use force, there will be no force; and whenever the US wanted force (until 2003), it secured it. As we see in Chapter 7, American power explains why Iraq was never offered carrots, as well as sticks, to disarm. The US sometimes got its way through laborious arm-twisting and bribing, but it almost always worked. From the Soviet collapse until late 2002 no powers dared get together to form a coalition to thwart the American will.

In fact, the thought did not often occur to them, since American power was hegemonic—routinized and mostly legitimate. As Martin Shaw points out, the US became the core of what he calls a "Western state." Violence had been abolished within this "state," or rather bloc of states, and shifted to its outer borders. The US could rely on support from Britain and (usually) France on the Security Council, plus the rest of Western Europe and the other Anglo-Saxon countries—and then from non-Western countries like Japan and its other East Asian allies. The US derived considerable authority from the leadership of this bloc of allies. Through them it also dominated the UN as a whole, so that the US/Western bloc became a nascent "global state."[1] So the US already possessed considerable informal imperialism, even within this supposedly multilateral system of sovereign states. The nation state system did not seem to offer much of an obstacle to American power.

This was because it had been the US and not the UN that had offered security to most of the world. The other states of the North had been under American protection since 1945, unable to defend themselves against communism without American help. America dominated security organizations like NATO and SEATO. Whatever their jealousies and resentments, states in the "free world" believed that their common interests ultimately lay with the US. In military as well as economic matters, American power was routinized and mostly considered legitimate. After the collapse of the Soviet Union, NATO was expanded eastward and former communist countries scrabbled for American favors. Especially in "hard" geopolitics global multilateralism often masked American hegemony.

Why would the US want more power than this? If this is called multilateralism, why bother with unilateralism? US intervention without the political mandate of the United Nations might also incur heavy costs in military, economic and ideological power alike. The mandate brings unconditional permission to use foreign bases, allied troops, the cash to fund the venture and, above all, legitimacy. Europe, not the US, paid most of the costs of rebuilding Yugoslavia; Germany, Japan and the Arab oil states paid for most of the 1991 Gulf War. UN legitimacy also reduces global opposition to any action. It particularly allows states to support actions which are unpopular with their own people, for they can hide behind UN ideological authority and say "We are reluctant, but it is the will of the world." Intervention goes much better for the US when formally multilateral.

The US knows this. Yet in 2002–2003 during the crisis over Iraq, it began to push and pull the Security Council as never before, to its limits. It bought smaller states, threatened others and publicly abused its tentatively dissident allies. Behind it lay a threat to abandon multilateralism altogether and to go to war with Iraq (almost) unilaterally. The US seemed confident in its bullying, but its foreign policy was now schi-zophrenic, oscillating between multilateralism and unilateralism. In late 2002 it emerged only with an ambiguous Resolution 1441 that it claimed would justify war without a further resolution if Saddam did not totally and swiftly disarm. Yet most of its allies and UN Secretary-General Kofi Annan interpreted the resolution as requiring a further UN resolution if an invasion was to be launched. To satisfy Tony Blair, the Bush administration tried for the second resolution in early 2003, but failed. It withdrew the proposed resolution when it became clear it had only four certain votes out of the nine needed from the 15-member Security Council. France and probably also Russia and China were prepared in any case to veto it even if by some miracle the requisite nine votes were forthcoming. An Anglo-Saxon invasion went ahead without explicit UN backing, including only American, British and Australian (plus 56 Polish) soldiers. This was as close to unilateralism as makes no difference. It was a virtual "clash of civilizations"—between Anglo-Saxon and global civilizations.

Part of the reason for failure lay in rising resentment at American withdrawals from international treaties plus its recent bullying and bribing tactics. Yet there was also a deeper reason. The very success of American hegemony over the previous period had played its part. Europe is now much less threatened by anyone. The American bases in the continent are mere shells of what they once were, and the US is considering closing more of them. France and Germany had taken the first steps toward a collective defense force—rather small, but then so was any threat to the continent. Elsewhere, Africa remained turbulent, but the US increasingly stayed out of it, as it did in South Asia as Indian power grew. There were no war threats in Latin America. Most of the world felt it did not *need* the American Empire. It certainly did not need protecting from a tinpot Iraqi dictator. Correspondingly, against such a small adversary, the US did not need Europe or anyone else. Uni-lateralism could work—though perhaps with considerable blowback.

The US saw two main zones of threat, North-East Asia and the Middle East. But in the Middle East American policy is increasingly at odds with that advocated by much of Europe and Russia, and has little resonance in the rest of the world; while North-East Asia, Japan, South Korea and Russia are also increasingly at odds with the US. Will Shaw's "Western" and "global" states break apart under the pressures of American unilateralism?

As Talcott Parsons noted, raw power, unlike consensus authority, is "deflationary." The more it is actually used, the more rapidly it deflates. If the US pursues Middle or Far Eastern adventurism which the other Northern states feel is not in their interests, they will probably not support it. It is not in their interests that the US runs amok whenever it pleases. Will the Northern states support an American Empire? Why should they, if they don't need it any more? Would the US ignore them and act regardless, thus endangering a multilateralism which had so favored itself? These questions were asked openly in early 2003, over Iraq. They were also being asked in private by the East Asian states about US policy to North Korea. The new imperialists might have over-reached themselves. Even the UN lap-dog began to bark. I examine these cases in Chapters 7 and 8.

Nonetheless, American political hegemony has been so secure that it might survive these half-baked challenges. A little more tact might soothe the worried brows of the allies, though tact is not a skill which Bush, Cheney, Rumsfeld and most of their Myrmidons have ever honed before. But geopolitically, the US *should* remain very strong, unless it carelessly blew this strength away.

CHALLENGE 2: EFFECTING REGIME CHANGE

Now I shift to challenges coming from within sovereign states. The scenario is that the US wishes to effect a "regime change," that is to remove an unfriendly government and replace it with a friendly one. During the cold war the US often succeeded in doing this, especially in Latin America, only occasionally through direct military intervention. Then, as the Soviet Union collapsed, it achieved spectacular success, yielding about 15 new, increasingly friendly post-communist regimes, simply by pressure exerted from afar. But the next decade saw only failures. The US identified seven "rogue states," all fairly small and far from powerful (except perhaps North Korea). It threatened them, sanctioned them, even bombed some of them. But all the rogues remained in place. Then it suddenly escalated, provoked by 9-11, and invaded Afghanistan and installed a new, friendly regime. Then it tried the same in Iraq. If successful, more interventions might follow. Threats against Iran and Syria began even before victory in Iraq was assured. Let us assume that the extraordinary offensive military power of the US gives it battlefield victory. If it wishes to instal a sovereign, friendly nation state, can it achieve this?

The minimal option would be Michael Ignatieff's "nation-building lite."[2] This means a short American occupation, training a local police force and army, rebuilding a few infrastructures, handing power over to a client ruler, and departing. This requires that the country already possesses some social and political cohesion, and that the overthrown regime was unpopular and the new regime popular. These conditions might not be found very often. Afghanistan is not yet such a case, as we shall see in Chapter 5. There the US and its client are forced to rule, not through "nation-building lite" but ethnic "divide and rule." Nation-building lite is here a cover for destroying the enemy and then getting out. It does not produce an effectively sovereign state. A sequence of several such interventions by the US would not bring more order to the world, but more disorder.

At the other extreme comes a permanent territorial American Empire. The last big attempts to do this were the Thousand Year Reich, the Greater Asian Co-Prosperity Sphere, and the Soviet Bloc—a rather chilling thought. The new imperialists say that the American Empire will be benevolent, but the Nazis, Japanese militarists and Soviets said that too. Only when Empires encounter serious resistance do they really reveal their dark side. Most Americans say they do not even want a territorial Empire. But the British, the French, the Belgians, etc. also claimed that. Initially, they said, they only wanted to trade. The lure of settler colonies or rich mineral resources pushed them further in some places. But elsewhere they said that only the pressure of rival Western Empires or native unruliness forced them further, into territorial imperialism. They said they still preferred to merely exact light taxes through native rulers, but unfortunately the unreliability of these supposed clients pushed them toward territorial Empire.

For the US to follow the same route goes against contemporary global norms and its own recent traditions. Oil might tempt it. But would any US government be prepared for the military routines of territorial Empire—permanent garrisons from which its troops would sally forth to crush risings and riots, American lives dribbling away through raids on isolated garrisons and patrols, punitive raids into rebellious areas, destroying villages, relocating populations into secure environments? Will it ease the burden of body-bags by commanding native levies, as the British and other imperialists did? Will the US repeat imperial ideological policies—mass education in English, conversions to Christianity, educating the children of local elites, even inter-marriage between Americans and locals? It did a little of this in the Philippines, but that ended in 1941. It began a little of this in Vietnam, but that did not end well. I doubt there will be American territorial Empire.

A more realistic American Empire might lie somewhere between these extremes, offering a major but temporary territorial presence to secure a loyal and sovereign client state. This was the stated aim in Iraq. There are successful historical examples to encourage the US. In 1945 the US occupied Japan and with its allies occupied Germany. The forces occupied the countries for several years, before retiring into bases from which they continued to project force against the perceived outside enemy. Japan and Germany then built up their own armed forces. From 1945 their civilian administrators worked alongside Americans, and they soon took charge of the whole civilian administration. The new regimes were also generously showered with dollars, assisting economic recovery.

The political strategy in Germany and Japan was to lay blame for the past very narrowly, on militarists and fascists. A few were executed or imprisoned, a few more banned from public life. The Japanese Emperor remained, and many who were deeply implicated in the old regimes staffed the administration. The allies then introduced labor and welfare reform to conciliate and compromise the class conflicts that had initially brought fascists and militarists into power.[3] Fascists and communists were repressed, but social democrats, liberals and conservatives were integrated into conciliatory political and industrial systems. The new regimes were popular, the countries democratized, and they developed the political parties and labor relations of Western democracies. They became loyal allies of the US.

This success was also founded on the locals' desperation for peace. 1945 came after six years of war for the Germans, more for the Japanese. They had been losing the war for at least two years, their cities were in ashes, and they had focused on merely staying alive. They felt enormous relief when the war ended. Almost no one wished to restart the war. Even former Nazis and militarists were glad to creep back into the new regime. The formidable human capital of the two peoples then rebuilt their devastated countries.[4]

Could this tremendous success be replicated? A six-year war against Russia or China, resulting in complete US victory over their devastated countries might be comparable cases. But this appalling thought-experiment would not be worth the risk, since nuclear holocaust might be the outcome. But for other, less powerful countries, problems paradoxically flow from a victory achieved too easily. The US would likely overcome the armed forces of each "rogue state" rapidly. Enemy forces might disintegrate and disappear so that conquered territory would be full of armed men and be more difficult to pacify. Victory would come before the local population became desperate for peace, and without changing the conditions that had brought the rogues into power in the first place. Saddam Hussein's ferocious rule did not result simply from his own whims. This is not an easy country to hold together. We cannot simply remove him and bring order to Iraq. Germany and Japan were ethnically homogeneous, and the allies offered genuine solutions to the class conflicts which had helped bring fascism and militarism to them. These solutions were devised from the allies' own experience in compromising class conflict. Regime change today would have to devise comparable solutions to the internal conflicts of today's nation states. Nowadays these are mainly ethnic and religious conflicts.

Everything turns on finding loyal clients who have effective sovereignty over the country. This is what Japanese and German elites provided. This was also the key in the permanent Empires of history. In reality most Empires ruled "indirectly," through native elites. We saw in Chapter 1 that their armies were mostly composed of locals, and this was also true of the civilian administration. In British West Africa the governors and district commissioners were British, and they had small mixed British/local staffs. But they ruled through local princes, chiefs and community councils whose "native administrations," including courts, public works, and tax-gathering administrators, greatly outnumbered the handful of British civil servants. Typically a commissioner plus one or two British political officers would rule over a territory of over one thousand square miles.[5]

In the Age of Empire imperialists did not have to attempt "nation-building" because the only nations were European ones. Colonies contained only village, tribal and regional networks of patrons and clients. You pledged allegiance to your kin and then to whoever could best offer your kin the most effective patronage. The British or the Belgians entered these networks as merely the most powerful patron. There was rarely dishonor in locals pledging allegiance to them, and interest could overcome it. The Baganda monarchy did well out of British rule in Uganda; the Tutsi monarchy and most Tutsi clan chiefs did well out of the Belgians in Rwanda. Not all went smoothly. Native elites excluded from rule often rebelled. The imperial response was a mixture of repression and divide and rule. But discontent was usually only local. "Third World" nationalism, aided by liberal, socialist and fascist ideas from Europe, only began to sustain broader-based rebellions in the twentieth century. Then they quickly dismantled the Empires—not a good omen for an American Empire.

Different clients emerged in the more "informal" American Empire stretching across the "Third World" during the cold war. This "war" blended Great Power rivalry with struggles between classes and political creeds. The USSR and China said they supported the world's workers and peasants through proletarian democracy. The US supported property and liberal democracy. Politically the US had the edge, since most people prefer liberal to proletarian democracy, but the US informal Empire was essentially ruled through the local propertied classes. It had powerful clients, normally accustomed to rule.

The system required some repression. The US intervened militarily against revolutionary movements or mildly leftist-leaning governments, confident it could then rule indirectly, through local oligarchies. Leftists denounced them as a *comprador burguesia* (a bought bourgeoisie), which was true enough. The US Army's School of the Americas at Fort Benning, Georgia, helped train their military and police forces in nasty counter-insurgency methods. It was not real democracy, but in the Age of Class Struggle, class interests usually produced loyal clients.

The Age of Empires is over, the Age of Class Struggle is in decline, though it has not passed entirely. As the last chapter showed, American economic policy favors the global rich at the expense of the poor, so it does find some support from the world's upper classes. Yet in the Age of Nation States, they are more constrained by its dominant ideology, nationalism. Aiding the US after it has invaded your country opens you to the charge of treason. It becomes more difficult to find clients, especially in democracies. Few of America's newer clients are democracies, since the people dislike and resist imperialism, and their regimes' support for the US needs bolstering by repression.

Since this Age is also beset by rival ethnic/religious claims to the nation, the US might play off rival groups against one another. In Iraq this would play off Shiite and Sunni Muslims and Kurds. The US invasion aimed to overthrow the Sunni clans dominating the Saddam regime. But dividing and ruling in traditional imperial fashion weakens social order. It is better to conciliate all the important groups, and the US recognized this—and so sought to restrain Kurdish aspirations for autonomy. But the US has no expertise in ethnic/religious conciliation. Quite the reverse. In 1945 the Western allies already knew how to conciliate class conflicts. The US has no solutions in its kit-bag for ethnic and religious conflict. In fact, as we shall see, its policies actually inflame tensions between Muslims and Christians/Jews, and between Arabs and the West. The effect of invasion on Iraq—a more modern country than Afghanistan—brings rival dangers, on the one hand intensifying ethnic conflicts, on the other hand intensifying a nationalism which would seek to defend Iraq.[6] Regime change through the bomb-bay is much more difficult than the new imperialists imagine. It may be impossible.

Nonetheless, this section has been somewhat hypothetical, since the US has no recent track record of even temporary territorial imperialism. It would have to develop the necessary skills from scratch. In Iraq, if it wished to become popular, it would also have to change its fundamental policies toward the Middle East. It is conceivable, though not likely, that it could do so. We shall see its initial success rate manifested in chapters on Afghanistan and Iraq.

CHALLENGE 3: DISLOYAL CLIENT STATES

But I move on, assuming that success has been achieved. The US and/or the UN has installed a client regime which keeps sufficient order to allow foreign troops to withdraw. How then is it *kept* loyal? Here we do have a long track record to go on, since the US has had many allies and clients. Allies such as the other Anglo-Saxons and most West Europeans are culturally so similar to the US their loyalty is almost unthinking. Shared fear works too. Japan and Germany stayed loyal because they feared the Soviet Union, and Japan also feared China. South Korea and the US have both feared North Korea, and the Colombian government and the US both fear leftist insurgents in Colombia. These have been fairly solid alliances based on a common sense of threat. But the cold war is mostly gone, and the US and its allies have very few enemies left.

Since the Middle East is where the US most needs clients today, I focus there. Unfortunately for the US, the region is culturally fairly alien to it, while only a few states are threatened by the states the US defines as its enemies. Most conflicts are either between American allies (e.g. Israel and Arab states) or between states which are both enemies of the US (Iran versus Iraq). This does not look promising, but I examine three of them to see if they are reliable clients.

Israel gets over a third of US total foreign aid. During the televised presidential foreign-policy debate of 2000, George Bush and Al Gore both mentioned only one ally by name, Israel. It no longer survives *because* of American support, since it is the strongest military power in the region. Nonetheless, Israel *should* be loyal.

Yet Israel is a sovereign nation state, with an ethnic and increasingly religious base to its sense of collective identity. Israeli governments primarily pursue the national interests of Jews against Arabs. Since most Jews still see themselves as greatly threatened, all governments have tended to strike out ferociously when perceiving even quite slight threats from Arabs. The US interest is to ensure peace, stability and free markets, especially in oil. As part of this, it guarantees the existence of Israel. But now that Israel is secure, the primary US goal should be to ensure a peaceful settlement of the Israeli/Palestinian conflict. That is why Presidents devoted so much time to the issue during the 1990s. Though the US could hardly be considered neutral in the conflict, it tried to act as an honest broker during actual negotiations. President Clinton came quite close to success.

The Bush administration abandoned this stance. Some of its members (especially Feith, Perle and Wolfowitz) abandoned it long ago. But Bush himself appears to have been pushed in this direction recently, and primarily by Ariel Sharon. Over the last two years Sharon has shown that he is in practice no mere client of the US. Ultra-confident of US support, he feels free to pursue Israel's national interests as he sees them, without reference to US policy goals. Together with other Israeli leaders, he seized joyfully on the American war against terrorism, immediately declaring that its war was his war too. They were very important in the US equating national (e.g. Hamas) with international (e.g. al-Qaeda) terrorists. Sharon quickly won Bush's confidence and friendship for his toughness on terrorism.[7] Since Bush lacks the concept of "state terrorism"—especially in an ostensible democracy like Israel—he finds it difficult to regard Sharon and Arafat as equally culpable of escalating violence and terror.

Sharon has played on this, persistently identifying Arafat as the main organizer of terrorism. In February 2002 he publicly regretted having let slip a chance to kill Yasser Arafat in Lebanon in the 1980s, saying "I am sorry we did not liquidate him." Next month he declared: "If the Palestinians are not being beaten, there will be no negotiations. The aim is to increase the number of losses on the other side. Only after they've been battered will we be able to conduct talks." He ordered his tanks into Palestinian territory, and said they would stay there "until all terror ended." His escalations were promptly matched by Palestinian extremists. The two were locked into a deadly tango, as their mutual escalations helped each other undermine the moderates within the other's camp. They both succeeded brilliantly. Even their agendas are almost identical: expel all the Palestinians/Jews. Israeli doves identify Sharon's minimal goal as "imprison the Palestinians in several enclaves ... each one surrounded by settlements, by-pass roads and the army." Each enclave can be self-managing, and he "does not care if they are called 'a Palestinian state.'" They identify a possible maximum goal as "expel them all from the country."[8] He has substantially achieved the minimal goal. Some say that his hope for Iraq is that an invasion will cause so much chaos among the Arab states that he can then freely pursue the maximum goal. Whether this is his actual goal remains unclear, yet his goals are not a recipe for peace, but for terrorism and state terrorism without end. The US interest is to pressure its client to abandon them. It could threaten to withdraw some of those immense quantities of aid.

At first it did voice some criticism of Sharon. On March 7, 2002, Colin Powell said to Sharon: "If you declare war against the Palestinians thinking that you can solve the problems by seeing how many Palestinians can be killed, I don't know how that leads us anywhere." A month later, after the first tank invasions into the West Bank and the sack of Arafat's headquarters, Bush himself said: "I ask Israel to halt incursions into Palestinian-controlled areas, and begin the withdrawal from those cities it has recently occupied." He added firmly: "Israeli settlement activity in occupied territories must stop." Colin Powell was sent to Israel to talk tough to both sides. This caught Sharon by surprise, for it came after weeks of statements which seemed to give him the green light to crush the Palestinians by any means necessary.[9]

Sharon paused, but after applying pressure through the administration's hawks, he decided to call the American bluff. He was under domestic nationalist pressure. Many thought that Sharon would fall if he accepted Bush's command, since the Jewish electorate would not stand for it. One journalist wrote:

> The US is Israel's only reliable ally and this relationship is extremely important, but as Construction and Housing Minister Natan Sharansky put it, the requirements for basic survival are even more critical. Following Pessah and Holocaust Remembrance Day, and on the eve of our 54th Independence Day, we are again determined to defend our lives and freedom as we did in 1948, 1967, and 1973.[10]

Since opinion polls supported this emotional evocation of the national interest, Sharon intensified his military incursions and allowed Jewish settlements in the West Bank to continue. Bush capitulated. On April 16, Colin Powell was in Israel trying to negotiate with both sides, but he was suddenly instructed to make no policy statements and return home immediately. He was furious at being so undermined and humiliated, but he complied.[11]

The administration resumed its more pro-Israeli line. In June Bush escalated to demand "regime change" from the Palestinians:

> Peace requires a new and different Palestinian leadership so that a Palestinian state can be born. Today, Palestinian authorities are encouraging, not opposing terrorism. This is unacceptable. The United States will not support the establishment of a Palestinian state until its leaders engage in a sustained fight against the terrorists and dismantle their infrastructure.

Get rid of Arafat and then we will help you, Bush was saying to the Palestinians. The speech marked a victory within the administration by Cheney and Rumsfeld over Powell. A State Department official confided: "We started the process based on the premise that there were two partners in the peace process and the efforts centered on how to get over their lack of trust. We ended up with the premise that there is only one partner."[12] Bush continued to say "no one has confidence in the emerging Palestinian government."

Arafat was not blameless, but nor was Sharon. Yet Bush was giving the opposite message to Sharon. On April 17 White House press secretary Ari Fleischer told reporters: "The president has, does and will continue to work directly with Ariel Sharon to achieve peace in the region. The president believes that Ariel Sharon is a man of peace." No one had called Sharon a man of peace before—he had opposed all the peace treaties, and in his army days had commanded forces committing major atrocities against Palestinians. A State Department official admitted, "We're getting hammered for that quote throughout the Arab world." Yet in May Bush added: "I'm never going to tell my friend the prime minister what to do on how to handle his business. . . . That's his choice to make. He's a democratically elected official." Arafat had also been elected, but he was not Bush's "friend." When questioned in June about Israeli tanks and bulldozers destroying the buildings of the Palestinian Authority, Bush replied, "Israel has the right of self-defense." Regime change was for the Palestinians, not the Israelis.

In December, receiving the Nobel Peace Prize for 2002, former President Jimmy Carter said:

> Until President Bush, every president, Democrat or Republican, has in my opinion played a balancing role as a trusted mediator. Now, though, it seems obvious that the present administration in Washington is completely compatible with the Israeli government and they have completely ignored . . . the Palestinian Authority.

The stupidity continued. In March, while invading Iraq, Bush announced a whopping $10 billion in aid to Israel and then appointed as the first postwar administrator of Iraq an ex-general with a pro-Israeli record. The whole sequence reveals that the US does not control Sharon. The reverse is true. Israel is the tail that wags the American dog.

This is utterly perverse. The region may be strategic, but not Israel. It does not have oil, it alienates the region's oil producers and it destabilizes the whole region. US deference to Israel could not have arisen because of sympathy for Jewish sufferings or for a democracy defying the odds against authoritarian states, for the US gave almost no aid to Israel when it was most under threat. Ninety-nine percent of US aid came after its victory in the 1967 war, and it has been jacked up every time Israel triumphed and the enemies weakened or lessened their hostility. It rose by 450 percent after the Israeli victory in the 1967 war, by 700 percent after the 1970–71 civil war in Jordan, by 800 percent after the Israeli victory in the 1973 war, and by 400 percent after the Camp David accords of 1978. The signing of US-Israel military agreements came only after Israel became the region's dominant military power, and after its neighbors had signed peace treaties with it. Israel was a rare ally for the US in the Middle East during the cold war. It also did covert dirty work for the US from the cold war to the Iran-Contra affair. But this seems small return for such enormous aid. US failure to control Israel is irrational.[13]

It particularly undermines the main interest of the US in the country, which is to conciliate the Israeli/Palestinian dispute. Failure to rein in Sharon radicalizes Palestinians and then all Arabs. In June polls showed that between 60 percent and 68 percent of Palestinians supported suicide bombings within Israel (up from 26 percent three years previously). A stunning 86 percent supported attacks against Israeli troops and settlers within the West Bank and Gaza Strip.[14] Sheikh Abdul Majeed Atta was radicalized into becoming a Hamas spokesman. He expressed a very common view: "Even small children know that Israel is nothing without America. Here American means F-16, M-16, Apache heli-copters, the tools Israelis use to kill us and destroy our homes." He noted that Sharon's offensive had produced the first "field unity" between Fatah, Hamas and other Palestinian militants. Islamists and secular nationalists who normally hate each other were becoming allies.[15]

Could Sharon's policy work? The maximal strategy of some on the Likud right is the complete ethnic cleansing of Arabs from a Greater Israel. Under the cover of Middle Eastern chaos—Hitler's phrase was under the cover of the "night and fog" of war—that horror might be accomplished, though with what future horrors for the region! But short of that, it is unlikely that such a resonant national liberation struggle can be battered into submission within Israel/Palestine, given the havens that the densely packed refugee camps and Arab towns provide. The militias need an inflow of only a hundred or so recruits per year, and Sharon is producing far more enraged young people than that. Since the Palestinians remain too weak to frontally attack the Israeli army, some of them will continue to try terrorism, and this will be matched by Israeli state terrorism. The civilian casualties on both sides will grow. Measured in this ghastly way, the Palestinians are becoming more effective, since now the ratio of their dead to the Jewish dead is down from 4 to 1 to 2.5 to 1, a fact that some Arab media outlets took some pleasure in announcing.

But most Palestinians and Jews must surely be alienated by it all, just wanting out of such a dreadful situation. But how can they accomplish this? Since 9-11 over 100,000 Palestinians have fled into Jordan, further destabilizing that country. Jordan's Foreign Minister Marwan Muashar said: "The demonstrations are getting stronger by the day. The street is literally boiling. We are being forced to take steps we don't want to take because people are angry and public opinion in the Arab world cannot be ignored." He was particularly critical of the demands being made on Arafat. "The leader is under siege and cut off from the outside world, and there are demands that he do more to stop the violence. It is ludicrous."[16] The blowback is felt throughout the Muslim world. Failure to control the Israeli client is enormously damaging. It greatly harmed the invasion of Iraq.

But now consider a second American client, the Palestinian Authority. It receives much less aid than Israel does, but it is struggling even to survive, and US aid is crucial in enabling it to provide its few basic infrastructure services. American pressure on the Palestinians has been enormous, and it includes threatening to withhold the aid. The US repeatedly demands that the Authority cease all support for terrorists. But the Authority does not—it would fall if it did. So the superpower then demanded regime change. But it cannot make this happen either.

Like Israel, Palestine is dominated by nationalism. Unlike Israel, it is feeble, constituting much less than a sovereign state. But despite its weakness, the US cannot pick its leader. Palestinians do that, through elections. In early 2002 Palestinian discontent over Arafat's ineffective and corrupt rule grew. Newspapers ran profiles of half a dozen men who might replace him. It was only a matter of time, some said. Then Bush's demands for regime change perversely strengthened Arafat and under-mined the opposition. His opinion-poll ratings rose sharply. It was obvious he would win the next election, planned for January 2003. But under Israeli military occupation, the Authority lacked the logistics even to hold elections. They were postponed to a date a hundred days after the Israelis left the West Bank and Gaza. Arafat remained in power. His authority shredded to pieces, he was forced to make some concession, and he eventually announced the appointment of a deputy, a prime minister. If he ever did usurp Arafat's authority, no doubt the US would claim responsibility. But in actuality, Bush the Younger had only pro-longed Arafat's rule. At the same time Sharon rode on Jewish nationalist war fever to his own electoral triumph. In this terrible dispute the US lacks control of either side, and things get worse.

Imperial options are constrained in an age of nationalism. At their height the British or Belgian Empires—if they seriously wanted peace and order in a region—would have divided and ruled among both Jews and Arabs or ruled through one and repressed the other. Their pre-ference would have been for the Arabs, since they have the oil. Not nice—but that is what real Empires do.

Israel might be considered a special case, because of its lobbies within the US. So what about a third client, Saudi Arabia, which has no such lobby? During the 1990s the US sold the Saudis $40 billion of advanced weapons systems and stationed over 5,000 troops there, some manning Patriot missile batteries to defend them. The US actually went to war in 1991 to defend them from Saddam Hussein. They should be loyal cli-ents.

They are indeed quite supportive over oil, stabilizing its price within the constraints of the OPEC cartel, though this is also self-interested behavior. But against US wishes, they bought long-range ballistic missiles from China and they even sought nuclear materials to fill them.

They also financed Islamists and jihadis, now defined by the US as the greatest threat in the region. Saudi money finances radical madrassa schools and mosques. The schools teach the purist, intolerant Saudi Wahhabi version of Sunni Islam, and its Deobandi equivalent in Pakistan and Kashmir. From this network emerged many jihadi fighters. When the Saudis realized this, they did not abort the whole project. Instead, they merely expelled their own jihadis abroad, which turned them into international terrorists. One of them was Osama bin Laden, and a further 15 were among the 19 bombers of 9-11. Even after the Saudis realized the enormity of their actions, they did not stop financing the schools and mosques, or act vigorously against Saudi financing of terror networks.

Like the rulers of any sovereign state, the Saudis pursue their own interests. Theirs are actually more dynastic than national. To preserve their dynasty they force local jihadis abroad while trying not to alienate local Islamists. They face the problem that conservative, intolerant Islam legitimates their own rule but also generates jihadi terrorism. They are a US ally but few of their subjects like the US (16 percent in one survey). To survive, they walk on a knife edge, acting deviously and not according to the American game-plan. A sixth-grade official history textbook vows "Arabs and Muslims will succeed, God willing, in beating the Jews and their allies." A US official confided: "When the Saudis get hectored about reform, they get their backs up and say, To hell with it—we're not going to do it."[17] Since they are sovereign, they do not have to. Despite the arms and the bases, the Saudis are not very loyal clients of the US. Some believe that the US attempt to grab Iraqi oil is partly an attempt to be free from dependence on Saudi oil. If so, it is only exchanging one difficult client state for another which is likely to be much more difficult.

Egypt and Jordan have taken greater risks on behalf of the US, and they have been well rewarded. So too has Turkey, the closest Muslim ally of the US. But they make no secret of their hostility to US Middle Eastern policies and they refused more than the most minimal cooperation with the invasion of Iraq. Any loyalty is decidedly conditional. Is Tony Blair uniquely loyal, willing to risk British public opinion, the unity of his own party, and even British lives, whenever Bush leads? Not quite. Australian Premier John Howard also does whatever Bush asks in return for his military protection against possible future threats from Asian states. Howard even borrowed a policy from the new imperialists in December 2002 when he threatened preemptive strikes against Asian countries harboring terrorists. Indonesia must be quaking! Servants like Israel, Palestine and Saudi Arabia are unreliable, Qatar and Djibouti can be bought. But *good* servants are hard to find nowadays—except among the Anglo-Saxons.

This is a sea-change in the world. Client states are nowadays much less reliable. Some states are disorderly, some fail altogether. But the US must not exaggerate its chances of being able to do much about them.[18] In interventions inside nation states, the US is a political pygmy. After inflicting military devastation on a country, it cannot easily bring political order—as we see in both Afghanistan and Iraq. "They make a desert and call it peace" was the description of the Romans which Tacitus put into the mouth of a Gaulish chieftain. He was wrong about the Romans, for after conquering, they built roads, aqueducts and sports stadia, brought in Roman settlers and assimilated the locals. The pay-off was that in a generation or two they ruled through locals who spoke Latin and thought of themselves as Romans. The Emperors came from all over the Empire, including Africa and Syria. The Europeans could not do that, let alone the Americans. The Roman Empire was in a different class altogether. American political powers are *schizophrenic:* in international politics they are large but oscillating unsteadily between multilateralism and unilateralism; and when trying to interfere inside individual nation states they are small. Faced with a world of nation states, the US does not have imperial political powers. The Age of Empire has gone.

NOTES

1. Martin Shaw, *Theory of the Global State*, Cambridge: Cambridge University Press, 2000. Shaw does not emphasize American power quite so much as I have done here.
2. "Nation-Building Lite," *New York Times* Magazine, July 28, 2002.
3. For the reasons why they came to power, see my book *Fascists*, Cambridge: Cambridge University Press, 2004.
4. Richard Merritt, *Democracy Imposed: US Occupation Policy and the German Public, 1945–1948*, New Haven, CT: Yale University Press; and John Dower, *Embracing Defeat: Japan in the Wake of World War II*, New York: Norton, 1999. South Korea did not fit this model. The US did not trust South Korean resistance forces and democrats, and ruled more directly, with the help of military and authoritarian

regimes. This helped precipitate a civil war, though eventually it led to a more democratic and peaceful South Korean ally.

5. See two books by Michael Crowder, *West Africa Under Colonial Rule*, London: Hutchinson, 1968, and *Colonial West Africa*, London: Frank Cass, 1978.

6. In North Korea an alternative nation state is readily available—a united Korea, led initially by South Korea. This may be how this confrontation will eventually end.

7. Doyle McManus, "Unlike Arafat, Sharon Won Bush's Trust," *Los Angeles Times*, April 14, 2002. But Ehud Barak, then the Labor Party leader, also made this equation. From 9–11 he was trapped in London by the cessation of airline flights and so appeared repeatedly that week on British television. Israel had long been involved in a struggle of civilization against barbarism, he kept saying, and now the US was too.

8. Anthony Lewis, "Is There a Solution?" *New York Review of Books*, April 25, 2002.

9. *New York Times*, March 7 and April 5, 2002.

10. Gerald Steinberg, *Jerusalem Post*, April 14, 2002.

11. This is the most graphic part of Bob Woodward's book, *Bush at War*, New York: Simon & Schuster, 2002, obviously leaked by Powell or his staff.

12. *Los Angeles Times*, June 27, 2002 and December 13, 2002.

13. Figures from Stephen Zunes, "The Strategic Functions of U.S. Aid to Israel," *Middle East Policy*, vol. 4, October 1996. The "strategic functions" he identifies seem unconvincing. Aid probably grew as the Jewish and Christian fundamentalist lobbies in the US grew, as the American military-industrial complex developed a strong vested interest in Israel, and as the new imperialists believed they were waging a common civilizational struggle against Muslims. Some neo-conservatives say that to facilitate the Second Coming of Christ the Jews must first control the Temple Mount. Other senior Republicans will not risk incurring their opposition by laughing. As American anti-Semitism declined, Jews became seen as a part of Western civilization rather than alien to it—unlike Arabs. But the irrational is not easy even for a sociologist to explain.

14. *Los Angeles Times*, June 20 and 28, 2002.

15. Peter Ford, "Why Do They Hate Us?" and "All Sides Close in on Arafat," *Christian Science Monitor*, September 27 and December 5, 2001.

16. *New York Times*, April 3, 2002.
17. *Time Magazine*, October 27, 2002.
18. Here I am in agreement with conservative Realist critics of the new imperialism like Gary T. Dempsey of the Cato Institute, "Old Folly in a New Guise. Nation Building to Combat terrorism," *Policy Analysis*, no. 429, March 21, 2002.

FOUR

THE IDEOLOGICAL PHANTOM

AMERICAN IDEOLOGICAL RESOURCES

Like all imperialists, American ones are self-righteous. The politicians utter impeccable ideals of freedom, democracy and human rights for the world, and they promise it material plenty. They say they have achieved this "American Dream" in the US and that they are now bringing it to the world. Colin Powell expressed this self-righteousness when lecturing the UN to heed the US because it was the oldest democracy in the world. When was he dating the beginnings of this democracy, I wonder? Was it perhaps the 1780s when only white male property owners had the vote, Indians were being exterminated, and people of his own skin color were slaves? Was it perhaps the 1950s when people of his own skin color still could not vote across parts of the country? In a survey of young people in five European countries, most agreed with the statement that Europe, not America, was the birthplace of democracy, enlightenment and progress.[1] But then, everyone is a little self-righteous.

American democracy today does not even seem in especially good shape. Only between one-third and one-half of American adults vote in national elections. Most members of Congress have to raise over a million dollars from business interests to get elected, and so inequality widens to a degree unparalleled anywhere else in the world. The media, especially television, from which most people get their news, are generally deferential to authority and rarely critical of their leaders in foreign affairs. American politicians rarely submit to sustained critical questioning from each other or from reporters—and the President almost never does. In Bush administration press conferences journalists typically ask a single question. When the question is evaded (which is always the case with difficult questions), they do not follow up. Questioning by the most famous TV interviewers, like Larry King and Diane Sawyer, is sycophantic by European standards. Britain's Jeremy Paxman (who once asked a cabinet minister the same question 14 times, after repeated evasive answers) would be fired after his first interview. NBC did promptly fire Phil Donahue, the one television network host who opposed the Iraq invasion. It also fired the veteran war reporter, Peter Arnett, who appeared on Iraqi television suggesting to the Iraqis that they tolerate foreign journalists in Baghdad on the grounds that their reports aided the US anti-war movement. All this self-censorship muzzles American democracy.

When the Iraq war started, television and radio generally presented the Pentagon view of the war, and not only because of "embedded" reporters. Theirs was what I called at the time of Britain's Falklands War with Argentina "spectator sport militarism," where the audience is incited to cheer on its own team at no possible risk to itself and with no real view of the actual horrors of war.[2] Television was dominated by obsession with war-gaming conducted by an endless supply of ex-military officers, and almost complete neglect of the wider issues of the war. American newspapers were more varied. Some, like the *Los Angeles Times*, retained more of the critical intelligence which characterized most British television and newspapers. The effects of globalization were manifest in contradictory ways. For some it gave an opportunity to trawl the web for different slants; but I suspect that more got their news uniformly slanted through the 150 newspapers and numerous television channels owned by Rupert Murdoch. In the US his Fox News Channel was especially militarist, and its ratings struggle with CNN seemed to pressure the latter in the same direction. Worst of all were the numerous American "talk radio" hosts who were inciting their listeners into raw hatred and violence against Iraqis and Muslims.

Some Americans are aware that democratic virtues must be earned. Joseph Nye, former Deputy Secretary of State, distinguishes between "hard power," compelling others to behave as we wish, and "soft power," persuading people to want what we want—because what we want embodies virtues. We must zealously preserve these virtues, he says. He believes that American values and so American soft power are globally welcomed. Only a few tyrants and extremists will hate the US and their "hard nuggets of hatred are unlikely to catalyze broader hatred unless we abandon our values and pursue arrogant and overbearing policies that let the extremists appeal to the majority in the middle." For Nye, an American Empire based on arrogance and force would do just that. Using too much hard power destroys soft power and becomes more and more costly to apply. From France, Emmanuel Todd noted that American policies flagrantly contradicted the universalism of values which is an essential requirement of Empires. He saw the increasing quasi-racial contempt for Arabs and the decline of genuine "anthropological" knowledge of Muslim societies and cultures as particularly acute sources of ideological weakness.[3]

In principle, most Americans would respect these warnings. Polls indicate that most Americans want to bring peace, democracy, human rights and economic development to the world. Most say that the US should give aid to help poor countries escape poverty and disease, that force should only be used sparingly and as a last resort, and that the US must only exercise a multilateral leadership role. A majority wants to strengthen the UN, denies that Americans are engaged in a war against Islam, and agrees that the real message of Islam—like all religions—is peaceful.[4]

After all, Americans are taught from childhood that US history embodies the triumph of these fine principles. The Founding Fathers bore them, the Civil War and the Civil Rights struggle eventually secured them. On principle, Americans are uneasy about Empire. But distaste for Empire also derives from Americans' lack of interest in the world. In a 2002 National Geographic Society/Roper Poll survey young people aged 18 to 24 in nine countries were asked a battery of questions about the world. Presented with a map of the world, only 13 percent of young Americans could find Iraq or Iran, only 17 percent found Afghanistan, and only 24 percent found Saudi Arabia. Thirty-four percent of the young Americans could find the Pacific island used on last season's "Survivor" TV show—and 89 percent could find the US. In their knowledge, the Americans ranked last but one of the nine nations surveyed, coming narrowly above Mexico.[5] Shouldn't imperialists rank first?

Palestinians tell of an apocryphal UN world survey containing the question "What is your opinion about the food shortage in the rest of the world?" They say the survey failed because in Africa no one knew what "food" meant, in Western Europe no one knew what "shortage" meant, in dictatorships no one knew what "opinion" meant, and in the United States no one knew what "the rest of the world" meant.[6]

Ignorance breeds fear. Countless Hollywood movies narrated alien attacks on peaceful American communities during the cold war, and they have recently revived. Forty-five percent of Americans believe intelligent aliens have visited Earth.[7] There are repeated national scares about invasive plant and insect species—"Africanized killer bees," "South American fire ants." These have the same subtext: harmless, peace-loving American (sometimes European) species are overwhelmed by more aggressive foreigners. There was the anthrax scare of 2001, the smallpox scare of 2002, the dirty bomb and duct-tape scares of 2003 (seal your windows against a chemical attack). The level of paranoia is hard for foreigners to understand, in this continental country so well-protected by its oceans and armaments. Reds have given way to terrorists under the beds. Americans arm themselves with handguns and tank-like SUVs. Only one in six Americans even have passports, and after 9-11 they travel abroad much less than before. Neighboring Mexico sees few American tourists outside of Americanized high-rise beaches. They see Mexico as dangerous, though the US murder rate is much higher.

Cultivating paranoia is a Bush the Younger specialism: sweeping arrests of Middle Easterners, repeated denunciations of foreign "evil-doers," calls for perpetual vigilance, the extraordinary precautions against the near-zero chances of a smallpox virus attack (several medical personnel actually died from this panic by being forced to take the supposed antidote), the repeated claims that Iraq, a battered, impoverished country of only 23 million people, half of them children, with a rag-tag army, constituted an "imminent threat" to the United States.[8] Since 9-11 terrorism in the US has been zero-intensity warfare. After 20 months it had not killed one more person in the US. Almost 3,000 people were killed on 9-11 itself, a terrible number. But in the same year in the United States there were 30,000 firearm-related deaths, 38,000 deaths in auto accidents, 150,000 deaths from lung cancer, and 250,000 rape victims. The US is one of the safest places of the world, except from other Americans.

But Bush the Younger's call to arms against Muslims appeared to be winning the ideological war within the US. Though most Americans initially said they would prefer a stronger United Nations, and an Iraq disciplined through the UN, Bush's approval ratings on "the war against terrorism" and the invasion of Iraq remained very high. In 2002 a quarter of Americans viewed Muslim countries favorably, a majority favored restricting or ending Muslim immigration, and two in three of them thought Muslims would be better off if they adopted American values.[9] The public had been made compliant with imperialism by fear of the alien unknown and an extraordinarily self-muzzling mass media. Few Democrats offered any opposition to the new imperialism, giving Bush a blank congressional check to invade Iraq as he saw fit—less because they agreed with him than because they believed the people did so. They were right.

But the second ideological war is the more important one. This is the one abroad, where the Empire is being established. Unfortunately for the US, this is not being won. In fact, the disconnect between the American and foreign media during the Iraq invasion became quite extreme. Americans were protected from the war's horrors; critics of the war ceased appearing in the media except in voiceless pictures of street demonstrators. American television seemed unable to accept the disconnect. It focused on France. Suddenly, from being an American ally and a rather respected (if somewhat snooty) culture, France was presented as an enemy, alongside Saddam. Yet most of the world argued as the French did.

Yet America's cultural resources deployed abroad are often rather thinner than they seem. The US was the first to develop efficient mass production of culture, and Hollywood and US television networks used to have a massive global lead. US movies do remain the most popular in foreign markets except in Bombay's Bollywood realm in Asia. But American movies and TV shows are now getting ideologically thinner. Since over half Hollywood's profits now come from abroad, it counters the stilting effects of subtitles and dubbing by reducing the number of words per minute. Narrative drive, action, sex and violence do not communicate much of a message. The major US television network shows present private life in an overwhelmingly apolitical way. They reinforce the style of the commercials, which now occupy 22 minutes per hour of air-time. Michael Schudson aptly called the message of advertising "capitalist realism." Without having any "master plan," it "glorifies the pleasures and freedoms of consumer choices in defence of the virtues of private lives and material ambitions."[10] Research also shows that people in other countries do not receive American cultural messages passively. Popular shows like *Dallas* and *The Bold and the Beautiful* are interpreted in very different ways in different cultures. In any case, what they depict is often so alien from the experiences of people in poorer countries that they are enjoyed as a fantasy world totally removed from real everyday life or politics. The material luxuries depicted, reinforced by local advertising, do make them go out and buy what they can, but if they were to adopt "capitalist realism," they would be extremely frustrated by their negligible purchasing powers.[11]

Indeed, American media are now becoming less popular around the world. TV sales abroad are declining, as consumers turn increasingly to locally produced shows. A 2001 survey of 60 countries revealed that 71 percent of their top 10 programs were locally produced. "The world-wide television market is growing," said the president of Walt Disney Television, "but America's place in it is declining." The US share of the world-wide web has also declined, from a half to a third during the 1990s. In 2003, 32 percent of internet sites are American, 28 percent European and 26 percent Asian.[12] The US does have the doubtful benefit of the world's fastest-expanding religion, Evangelical Protestantism. American universities do attract the most foreign students; and American borders do allow through the most immigrants. The English language is the lingua franca of modernity, and the world's educated classes increasingly speak it with an American accent, though it is the language of business, not of the heart or political mobilization. American media are rather patchy, better suited to business profit than imperial legitimacy, or to communicate Nye's "soft power."

American ideals do sometimes shine through the world. In 1989 Chinese students constructed icons of democracy in Tiananmen Square, Beijing, and in Shanghai as well, based on the Statue of Liberty. But when the US is perceived as not living up to its ideals, we see parodies. After Bush's "axis of evil" speech, tens of thousands of demonstrators shouted anti-American slogans in Teheran. A giant effigy carried at the rally was a Statue of Liberty with rockets instead of spikes in her crown and with a skull for a face. Instead of a torch in its right hand, it held up a bomb; in its left, a book with a star of David, representing Israel. Many of the demonstrators were pro-democracy anti-fundamentalists. "I didn't hate Bush before, but now I really hate him," exclaimed a reform-leaning young woman. "He's damaging everything. He has hurt the reformers, and is bringing all the hard-liners together."[13] A later cartoon in *Al-Ahram* showed the Statue using her torch as a flame-thrower, its fire covering the world with black clouds.

Surveys indicate that the world admires American science and technology, loves the general values of democracy, freedom and human rights, and likes the American version of them, though rather less strongly (reservations were commonest in Western Europe, Russia and Muslim countries). It likes "Americans" more than "the United States." It consumes American popular culture though many of the more educated and the Muslims complain about "cultural imperialism." They eat hamburgers or fried chicken, but mainly as convenience foods—and Americans themselves are appropriately queasy that fast food should symbolize the country. But the approval rating on most of these items is now slipping, and there is rising criticism of US government policies, especially in encouraging widening inequality in the world. They believe the US does not help solve the world's most pressing problems, and they deplore American unilateralism and militarism. They especially dislike US policy toward Israel and Iraq.[14] These are quite ambivalent views, poised for the US government to influence positively or negatively. But what are their ideological challengers?

CHALLENGE 1: ETHNO-NATIONALISM

The ideology which lies behind the nation state is nationalism, now the world's dominant ideology. Unfortunately, nationalism comes conflict-laden. The international system manages to regulate most conflicts between nation states. But not conflicts within them.

Here I draw upon the results of my own extensive researches on ethnic cleansing.[15] The underlying problem is that claims to "rule by the people" and "national self-determination" confuse two distinct meanings of "the people"—the *demos* of democracy and the *ethnos* of ethnicity. President Woodrow Wilson famously confused the two when he declared that "national self-determination" should be the principle underlying the peace treaties ending World War I. He meant each ethnic group should be allowed to have its own separate democracy. This is a rather dangerous principle. It gives democracy a dark side, whereby claims made by one ethnic group for its "own state" are made at the expense of other groups. Poland for the Poles, Croatia for the Croats, Rwanda for the Hutus (which Hutus believe would be legitimate, since it would be a "majoritarian democracy"). In response, dominated groups claim their own political rights. If denied, they claim their own separate states. This sets off ethno-nationalist wars.

My research shows that the most dangerous situations are those in which two different ethnic or religious groups lay claim to their own state over the same territory, and where the claims have both historical legitimacy and a chance of being achieved. This normally involves the weaker side being assisted by ethnic or religious comrades in neighboring states or by a neighboring state with its own geopolitical motives. Otherwise the weaker side will submit and accept discrimination rather than fight, which is the most common outcome of ethnic conflicts. Ethno-nationalist conflicts from the Balkans before World War I to Rwanda in the 1990s to ongoing conflicts in Palestine, Kashmir and Chechnya all fit this model. So peopling the world with nation states tended to move violence to within states. The dominance of the ideal of "rule by the people" meant that during the nineteenth and twentieth centuries it became more difficult to devise multi-ethnic democracy. Wilson's principle of national self-determination did underlie the peace treaties of 1918–1920, and Eastern Europe was peopled with new nation states in which one ethnic group comprised over 70 percent of the population, and oppressed the minorities—especially the Jews.

But then the zenith of socialism across the mid-twentieth century damped down ethno-nationalism. So to a lesser extent did Western secular liberalism. The communist countries claimed nations were less important than classes. "Third World Socialism" asserted that the populations of underdeveloped countries formed a single "class" exploited by the rich capitalist nations. In this case either each nation might consider itself a "class" or whole groups of nations might make the claim, generating pan-regional movements like African Socialism or Arab Socialism. But then socialism declined. The collapse of the USSR and Yugoslavia produced ethno-nationalist conflagrations. Third World Socialism declined more gradually. African and Arab Socialism broke up into numerous corrupt, authoritarian states, failing to produce social and economic development. So indeed, did many Third World liberal and centrist regimes. These failures weakened the milder socialist, liberal and secular versions of nationalism and deepened ethnic and religious divisions. Ethno-nationalist wars and civil wars surged steeply upwards in the early 1990s, though perhaps leveling off since then.[16] They remain as the source of most of the world's disorder.

Any global American imperialism must now confront self-styled "freedom fighters," defining "the people" in ethnic or religious terms. Palestinians, Kashmiris, Tamils, Chechens and the many other "national liberal fighters" of the world are not reactionaries struggling against modernity. Rather, they want to achieve what others have achieved, their own nation state. Ethno-nationalism is rooted not in antiquity but in modernity, and it spreads across the world as part of globalization. Ethno-nationalists are not likely to go away. Against repression they mobilize resonant ideals of national self-determination. They consider themselves patriots, acting in the name of the people, and patriots are even willing to die for their cause.

Photographs of the 28-year-old divorcee Wafa Idris showed her as sparkling with vitality and charm. But on the morning of Sunday, January 27, 2002, she went shopping in Jerusalem, and as she left a shoe-store, she exploded a bomb strapped between her breasts. She killed herself and an 81-year-old Israeli man, and wounded 80 others. At this moment she became the first female suicide-bomber of the Middle East. Wafa was born and lived in a refugee camp near Ramallah. She volunteered as a Red Crescent worker there, and had grown used to dealing with intifada casualties. Like most of the Palestinian bombers, she was a secular Palestinian nationalist, not a fundamentalist. Her work experience preyed on her mind. Her brother Khalil said afterwards, "She used to tell me, coming home from work, about what she saw that day—someone lost a leg, or a brain on the ground, or a child killed. All these things accumulated." An elderly woman relative confirmed this, "She came home from work every day and told us what she saw: a wounded child, a youth whose brains were spilled by a bullet, a young man with a bullet in his heart, eyes that were red from tear gas." "Why go through all that, and for no pay?" her mother had asked her. She says Idris answered, "For our country and our people."

Her older sister-in-law Wisam said that when they saw television pictures of a suicide attack, Wafa would say, "I wish I did that." Wisam would reply, "No, no, no, you are too young, you have much to do with your life." Wisam said that Wafa's example would "encourage other girls to commit such acts," though she added uncertainly, " I don't know if this is the right thing or not." Wafa's mother seemed to have no such doubts, declaring, "we're proud ... I wish every man, every woman would do the same, be a martyr." But as the reporters left, her composure broke and she wept. "I lost my daughter," she wailed.

Yasser Arafat promptly declared: "The Fatah movement proudly glorifies its heroine martyr, from the Alamari Camp, the martyr Wafa Idris." Others hailed her as a feminist martyr. Commented an Egyptian journalist, "Wafa Idris elevated the value of the Arab woman and, in one moment, and with enviable courage, put an end to the unending debate about equality between men and women." A Jordanian journalist contrasted Wafa favorably to other educated young Arabs, saying that she "never dreamed of owning a BMW car or having a cellular phone. Wafa did not have makeup in her suitcase, but, rather, enough explosives to fill the enemies with horror."

Over the following months three more young Palestinian women followed Wafa's example. "I decided to become the second female bomber and continue on the same path of Wafa Idris," said 22-year-old Darin Abu Eisheh, a top English Literature student at Al-Najah University in Nablus. "Our role will not be to shed tears for the killing of our fathers, husbands and brothers, we will now turn our bodies into human bombs to destroy the Israeli security theory." These were her last words on a video before exploding herself at an Israeli checkpoint, wounding three Israeli soldiers. She was a Hamas member, believing that Muhammad himself had authorized women to join the holy war. But since she was unable to convince Hamas of this, she had turned to the secular Al-Aqsa Martyrs Brigade for her training.[17]

Why did Wafa and Abu do it? They were not "fundamentalists," expecting to enter paradise. The answer they both gave was simple: patriotism, "for our country and our people." We must come to terms with that simple answer. To call these young women "evil" does not help analysis, for such moral absolutes tend to forestall exploration of motives and causes. If we want a better world, we have to understand people like Wafa and Abu. As we see in Chapter 6, most suicide-bombers have been nationalists, not fundamentalists. The immortality offered by sacrifice for the nation is much more real than any religious notion of heaven. The freedom fighter has enormous social status among her own community. It is what little children want to be. Charles Dharapak's famous photograph shows two Palestinian tots, about eight years old, in their best clothes, with bandanas around their heads, cradling Kalashnikovs, being coached in how to fire them. Al-Jazeera television has shown video footage of several such role-modeling sessions.

Nationalist immortality is assured. Examine our children's history textbooks, or the statues in our squares, or our anthems and poems. Our past martyrs *are* immortal, since we remember and honor them today. Today's bids for martyrdom are low risk, since almost all national liberation struggles do win either their own nation states or some degree of political autonomy. The dead terrorists from the Stern Gang and Irgun of the 1940s are honored as Israeli martyrs, and one survivor made it as far as Prime Minister (Begin). Sharon and Arafat both expect to be remembered as honored patriots, for they believe they are defending their people. So does Saddam Hussein. Will all his sins be forgiven if he goes down as a martyr, fighting bravely against the infidel imperialist bombers? Very likely.

I do not want to glamorize "freedom fighters". The wars they fight are normally very dirty ones, since they are civil wars. They often commit atrocities against their own community. They kill moderates who wish to come to terms with the oppressor. As guerrillas, they need to hide amid their own community, but many of its people are reluctant to get involved, and some may side with the supposed oppressor. Guerrillas use their own community as "civilian shields" in a general sense and will coerce those who attempt to flee from this role. They also face the perennial problem of being denounced by informers, loyal to or bribed by the oppressor, and so they execute supposed "traitors." In such conflicts people on both sides characteristically use ideology as a pretext to settle personal scores against neighbors. They denounce them as traitors because they bear them or their family or village a personal grudge. Freedom fighters, like states who fight in the name of freedom, often violate human freedom. They necessarily infringe the Geneva Conventions, which were designed to deal with interstate wars in which soldiers are clearly identified by their uniforms and formations. During the Vietnam War the US decided to be flexible and treat Vietcong guerrillas as prisoners of war whether or not they wore uniforms. Some countries (though not the US or Iraq) then adopted a protocol to the Conventions whereby fighters in "wars of national liberation" would be considered legitimate combatants, whether or not they were uniformed or bore arms openly. Obviously fighters who are too militarily weak to openly identify themselves will play by different rules.

But they do endure. Chechens keep on fighting, despite all they suffered under the Tsars and the Soviets. Stalin deported and dispersed the entire nation. Twenty years later, they returned to their homeland, and after a pause some of them resumed fighting. President Putin subjects them to considerable state terrorism. In Grozny, the devastated Chechen capital, the traumatology unit was forced to flee from the city's main hospital. Its strategic location, commanding a firing zone down Grozny's main street, had made it first a rebel and then a Russian base. Salman Yandarev, chief surgeon in the hospital's new location, says: "We spend all our lives at this hospital and we see all the troubles that lay as a burden on our patients, so it gives us a heartache. I keep saying that tomorrow or the day after it will get better. I returned here in April of 2000 and I keep waiting, but a year passed, and now another year has passed, and there has been no change." Another doctor told *Médecins du Monde* "War or not war, we no longer know what it is now, how we should call it."

Yandarev supports neither the rebel leaders nor the tactics of the Russian military. Men with honor could have settled this conflict, he says. He concludes wearily,

We have fewer traumas now caused by explosives. But we have more bullet wounds. Maybe they have run out of mines, or the people are choosing their path more carefully. You have this alarming sensation inside you. In broad daylight, you can face death more peacefully, but at night, you are all alone. You never know who will burst into your house, and you keep thinking: when will dawn come?

A nurse is bitter about the Russian troops:

Everybody knows that here there are only refugees, and not fighters. So why do they bombard? They wage this war all alone. Nobody is fighting them. They fight all by themselves. We never saw that during the first war. Never saw that. The women cry, and everything is falling, walls, and we can't help our children.[18]

But military repression will not bring dawn. Putin is thankfully no Stalin, and Stalin failed. As Dr Yandarev says, conciliation is the only solution to ethno-nationalist conflict. If the United States is to ensure global peace and order, a *pax americana*, it must become the global conciliator.

These cases are the ones that make the world's headlines. They tug at our rival sympathies—for Israelis or Palestinians, Irish Catholics or Protestants. The US must free itself from such bias if it wishes to bring peace and order. Yet these highly organized struggles are not impossible to settle. We know roughly the solution to the Palestinian conflict—two states recognizing each other, some power-sharing in Jerusalem, compensation to Palestinian refugees but no automatic "right of return," and withdrawal of Israel from well over 90 percent of the "occupied lands." It is just a question of getting from here to there. But both sides are getting war-weary, just as the contenders did in Northern Ireland and Sri Lanka. Conciliation could happen, and the US can provide assistance, as it did in Ireland after it freed itself from the normal bias of Americans toward the Catholic cause.

The more intractable cases are where ethno-nationalist ideals have debased much further in the true "black holes" of ethno-nationalist violence. In the ongoing Congolese civil war, it is estimated that between three and four and a half million people have died since 1994, easily the most devastating recent war, yet one that barely makes it into our mass media. In 2002 the Eastern Congolese city of Goma was hit by the four horsemen of the apocalypse. First, Hutu *génocidaires* fleeing from Tutsi vengeance in Rwanda seized the town. Then predatory army units arrived from neighboring states, attracted to the area by its precious metals—coltan, tantalite and gold. The "Congolese Rally for Democracy, Goma Faction" (RCD-Goma), supported by Tutsi army units from Rwanda, seized the town. Then cholera ravaged the overcrowded and undernourished population, followed by molten lava from a volcanic eruption sweeping through it.

The RCD-Goma government lacked the resources to rebuild the city. The Rwandans and Western corporations pocketed most of the profits from metals. Tax collector Mitima Mvonabandi received no pay, so he traded tax exemptions with local merchants. "Many of them don't declare the full value of their goods," he said, "I don't tell the RCD, and they help me feed my six children. It's a fair trade."[19] This is a failed state in action.

They are present in an increasing number of African countries. Elites mobilize ethnic and regional grievances to loot local resources and sell them to foreign corporations, in the name of the people. They give local youths Kalashnikovs, and the youths torture, rape and kill. The government strikes back. Then malnutrition and HIV/AIDS infection threaten the people's survival. "We are afraid and suffering too much," said Musu Guah, a Liberian refugee, her children visibly suffering from malnutrition. "People are afraid of the dissidents and afraid of the government. They knock on the door, even in the daytime, to say they need manpower to fight, and the men disappear." Marie Gono clutched her small children in flight and said: "There is terrible, terrible fighting, all the time now. First the rebels come and say we support the government and kill people. Then the government comes and kills people because they say we are trying to take power. What kind of power? We have no power."[20]

Such ethno-nationalist struggles in failing economies and states generate local terrorism, but they rarely direct it against outsiders. There is no reason why the US should be involved on either side in such wars. A benevolent Empire would offer conciliation, economic aid, and some controls over foreign states, corporations and the arms trade. That is a tall order. A more cynical Empire would merely stay well clear. In Africa the US offers a little aid and occasional conciliation, but generally takes the cynical line. Even the new imperialists accept that there are limits to American power. For the most part ethno-nationalism only exposes the limits of the *pax americana*. Only where the US actually intervenes does it become an actual challenger.

CHALLENGE 2: THE RISE OF RELIGIOUS FUNDAMENTALISM

I have so far grouped ethno-nationalist and religious conflicts together, and the two do often bolster each other. In Palestine/Israel and Kashmir/India, for example, religion strengthens the sense of identity of the rival contenders. There is an added nationalist complication, especially among Arabs, since nationalism may be attached to either the individual nation state or to the Arab people as a whole. Iraqis may fight imperialism in the name of the Iraqi or the Arab people. I shall call the former nationalists and the latter pan-Arabists. But the spread of the major world religions creates a third, even broader identity. Christianity and Islam span across many countries. The Muslim faith thus also bolsters a pan-Islamic sense of identity, alongside and conflicting with nationalism and pan-Arabism.

Since socialism was godless, and liberalism was secular, their decline led to a religious upsurge. Religions claimed to offer yet another "Third Way," this time between failed Marxism and failed Western materialism. We have become obsessed with "Islamic fundamentalism." But similar movements arose among Hindus, Sikhs, Buddhists, Jews and Christians. The revival had actually begun in the last days of colonialism but stagnated until the first secular wave of post-colonial regimes began to fail. Religious extremists then denounced them, saying they had abandoned the religious soul of the community to embrace foreign, godless ideologies. The degeneration of the Congress Party in India encouraged a "purer" Hindu nationalism, some of whose adherents began to attack Muslims. In the Muslim world American interventions brought Islamists to denounce corrupt, oppressive Muslim regimes who were the servants of American imperialism.

Samuel Huntington rightly perceived a religious "fault-line" emerging between Islam and other religions, but he offered little explanation for this.[21] The main reason is that Islam has long sustained resistance to foreign imperialism. The Ottoman Empire, finally becoming the Turkish Republic, was never conquered by the West, nor was Persia/Iran. For centuries Muslim peoples in the Caucasus proved the most effective rebels against Russian, and then Soviet, imperialism. After World War I, most of the Muslim Middle East was subject to only indirect "protectorate" rule by Britain and France, and resistance continued. Muslim countries were generally among the first batch of countries to achieve independence from the colonial powers in the twentieth century. In October 2001, Osama bin Laden declared that for over 80 years Islam had been "tasting ... humiliation and disgrace, its sons killed and their blood spilled, its sanctities desecrated." His "80 years" refers to the granting of Arab protectorates to Britain. Then the US took over from Britain as the hated imperial power. Bin Laden's ideology is not nationalist but it is deeply anti-imperialist, like most Islamism and Arabism alike.

This characteristic is reinforced by Islam's persistent ability to generate "warrior sects." In the past they swept in from the desert to conquer corrupt and repressive Muslim states and re-establish the purity of Muhammad's teachings. The cycles of conquest between warrior tribes and settled city states was first identified by the sociologist Ibn Khaldun in the fifteenth century. Ernest Gellner noted similar patterns recurring right into the twentieth century. The Wahhabis were a modern version of the purist warrior sect, and then they settled down into comfortable, corrupt rule of Saudi Arabia—just as Ibn Khaldun would have predicted.

Today some Muslims urge a return to the purity of Islam established in Muhammad's own time. The key, they say, is to impose Sharia, Islamic law, on the Muslim community as a whole. In principle this would revive the old caliphate, a single pan-Islamic state, though no one has claimed the caliphate since the collapse of the Ottoman Empire. Following most scholars I call these Muslims *Islamists* rather than fundamentalists. Some of them also revive the anti–imperial warrior tradition, adding the duty of *qital*, meaning "combat against enemies," to the broader duty of *jihad*, meaning only "struggle/striving in the name of Allah." They focus on the Koran's repeated injunctions to resist oppression—"for oppression is even worse than killing" (2:191), so "fight against them until there is no more oppression and all worship is devoted to Allah alone" (2:193). I label them *jihadis*—holy warriors. They denounce Muslim rulers as "apostates," setting aside the normal koranic injunction against overthrowing a Muslim ruler. Apostate regimes and infidel imperialists are seen as locked together in an oppressive embrace. They attack them both.

But though their movement is formally transnational, they are also molded by two nationalisms, of the Arabs and their own nation state.[22] In recent years nationalism was the strongest of the three. Engrossed in a local political struggle, in practice they forgot the caliphate and pan-Arabism, becoming jihadi nationalists. This is what happened to the Palestinian Hamas and Islamic Jihad, and the Lebanese Hezbollah. The more moderate Muslim Brotherhood, organized right across the Middle

East, also tended to fragment into a series of national chapters, each pursuing local issues. This led its chapters into actually supporting different sides in the 1991 Gulf War. Islamic unity becomes fractured as nationalism and Islamism undercut one another.

A few Islamists do remain more internationally orientated. They are aggressively anti-American and anti-Jewish—both relatively new features of Islam. But their word for the Americans is an old term of Muslim abuse—"Crusaders." Fundamentalist movements among Hindus in India and Buddhists in Sri Lanka lack this internationalism and tend to be simply nationalist. But within all the major religions, conflict also pits fundamentalists against a motley assortment of moderates, mystics, seculars and religious conservatives, for all religions are extremely varied.

Jihadis are sometimes rather ordinary men. Mohamed Atta was born in 1968, the son of an Egyptian lawyer. He was clever, quiet, shy, serious and perhaps a little spoiled. He studied architecture at Cairo University and excelled at the technical side of the work, but was not much interested in design. He was therefore refused entry into the graduate school in Cairo. He went instead to Germany. So far he had revealed no political commitment and nothing beyond strong Muslim piety. In Germany he studied urban planning at the Technical University of Hamburg, obtaining his PhD in the summer of 1999. As we shall see in Chapter 6, most international terrorists were trained in the technical subjects.

German acquaintances described him as having narrow interests, almost no sociability, and puritanical Islamic beliefs. Women made him uncomfortable and he despised the laxness of Western moral standards. With his family's help, he went on pilgrimage to Mecca in 1995, an unusual privilege for one so young. The practical work for his urban planning dissertation took him to both Aleppo and Cairo, where he became very frustrated at the local planners. Either they destroyed the Islamic architectural heritage with modernist urban redevelopment or they sought to turn it into what he called "an Islamic Disneyland," the result he said of subordination to the United States. By 1998 in Germany he was consorting with radical Muslims and attending a radical mosque. But his apparent leadership of the 9-11 bombers came as a complete surprise to everyone who had met him. One biography ends: "There is something deeply unsatisfying about this. We want our monsters to be monstrous. We expect them to be somehow equal to their crimes. We want them to be extraordinary." Mohamed Atta was in contrast rather ordinary. But he was "a perfect soldier," not a patriot-soldier like Wafa Idris, but a soldier in a religious international brigade.[23]

Islamism and jihadis rose as socialist and liberal secularism declined, from about 1970 onward. They mobilized behind what Madoudi, the Pakistani inspirer of much modern Islamism, termed "theo-democracy"—a sovereignty resting not in the state but in the *umma*, the whole religious community, conforming to the Koran. So they are populists, invoking the people against repressive and corrupt states, some fairly secular like Egypt, others purporting to be religious, like Saudi Arabia. They recruit young educated dissidents, and they also organize community education and welfare programs among the poor, especially the refugees. These two "core constituencies" are not particularly large, but they enjoy much sympathy from Muslim peoples alienated from their governments. The Iranian ayatollahs had come to power by identifying the Shah as a corrupt, repressive American client (which was true). Armed struggle against Soviet imperialism in Afghanistan then created an "international brigade" of fighters, sympathy across the whole Muslim world, and Osama bin Laden. They succeeded in throwing out the godless communists. The new American imperialists should pause before giving *jihadis* another popular infidel target.

Ismaili Shatti is a moderate Kuwaiti Islamist. He generally supports the US presence in his country, but notes that Islamists now dominate the Kuwaiti parliament. He says they have faced little competition since the collapse of nationalist and socialist movements in the region. He sees the only alternative today as "liberal democracy—the West. And people do not like how the West has been treating us."[24]

We should not overestimate jihadi powers. Islamist regimes tend to establish harsh religious dictatorships, as in Iran, Sudan and Afghanistan, and this reduces their popularity. The surveys conducted by Riaz Hassan in Egypt, Indonesia, Iran, Kazakhstan and Pakistan reveal that trust in both Islam and the state is lower where the state is more Islamic. Trust is higher in the more secular states. He concludes that, for their own sakes, Islam and the state should avoid each other![25] As we shall see in Chapter 6, jihadis also alienate most people through extreme violence, as they did in the early 1990s in Algeria and Egypt. Islamism and jihadis were declining from the mid-1990s. But then US actions began to revive them.

In Africa Islamism thrives on genuinely popular grievances. Nigeria lies on Huntington's Christian/Muslim "fault-line." In some northern provincial states Sharia law has been introduced. Its supporters say it will stop corruption and crime, which have become major social problems. Muslims are flocking into towns where the Sharia operates, and the authorities claim it has reduced the crime rate. But Christians resist. As across most of the African "fault-line," the divide is also ethnic. In February 2002 over a hundred people were killed during four days of rioting in Lagos between Muslim Hausas and Christian Ibos. "They killed my father and they raped my mother before they killed my father. They slaughtered him," said a Muslim man, drawing a line across his own throat, "They put the knife there." Violence also flared in Kaduna. A fashion reporter had published an article satirizing Muslim complaints that a Miss World beauty pageant held in the country promoted sexual promiscuity. She had asked, "What would Muhammad think? In all honesty, he would probably have chosen a wife from among them." This was the spark, though not the underlying cause, igniting Muslim/Christian riots. After four days local police counted 215 bodies.

Sanusi Umoru, a Muslim man, lost his brother and could barely speak. "What do you want me to say?" he replies angrily. "I leave everything for Allah. It is very painful but we can't question God." A Christian, Ilya Haruna, said:

> I was returning from work and before I got to my house, I was accosted by a group of people. I knew all of them because they are all my friends. They shouted at me to stop, saying unbeliever, unbeliever. One person struck me on my head with a sharp object ... the rest just descended on me and I struggled and ran away from them with blood gushing out from my head and hand.

But the mob attacked his family home and four of his family were burnt alive.

A few Nigerian Muslims admire Osama bin Laden. A young man declares:

> Anywhere Muslims should love Osama. America does not love Islam. So I'm happy about what happened to America, and I feel more should happen so that America can feel the impact of what it does to others.

But this is just moaning. Nigerians are not likely to attack America. After all, America does not threaten or attack them. Even though Islamism is very popular among Nigerian Muslims, it does not generate international terrorism.

Across parts of Eurasia it is different. There the US takes sides—with Jewish and Christian states, and with secular and conservative Muslim states against "fundamentalists." And so it finds itself engaged in a highly selective ideological war against some ethno-nationalists, most Islamists, most Arabs, almost all jihadis and an increasing part of the entire Muslim population of the world. Some of its enemies are deeply rooted in popular ideologies. It would have great difficulty in defeating them all. But we should note that they themselves are deeply divided. Islamists, pan-Arabists and nationalists should have a little more in common with one another than they do with the United States. Their conflicts with the US, mediated by local states struggling to contain all their pressures, is more likely to result in chaos than a conflict between civilizations. As we see later, that is what was happening, but now the new American imperialists are driving them all together. But the rival challenges rather than any single "fault-line" could potentially lead to disorder.

CHALLENGE 3: THE DECLINE OF IMPERIAL IDEOLOGY

The new imperialists say American power is much greater than that of Britain or France in the nineteenth century. They are right if we compare individual countries. The US is more powerful than Britain, much more powerful than France. But Britain and France were not go-it-alone imperialists. Despite fighting wars against each other, they were partners in a much broader "civilizing mission" launched first by Europe, then by the West, on the rest of the world. The US joined in at the end of the nineteenth century in Cuba, the Philippines, China and elsewhere. This Western imperialism was much more formidable than the US is today, militarily, politically, economically and especially ideologically. From the point of view of the rest of the world, Britain, France, Belgium, Russia, the United States, etc. all looked culturally the same. When viewed collectively, there was simply no escaping their power.

Culturally, the West represented modernity, progress, power. Its culture was so powerful that native elites all over the world knew they needed much of it, even while they fought for liberation. The West also controlled the means of long-distance communication. In Africa the British, the French, the Belgians, the Portuguese, the Germans, the Italians could all communicate easily; while the "Africans" (our term, not theirs) in different regions of the continent could not easily communicate with one another. A Western communications monopoly prevented them organizing collective resistance at other than a local level. It needed splits among the imperialists themselves for bad news to get out. Occasionally, the split would be between the civilian and military imperial authorities. More often it would be clerics and missionaries who publicized imperial atrocities. A bishop, Las Casas, blew the whistle on the *conquistadores* in Mexico, the Rhineland Missionary Society on the German genocide in South West Africa.

Our splits today are much worse than theirs, since democratic values dominate today's world, and America itself. If the US deviates from them, this is publicized and denounced. UN officials sometimes do not mince their words. NGOs and the emerging "transnational civil society" also blow the whistle. Human Rights Watch is a very American organization. It has a very corporate structure and (like any US politician) it is deferential to its major donors. But it proclaims quintessentially American values of the sanctity of the individual, especially against state oppression. HRW has built up credibility for frank and unvarnished reports of human rights violations.[26] It denounced Milosevic, the Taliban and Saddam Hussein. In October 2001, Colin Powell felt moved to say, "The NGOs are such a force multiplier for us, such an important part of our combat team." But HRW cannot be reduced to being the 201st Airborne Division, for it also keeps watch on the conduct of the US and its allies. Whether it is US bombing of civilians or condoning massacres by its Afghan allies or treatment of prisoners in Guantanamo Bay, HRW makes the White House squirm, and its critical reports are headlined across the world—though this prophet is becoming less honored in its own country.

In response, the new imperialism has adopted a military model of information flows—hierarchical, secretive and censoring. In recent wars it has controled war zones through the press-pool system, cutting down the freedom of movement of reporters. It cooperates most with "loyal" media. The nadir was reached with the unabashedly militaristic ABC television "reality show," "Profiles from the Front Line," a series chronicling the everyday duties and constant successes of US soldiers in Afghanistan, made with full Pentagon cooperation. In the Iraq war the Pentagon adopted the strategy of "embedding" reporters amid American troops. If the reporters leave their assigned unit, they are defined as AWOL and deported. They see the war only from the perspective of the soldiers, whose privations they share and understandably sympathize with. Compared to Afghanistan this resulted in a decline in their ability to hire local interpreters and interview local civilians. Except for those in

Baghdad (who had their own Iraqi minders), we learned little from them about Iraqi civilian experiences and casualties. As usual, the Pentagon provided minimal information about civilian casualties. This worries some American reporters, and it infuriates foreign reporters. The graphic and harrowing pictures and stories of the dead and the bereaved presented on Al-Jazeera television were broadcast around the Middle East in the case of Afghanistan and around almost the whole world in the case of Iraq. Al-Jazeera, followed in Iraq by other Arab networks, had no historical precedents in previous Empires, where the world did not hear the voice of the victim. Now alternative versions of the truth will out. Weapons of mass communication level the visibility of the playing-field.

This is recognized by the Pentagon itself, which has become much more conscious of the damage to its case which civilian casualties bring. Indeed, US military personnel now do try hard to reduce them, insofar as its overriding concern with "force protection" (the safety of its own soldiers) allows. As we see in Iraq, however, this contradiction between concern for civilians and its own soldiers produces incoherent military tactics and more ideological evasions.

But the world outside is well aware of the contradictions of American Empire. It sees that the American Dream becomes the American *Phantom*. It dances in front of people's eyes, but when they advance toward it, it flickers, recedes and disappears. American democratic values are flagrantly contradicted by an imperialism which is strong on military offense, but weak on the ability to bring order, peace and democracy afterwards. The American economic programs discussed in Chapter 2 also help keep affluence out of reach of much of the South.

In the age of nationalism the peoples of the world are held responsible for their own destinies. Outside intervention must be justified by extreme conditions, as the UN Charter states; and intervention must be quick and beneficent. This is a higher standard than the Roman, British or Belgian Empires could ever have met. The first years of their conquests were usually mired in the blood of civilian casualties, but this mattered little. Today the world's dominant ideologies, carried through the mass media, contradict *any* imperialism. That is the fundamental ideological problem confronting the new imperialists. Though in the Middle East nationalists, pan-Arabists and Islamists may be quite weak and divided, many in the world look sympathetically on their plight, and even some in the supposed imperialist camp lack heart and soul for the task of oppressing them.

NOTES

1. RYPE Report, available at *www.alli.fi/nuorisotutkimus/rype2/4/ 2_5.html*. Of course, Europe was also the birthplace of a lot of undesirable things too. Strictly speaking, New Zealand is the world's oldest democracy, enfranchising all women, alongside all men, in 1899, before anyone else.

2. In "The Roots and Contradictions of Modern Militarism," in my book *States, War and Capitalism*, Oxford: Blackwell, 1988.

3. Joseph Nye, *The Paradox of American Power*, Oxford: Oxford University Press, 2002; Emmanuel Todd, *Après L'Empire*, Paris: Gallimard, 2002, ch. 5.

4. See, for example, the German Marshall Fund/Council on Foreign Relations poll, *www.worldviews.org/*.

5. See *www.nationalgeographic.com/poll*. In a Leger Marketing poll of October 7–13, only 8 percent of Americans knew the name of the Prime Minister of Canada, and 21 percent knew the name of the Canadian capital. In contrast, 90 percent and 88 percent of the Canadians knew the names of their neighbor's president and capital.

6. With thanks to Baruch Kimmerling for this story.

7. Poll conducted by *Popular Science*, 2000.

8. The alternative, that Bush himself believes this, is more worrying. He seemed worryingly sincere in his 2003 State of the Union Speech when he again identified Iraq as an imminent threat. A paranoid President of the United States would be worse news for the world than a liar.

9. See *www.USATODAY/CNN/Gallup Poll*, March 1–3, 2002.

10. "Advertising as Capitalist Realism," in *Advertising: The Uneasy Persuasion*, New York: Basic Books, 1984, p. 218.

11. Lila Abu-Lughod, "The Objects of Soap Opera: Egyptian Television and the Cultural Politics of Modernity," in Daniel Miller, ed., *Worlds Apart. Modernity through the Prism of the Local*, London: Routledge, 1995; Tamar Liebes and Elihu Katz, *The Export of Meaning: Cross-Cultural Readings of Dallas*, Cambridge: Polity Press, 1993.

12. Suzanne Kapner, "Pax Americana? Not in World TV Market," *Straits Times* (Singapore), January 3, 2003; "Faiblit la domination de l'Internet de la part des US," *www.GSMBOX.fr*, June 8, 2000.

13. Scott Peterson, "Death to America Is Back," *Christian Science Monitor*, February 12, 2002.

14. The Pew Global Attitudes Project, *What the World Thinks in* 2002, Washington, DC: The Pew Center for the People and the Press, 2002; The German Marshall Fund/Council on Foreign Relations poll, *www.worldviews.org/*; "How the Japanese, South Koreans and Chinese View the Post 9-11 World and US Military Action," *The Harris Poll*, no. 63, December 26, 2001. The decline in perception of the US continued in the Pew Global Attitudes Survey of 2003.

15. Michael Mann, *The Dark-Side of Democracy: Explaining Ethnic Cleansing*, Cambridge: Cambridge University Press, 2004.

16. Ted Gurr and his associates argue for a recent decline in *Minorities at Risk: A Global View of Ethnopolitical Conflicts* and *People versus States. Minorities at Risk in the New Century*, both published in Washington, DC: United States Institute of Peace, 1994 and 2000. But M. Sollenberg and P. Wallensteen detect only a recent leveling-off in "Patterns of Armed Conflict, 1990–2000," *Stockholm Institute of Peace Research Yearbook*, 2001, Appendix 1A.

17. Details of the two young women from *www.MEMRI.org/news*, February 22, 2002; and *New York Times*, February 11 and March 1, 2002.

18. Patrick E. Tyler, "Chechen Civilians Are Casualties of Random Acts of War," *New York Times*, February 10, 2002; and *www. medecinsdumonde.org*.

19. *Los Angeles Times*, February 5, 2002.

20. "Inter-Agency Co-ordination for Liberia," *UN Office for the Coordination of Humanitarian Affairs* (OCHA), November 26, 2001; Douglas Farah, "Fighting Flares in Liberia and Threatens Ivory Coast," *Washington Post*, August 6, 2001.

21. *The Clash of Civilizations and the Remaking of World Order*, New York: Simon & Schuster, 1966.

22. I here draw on the work of Olivier Roy. See his *The Failure of Political Islam*, Cambridge, MA: Harvard University Press, 1994.

23. Terry McDermott, "A Perfect Soldier," *Los Angeles Times*, January 27, 2002.

24. *Los Angeles Times*, December 2, 2002.

25. Riaz Hassan, *Faithlines: Muslim Conceptions of Islam and Society*, Oxford: Oxford University Press, 2002.

26. That is, of violations of their civil and political rights. Human Rights Watch is much less concerned about economic exploitation.

FIVE

THE WAR IN AFGHANISTAN

The terrible events of 9-11 generated worldwide sympathy for the US. Almost all heads of state sent condolences and pledged assistance in hunting down the terrorists. The Bush administration, sensing the mood, seemed happy to consult widely. The UN Security Council unanimously passed a resolution requiring all member countries to pursue terrorists and the financial systems supporting them. NATO invoked Article 5 of its Charter, declaring 9-11 as an attack on all 19 NATO states. The Organization of American States followed suit. Almost no states were to reject requests for assistance from the US over the next months.

The Bush administration immediately identified Osama bin Laden and his al-Qaeda network as the culprits, and few outside the Middle East doubted this. Bush said he wanted bin Laden "dead or alive," and though many found this primitive, they could understand the desire for vengeance. On September 15 President Bush gave the Taliban regime of Afghanistan an ultimatum: hand over bin Laden and close his camps, or face the consequences. Pakistani diplomats personally conveyed this to the Taliban. Afghanistan's Grand Islamic Council did recommend that head of state Mullah Mohammad Omar persuade bin Laden to leave, and CIA Director George Tenet believed the Taliban might split. On September 18 the Foreign Minister said it might extradite bin Laden if the US provided "solid and convincing" evidence of his involvement in terrorism. But Bush told Congress "there will be no negotiations or discussions ... there's no need to discuss innocence or guilt ... we know he's guilty." The Taliban ambassador to Pakistan twice repeated the request for evidence. Discussions were proceeding between Pakistani diplomats and clerics and the Taliban. They agreed that bin Laden would be handed over to an Islamic court in Peshawar, Pakistan. That court could then decide whether to try him or hand him over to the Americans for trial. But Pakistan President Musharraf vetoed the deal, after US pressure.[1] The US said its demands were "clear and non-negotiable."

This intransigence was the first US mistake. The US was utterly convinced of the rightness of its cause and of its military power to attain it. But foreign policy is not about righteousness—that was the Taliban's mistake also. It is about winning, and this depends partly upon winning hearts and minds, and depriving the enemy of them.

The primary concern of the US should have been to capture bin Laden and his aides and bring them to trial. Bombing suspects and bystanders to death is not the normal strategy in a murder inquiry. The US should have provided evidence and done more negotiating. British Prime Minister Tony Blair, faced by more parliamentary criticism, produced a dossier of evidence on October 4, though it contained some holes. The US could have provided much more evidence. Secretary of State Colin Powell favored this, arguing it would win more allies. CIA Director Tenet added that it might help the Taliban split. But Defense Secretary Rumsfeld strenuously opposed producing a dossier, saying it would set a dangerous precedent for future military interventions when the evidence might not be so extensive. His argument won the day, especially after Pakistan became the first Muslim state to accept the US case—it got aid instead of evidence![2]

Whether the Taliban would have accepted negotiations or evidence is less important than whether the world—especially the Middle East—would be swayed toward or away from the US case. The statement "there's no need to discuss innocence or guilt ... we know he's guilty" would lead most to doubt the standards of American justice, an impression furthered by US announcements that terrorists would be tried before special military tribunals, not regular lawcourts. The consequence was skepticism about American claims which were probably true.

Negotiations might have continued. The next demand might be, hand over al-Qaeda leaders to a neutral country—Switzerland or Finland perhaps, or a moderate Muslim country like Malaysia. Or the UN might set up an International Criminal Tribunal for Terrorism. But the US was by then rejecting all extensions of the international criminal law. An alternative would be to discreetly bribe the Taliban. The US might have appeared reasonable, not simply the world's bully, brandishing its bombs. If the Taliban rejected all evidence and compromise, the US would win the international high ground for military action. Negotiations were not prejudicial to a military response, which took a month to prepare anyway. Even *appear* to negotiate, and the US would get more general support for its coming war. If alternatively bin Laden and his gang were handed over, that would be good, since the US had no vital interest in the Taliban other than that they stop harboring terrorists. But the US spurned all negotiations.

Gallup polls in 37 countries in late September asked the question, "In your opinion, once the identity of the terrorists is known, should the American government launch a military attack on the country or countries where the terrorists are based, or should the American government seek to extradite the terrorists to stand trial?" Only in the US, Israel and India (these two countries were already warring on terrorists) did majorities favor the military option. Around 80 percent of Europeans and 90 percent of South Americans favored extradition and trial, as did 80 percent of Bosnians and 69 percent of Pakistanis, the only Muslim countries surveyed.

The US started with such enormous sympathy that its failure to negotiate did not seem damaging. Most allies pledged support, as did rivals like Russia and China with their own terrorist agendas to pursue. Regional powers as varied as Russia, the Central Asian "stans," China, India, Pakistan, Saudi Arabia and Turkey all gave assistance, usually permitting bases and flying rights in their countries. Some were bribed. Once the war started, and the extradition/trial alternative was dropped from polls, far more Westerners supported the war—though most Germans and Russians did not, and most people everywhere deplored its civilian casualties. However, the countries who sent troops to assist the US were almost all Western, and only the Anglo-Saxons—Americans, British, Canadians and Australians—did any serious fighting.

The Muslim world was quite hostile. Bin Laden had declared that the US sided with repressive Muslim regimes, killed Iraqis, stationed US troops on holy Muslim soil, and supported Israel against the Palestinians. All these allegations were widely believed, because they were true. A few Muslims danced in the streets at the news of 9-11 but most preferred to believe that Muslims could not have done it. Bush referred to his counter-attack as a "crusade," hardly the way to endear himself to Muslims. The American media also tended to answer the question, "Why do they hate us?" by referring to the nature of Islam or fundamentalism. There were nasty incidents in the US against Muslims. All this was widely reported in Muslim countries.

Many Middle Easterners analyze this in terms of Arab elites versus "the Arab street." They usually note that though "the street" demonstrates and stones US embassies, the elites are anxious for American aid and wary of the street. In public elites condemn US aggression but in private they tell the US not to worry. Together the elites and the US sit out the mob, and the trouble soon dies down. Of course, this is a little oversimple. Social-psychological studies show that ordinary people rely heavily on "opinion-leaders" drawn from their friends and kin, who are more informed, articulate or literate than themselves. The opinion-leaders can especially influence their views on abstract issues which do not directly concern them—like most politics. "Elites" in this sense exist at all social levels. Middle Eastern opinion-leaders tend to acquire knowledge through sermons, the radio, TV and the newspapers, though they rein-terpret new information in terms of what they think they know already.

Since we know little of Middle Eastern opinion-leaders at the lower social levels, we generally rely on the comments of those drawn from the intellectuals. Consider these men, for example. A leading Arabic newspaper published a poem addressed to a dead Syrian poet. It ended:

> Children are dying, but no one makes a move.
> Houses are demolished, but no one makes a move.
> Holy places are desecrated, but no one makes a move ...
> I am fed up with life in the world of mortals.
> Find me a hole near you. For a life of dignity is in those holes.

Was this an alienated young Arab preparing for martyrdom, asks *Christian Science Monitor* reporter Peter Ford? No, the poem was written by the Saudi ambassador to London, scion of a wealthy Saudi family.[3] Consider also Muhammad al-Mulaifi, head of the information depart-ment at Kuwait's Ministry of Islamic Affairs, interviewed a year after 9-11. Kuwait is a US ally, not a radical state, and this man is no radical fundamentalist. But, he told US reporter Craig Smith, "I would be lying if I said I wasn't happy about the attack. Only then did we see America suffer for a few seconds what Muslims have been suffering for a long time." He added that he had attended several parties held in celebration of 9-11.[4] Given the way it started its campaign, the US would have problems with such opinion-leaders.

The war deepened Muslim hostility. Gallup conducted a poll in nine Muslim countries in December 2001 and January 2002. A massive 77 percent of all respondents said US military action in Afghanistan was morally unjustified. There was not much difference among the nine countries. The highest disapproval came from Indonesia (89 percent), the lowest from Turkey (59 percent). The nine countries contained 40 percent of all the world's Muslims, and the most hostile countries (Iran, Iraq and Libya) were not included. Sixty-seven percent of the sample said the September 11 attacks were also morally unjustified (only 9 percent actually approved of them), though 61 percent refused to believe they were carried out by Arabs. Many supported their view by pointing to US failure to produce a dossier of evidence on bin Laden, and its failure to negotiate. Yet again they are bombing rather than discussing, it was said.[5] Nonetheless, a short, sharp war resulting in victory, with few civilian casualties and a good aftermath might quiet such criticism.

VICTORY—AT A COST

Most Americans believe the war was a tremendous success. Victory was achieved quickly, the Taliban regime overthrown, al-Qaeda dispersed. Radical Islamists in neighboring Pakistan accepted it as a defeat and seemed demoralized. After the fact, some scoff at the backwardness and weakness of the Taliban. Yet most had expected a more difficult campaign. Had not the Russians been bogged down there for ten years before retreating ignominiously out of the country?[6] Was not this ideal guerrilla country, with half the men toting guns, able to live off the land and hide in mountain caves? We thought the Bush administration wise to quietly order up thousands of body-bags.

But they were not needed. This was a short war involving very few Americans. There were essentially no ground troops until after victory was assured. A hundred and ten CIA officers and 316 American Special Forces personnel on the ground, plus massive aerial bombardment and foreign allies on the ground, achieved victory at the cost of only 15 Americans killed by hostile fire by March 2003, plus 55 killed in accidents and "friendly fire." There were also 20 casualties among the Western allies, though only 5 were inflicted by the enemy. The Taliban army was routed, al-Qaeda scattered. All is not well in the aftermath, but the battlefield victory was swift and overwhelming. It encouraged Bush the Younger toward his next imperial campaign, in Iraq. The American media moved on, forgetting about Afghanistan. The path of Empire is not always popular, but victory seems to trump all.

The primitive military technology of the Taliban meant they could not resist US domination of the skies. "Smart" weapons had come onstream, pilotless Predators roamed across the skies, and Special Forces spotters on the ground used global positioning systems and satellite phones to direct the bombing. CIA agents spread out among the Afghan warlords with suitcases stuffed full of dollars, amounting in all to $45 million. A major warlord might get $1 million, a minor one $50,000.[7] But the US also had important allies—Pakistan which had cut off the possibility of resupplies to the Taliban, and the Afghan Northern Alliance warlords controlling a quarter of the country. When aerial attack and shortages of supplies destroyed the Taliban will to resist, the bribed warlords marched into Kabul.

Most reporters preferred a simpler story. They ascribed victory not to the suitcases but to the high-tech "revolution in military affairs" (RMA). They hailed it as a "bull's-eye" "finely tuned," "low risk," "stealth" war, characterized by "pinpoint bombing," "information-heavy combat weapons" that were "precise at hitting targets." Headlines declared: "Technology brings new style of warfare," "War ... demonstrates air power's new ability," "Pinpoint air power comes of age," "High-tech US arsenal proves its worth."[8] General Tommy Franks agreed, telling the Senate Armed Services' Committee: "This has been the most accurate war ever fought in this nation's history." The military strategist Michael O'Hanlon was slightly more circumspect, hailing it "A Flawed Masterpiece."[9]

Some of the bombing was very smart. John Hendry described the turning point of the war, when US airplanes shifted from attacking fixed targets to Taliban troop concentrations.

> Like most Northern Alliance generals, Abdul Rashid Dostum's experience with Russian bombers during the Soviet invasion of Afghanistan in the 1980s left him skeptical about calling for help from the air. You never knew when—or even where—the bombs would hit.
>
> But on Nov. 8, he had no choice. It had been days since his rebels won their first victory in Mazar-i-Sharif, and he was watching Al Qaeda fighters amassing to retake the northern city of Kunduz. "We need some air," he told a young US Air Force special operations lieutenant.
>
> Within 20 minutes, the eyes of Afghanistan's most feared warlord widened as a succession of fireballs erupted over an expanse the size of a football field, killing 259 Al Qaeda fighters and taking out a command center, artillery and armored vehicles.
>
> "You've got to be kidding," Dostum said. He hadn't expected the strike for a day or more.[10]

His account was confirmed by an ordinary Taliban soldier. Fada had liked his job as a driver and paymaster along the front line, since he could siphon off the Taliban soldiers' pay. "I changed my hat to a turban and I was a Talib!" he crowed. But he was about to change sides again: "The first time I saw B52s dropping bombs so exactly, I knew the Taliban were finished. For three days the Taliban tried to use anti-aircraft guns but then Mullah Omar said it was useless, and they could only wait for God to kill the B52s in the sky."[11] Fada promptly switched sides again, and is now in the new Afghan army.

But not all the bombing was surgical. It cannot have been, since it produced many civilian casualties. Their number is important militarily, in affecting tactics in any future wars, ideologically, in the winning of hearts and minds, and morally, in judging the rightness of the war. It influences the perception of whether the US acted as a "state terrorist." Some bombing clearly is state terrorism. That is the correct term for the Allied fire-bombing of Dresden or Tokyo and, more arguably, of Hiroshima and Nagasaki. They were intended to kill civilians, to induce general terror among the enemy population. One may justify them as a means of ending the war quickly, but this is also the claim of terrorists when they bomb.

The US did not engage in terror bombing in Afghanistan, since it did not deliberately target civilians. The problem of its bombs, like Sharon's tanks and missiles in Palestine, is only that they cannot distinguish accurately between military and civilian targets, so that civilians *will* get killed, routinely, even though they were not specifically targeted. Whether we call Sharon or Bush state terrorists will be a borderline decision depending on the care they take in making distinctions, the contrition they show afterwards for "mistakes," and their eagerness to correct them. Sharon fails these tests. Did the Pentagon too?

Since the issue is so highly charged, the numbers are controversial. Obviously, we can't know the exact casualties. Most US reporters said civilian casualties were in the range 1,000–1,300, which is quite low— disquieting, but in military, ideological and moral terms perhaps accep-table for the liberation of an entire country. This figure is still being bandied about in US news media as the authoritative figure. But it comes from a single estimate made by Carl Conetta, made when the war was only about two-thirds finished. Conetta also discounted all non-Western reports of deaths, mainly by Pakistani newspapers and Al-Jazeera tele-vision. But could only Western journalists have professional detachment? More mundanely, could they be all over Afghanistan at once?[12]

One study was more comprehensive. Marc Herold included non-Western sources, weighted his sources in terms of their likely accuracy, and only accepted figures which were confirmed by at least two independent sources. He responded to detailed criticism on some particular incidents by correcting his figures downward. Thus his early estimate of casualties incurred by the end of 2001 was actually much higher than his final total for the entire war. His research is demonstrably the best available.[13] We must accept it until something better comes along. It is perhaps the duty of the US government to provide a better report, but information is not its strong point. Herold's final estimate for Afghan civilian deaths directly inflicted by US action, October 7, 2001 to July 31, 2002, is between 3,125 and 3,620. I will be conservative and reduce it to the rounded figure of 3,000, though some people with local knowledge say it should be much higher. A de-mining expert in Afghanistan said, "you can probably double Herold's figures because so much goes unreported here. Most Muslims are buried within six hours of death. There's no need to report births or deaths here and the hospitals do not have anything on the dead."[14]

But Conetta noted that even his lower estimate meant that the rate of civilian casualties per bomb delivered must have been at least twice what it had been in Kosovo and Serbia two years earlier. Overall, US bombing had become *less* smart, directly contradicting General Franks.[15] If we go instead for 3,000 deaths, then the Afghan civilian casualty rate per bomb dropped reached over six times the Kosovo/Serbia level. It would be higher still if we added people killed after supposed victory by unexploded bombs and land-mines. About 5 percent of cluster bomblets land unexploded, and many of these exploded on human contact later.

The total would be much higher if we added Afghans dying of disease and malnutrition caused by war dislocation. Conetta said these were over 3,000. Médicins Sans Frontières studied two villages and a displaced-persons camp in Faryab province and concluded that the mortality and infant mortality rates doubled between August 2001 and February 2002. This would yield a higher death rate. The number of refugees and the number of people without food had also substantially increased. The pattern seemed similar across all northern Afghanistan.[16] *Overall* civilian losses must have been close to 10,000—triple the deaths inflicted by 9-11. This looks like state terrorism committed as revenge for terrorism, and like most revenge it exacted much more blood than the original provocation.

But we still need one more statistic, of deaths inflicted on enemy soldiers. If only 2,000 soldiers died, fewer than the civilians, this would be very inaccurate bombing; if 50,000 enemy combatants died, then this would be unusually accurate for a modern war. The only estimate seems to be Conetta's, of 3,000 to 4,000. But this means that well over half of the dead were civilians, completely destroying the notion that this was a "smart," precisely targeted war. In fact it would be a fairly typical war of the last hundred years. We should add that very few of the Taliban conscripts would have had any idea beforehand that they were enemies of the United States. Many of them were "innocents." War is an extremely blunt instrument of justice, since it kills far more of the innocent than the guilty.

But do any of these figures matter—except to the victims? Is not war always murderous? The number of casualties has not much mattered in the US, but it has in other countries, for both Herold's total figure and Conetta's bombing rate figure are widely cited. The Egyptian newspaper *Al-Ahram* is generally pro-Western. Faiza Rady wrote a piece on Herold's findings.

Afghan killing fields

There has been no official count of the number of civilians killed in the first eight and a half weeks of US bombing on Afghanistan, and the Pentagon has falsified the facts about its war. But one American academic is setting the record straight.

He then presents Herold's figures in detail as fact. Also in *Al-Ahram* Iffat Malek said:

The bottom line is that the [US] media and others are judging this war to be a success because there is a hierarchy even in death. Thousands of Americans were killed on 11 September—universally regarded as an awful tragedy. Thousands of Afghans have been killed since 7 October and for their families their deaths are an equally awful tragedy. However, for the West, and in particular America, these people are little more than a statistic. If the same value was placed on Afghan as on American lives, no one would be calling this war a success.[17]

This is nothing compared to the reporting in more popular Arab newspapers. They talk about "the terrorist Bush" (or Rumsfeld, or Cheney, etc.).

The civilian casualties were caused by the imprecision of large-scale aerial bombing, target selection and faulty intelligence. These suggest that some weapons are not smart, that none of them can be smart enough, and that we may not be as smart as our weapons.

The US still dropped many "dumb" bombs. Navy spokesmen said that, whereas under 10 percent of bombs dropped in the 1991 Gulf War had been "smart," 60 percent were smart in Afghanistan.[18] Most were actually "dumb" bombs "smartened" with a satellite-guided tail-fin kit (the JDAM). But that still leaves 40 percent which remained dumb. The Pentagon claimed that 75–80 percent of all bombs hit their targets, meaning that 20–25 percent missed. Cluster bombs, "daisy-cutters" and mines were the least discriminating, killing lots of civilians. Dozens died when a 1,000lb cluster pod spilt its 202 bomblets across a mosque and hospital complex in Herat.[19] The giant "daisy-cutter" bomb is designed to detonate above the ground, which prevents its shock being absorbed by the earth. It can clear a three-mile area—and not just of daisies. Reporter Tim McGirk describes the effects:

> I'm at the border when [an] ambulance screeches by, coming from inside Afghanistan. On a narrow stretcher in the back of the ambulance lies an Afghan, Hekmatullah, 22, gasping with pain at every bump. He had the awful luck to be living not more than 200 yards from a Taliban ammunition dump near Kandahar. Hekmatullah was sleeping in his courtyard the night when American bombs struck. The ammo depot erupted like a volcano, spewing bullets and rockets everywhere. Hekmatullah's house cracked apart like an egg. So did Hekmatullah. A bullet shattered his leg, and another lodged itself inches from his spine. His brother Abdul Halim rushed him to Kandahar hospital. But that night there were dozens of wounded, lying in the corridors on a stinking, bloodstained floor, and the doctors had fled during the night's bombing. Under the circumstances, I couldn't bring myself to explain about "collateral damage." . . . I felt awful about it. All the beds around Hekmatullah were filled with Afghans injured in the bombings. Not one of them was a Taliban.

McGirk saw only the wounded, not the dead. They had already been buried. He continues:

> Afghans still don't understand what this war is really about. They can't comprehend the enormity of what happened on Sept 11, nor why our wrath has fallen on them. Remember: the Talibans don't believe in TV or news-papers. Afghans haven't seen those horrifying images of the World Trade Center and the Pentagon. An aid worker friend was in Afghanistan at the time, trying to explain the dimensions of the calamity to Afghans. They couldn't understand what the fuss was about. They thought the World Trade Center was a few shops at a caravan crossing. No building in Kabul is over four stories high. They simply couldn't imagine what a skyscraper was like.[20]

The Navy spokesman claimed that 90 percent of smart bombs hit their target. That sounds a lot but even 10 percent can cause mayhem. The Pentagon calculates the "Circular Error Probability" of JDAMs at 32–42 feet. That means that 50 percent will drop within this distance of the center of the target, but 50 percent will fall outside it—though usually not far outside. The Pentagon knows in advance that even some smart bombs will hit civilians, even if none are actually so targeted.

But the dumb bombs are *deliberately* imprecise, since they are used for clearing massed troops, and demolishing fortifications, communications and utilities infrastructures and mine fields. Armies will continue to use them for these purposes, and so massive civilian casualties will continue. If Pentagon spokespersons deny the civilian dead, or attribute deaths only to mistakes, then they dissemble. Modern war is state terrorism. The *point* of such indiscriminate bombs is to terrorize the enemy as a whole into submission, including its support population. That is what war is about. It is not the same as justice.

The same tactics were being used a year after the war was supposedly over. Baghran is a mountainous region in the north of Helmand province. It was still a source of concern for US soldiers who were tracking movements of suspected local rebels. As special forces were reconnoitering a mountain valley, they came under attack and called in airstrikes. Planes bombed again next day for eight hours. US army Colonel King said that B-1s and B-52s dropped nearly 20 2,000-pound bombs on the area. He said he had no information about any civilian casualties. But Haji Mohammad Wali, an aide to the provincial governor, said that at least 17 civilians had been killed. Their relatives had come crying to the district headquarters.[21] The same thing happened in April 2002, when 11 out of a family of 12 were wiped out by bombers mistakenly believing their home was a Taliban headquarters. Just picture it—in the first incident 20 2,000-pound bombs dropped from a great height on areas containing a handful of rebels and many civilians! In the second incident two such bombs dropped on a single house! *Of course* more civilians than soldiers will be killed.

In fact most US bombs were aimed at buildings or compounds jammed right up against civilian structures, for Afghanistan's government infrastructures had been devastated by decades of war. The Taliban used what buildings they could find, and Taliban and al-Qaeda soldiers often shared them with their families or other non-combatants. Few Afghans wore full uniforms, and half Afghan men carried guns. So even smart bombs might not discriminate soldiers from civilians. But is the

Pentagon not to bomb at all? Then it could not have won the war at such low cost to US forces. What state would act differently?

All over the world guerrillas try to "live among the people like fish in the sea" so that the enemy cannot distinguish them from the sea of bystanders. Bombing in Vietnam produced hundreds of thousands of civilian casualties. Even RMA smart bombing will produce thousands of civilian casualties, including the babies and 85-year-olds that Pentagon spokespersons so dread having to explain away. Anyone fearing devastating US attack will imitate guerrilla tactics and move his troops close to civilians. This is what Saddam Hussein did in Iraq. Wouldn't you do the same if you thought it might deter devastating bombing? This is likely to remain a stubborn reality of US wars against enemies with much lesser military capabilities than our own. The carnage results partly from their tactics, but it is Americans who are bombing the babies. In any case, the notion that we fight fair, raining down the bombs from the heavens, while they fight dirty, hiding behind civilians, is ridiculous.

The third problem, intelligence failure, resulted in bombing civilians whom we thought were soldiers. These were mistakes but they were systemic, built into the high-tech, muscle-bound nature of the military, and its reluctance to risk American lives. RMA downgrades basic soldier skills.[22] Lightly equipped scouts with field and language skills are best at distinguishing civilians from soldiers in the war zone. These are high-risk activities, involving slipping through the war zone, often over enemy lines. But the Pentagon seemed to prefer a different kind of soldier. Just before the Afghan War started, the US press carried a Pentagon-fed illustration of a soldier who looked like a cross between Robocop and an Imperial Storm Trooper. He was heavily armored, slow and lumbering, helmeted and visored, showing no human face to the world, communicating to the skies through GPS, but to the locals only through a recorded amplified announcement: "Clear the area or you face death." His night-vision superiority was exercised when the locals were tucked up in bed. This soldier was alien to the people and territory he was seeking to conquer and pacify.[23]

Qais, a commander in the new Afghan army, was also drawn to Hollywood metaphors for the American soldiers:

They drove around Kabul in big APCs, which looked like mechanical dragons filled with soldiers that were foreign and square-jawed. They were covered in equipment, sunglasses, helmets, microphones attached to the helmets that curved in front of their mouths, radios on their hips, enormous

M16s across their shoulders, black polished boots on their feet. They looked like they had come to invade Mars. They looked like Hollywood soldiers who had found themselves suddenly on the Planet of the Afghans. ... The soldiers had mirrors instead of eyes and seldom descended from their vehicles.[24]

Critics say US intelligence suffers by valuing technology over people. Frustrated at depending on CIA operatives, the Pentagon expands high-tech ventures like "Gray Fox," low-profile eavesdropping planes—intelligence from afar.[25]

Inside the technology were frightened, angry men who sometimes made mistakes. One spotter gave the bombers his own coordinates as the target. He came to a ghastly end, along with two other Americans and six Afghans. Afghan President Hamid Karzai escaped death in this incident, but his nephew did not. In another mistake four soldiers became the first Canadians to die in battle since the Korean War when a US F-16 precisely but fallibly targeted them. Evidence given at the trial of the pilots revealed that they and other pilots were routinely given stimulant drugs to keep them awake during long flying hours. The spotter who twice brought down bombs on the Red Cross Center in Kabul was more consistently fallible.

As US forces began to arrive on the ground in the later stages of the war, they also became implicated. Robert Fisk's narrative of events in the village of Hajibirgit begins at midnight on May 22, 2002.[26] Everyone was suddenly awakened

> by the thunder of helicopter engines and the thwack of rotor blades and the screaming voices of the Americans. Haji Birgit Khan [the 85-year-old village leader] was seen running stiffly from his little lawn towards the white-walled village mosque, a rectangular cement building with a single loudspeaker and a few threadbare carpets. Several armed men were seen running after him. Hakim, one of the animal herders, saw the men from the helicopters chase the old man into the mosque and heard a burst of gunfire. "When our people found him, he had been killed with a bullet, in the head," he says, pointing downwards. There is a single bullet hole in the concrete floor of the mosque and a dried bloodstain beside it. "We found bits of his brain on the wall."
>
> Across the village, sharp explosions were detonating in the courtyards and doorways of the little homes. "The Americans were throwing stun grenades at us and smoke grenades," Mohamedin recalls. "They were throwing dozens of them at us and they were shouting and screaming all the time. We didn't understand their language, but there were Afghan gunmen with them,

too, Afghans with blackened faces. Several began to tie up our women—our own women—and the Americans were lifting their burqas, their covering, to look at their faces. That's when the little girl was seen running away." Abdul Satar says that she was three years old, that she ran shrieking in fear from her home, that her name was Zarguna, the daughter of a man called Abdul-Shakour ... and that someone saw her topple into the village's 60ft well on the other side of the mosque. During the night, she was to drown there, alone, her back apparently broken by the fall. Other village children would find her body in the morning. The Americans paid no attention. From the description of their clothes given by the villagers, they appeared to include Special Forces and also units of Afghan Special Forces, the brutish and ill-disciplined units run from Kabul's former Khad secret police head-quarters. There were also 150 soldiers from the US 101st Airborne ... the Americans were obsessed with one idea: that the village contained leaders from the Taliban and Osama bin Laden's al-Qa'ida movement.

A former member of a Special Forces unit from one of America's coa-lition partners supplied his own explanation for the American behaviour when I met him a few days later. "When we go into a village and see a farmer with a beard, we see an Afghan farmer with a beard," he said. "When the Americans go into a village and see a farmer with a beard, they see Osama bin Laden."[27]

Mohamedin continues: "the Americans were also firing bullets. Several peppered a wrecked car in which another villager, a taxi driver called Abdullah, had been sleeping. He was badly wounded. So was Haji Birgit Khan's son."

A military spokesman claimed that US soldiers had "come under fire" in the village and so killed one and wounded two "suspected Taliban or al-Qa'ida members." "The implication—that 85-year-old Haji Birgit Khan was the gunman—is clearly preposterous," says Fisk. "The two wounded were presumably Khan's son and Abdullah, the taxi driver. The US claim that they were Taliban or al-Qa'ida members was a palpable lie—since both of them were subsequently released."

Fisk says the soldiers took away 55 village men and confiscated all the weapons in the village. The captives were bound, helicoptered to Kandahar, interrogated (some stripped naked), and staked to the ground in cages for five days. Finally, the Americans accepted they were innocent. They apologized, recompensed them with a few dollars, and took them back to their village. "But," Fisk continues,

> there was a far greater tragedy to confront the men when they reached Hajibirgit. In their absence—without guns to defend the homes, and with

the village elder dead and many of the menfolk prisoners of the Americans—thieves had descended on Hajibirgit. A group of men from Helmand province, whose leader is Abdul Rahman Khan—once a brutal and rapacious "mujahid" fighter against the Russians, and now a Karzai government police commander—raided the village once the Americans had taken away so many of the men. Ninety-five of the 105 families had fled into the hills, leaving their mud homes to be pillaged.

Abdul had told the Americans this was a Taliban village, so that his men could pillage it. "Today," Fisk concludes, "Hajibirgit is a virtual ghost town, its village leader dead, most of its houses abandoned. The US raid was worthless."

This became a familiar litany across Afghanistan. Villages, convoys and no less than three wedding parties were bombed or raided because of trigger-happy American planes and soldiers or false testimony from rival Afghan leaders. Only two died in Fisk's village, but in Qalaye Niazi the estimates range from 32 to 107. In Oruzgan 15 to 21 were killed and the survivors allege they were imprisoned and beaten by Americans interrogating them. In Mudoh 50 died. "I curse America," said a survivor, kneeling over his wife's grave. A US soldier declared, "It's impossible. They all look the same and they all carry guns." A British soldier said, "if you carry a gun, as half Afghan men do, and point it at one of the coalition special forces, you will inevitably die quickly and once you've been shot, you are al-Qaeda/Taliban by definition."[28] The Arabic newspapers did not much embroider such stories. They took the basic story from the news agencies, tended to go for higher estimates of the dead and called the victims "martyrs" and the perpetrators "terrorists." They also often gave reasons why the mistake was made—saying, for example, that five cars were seen in front of a house making the Americans think they were Taliban leaders.[29] Add trigger-happy panic, misinformation from warlords—some with American satellite phones—and massacres result. US forces were poorly equipped for imperial pacification. The wedding-party incident generated serious blowback. A year later local rocket attacks on US troops were attributed to bereaved relatives.

Rumsfeld apologized to the Canadian government for the death of its soldiers, and there was later a trial of the American pilots who made the mistake. To apologize and seek justice for the Canadians but not the Afghans seemed like racism. Rumsfeld eventually voiced brief regret for the attack on the wedding party, adding that such mistakes were "inevitable." He said another incident was "unfortunate" but "no "mistake," since US forces had been fired on first—though all the Afghan witnesses deny this. Rumsfeld added, "Lets not call them innocents. We don't know quite what they were." He revealed that US forces were under orders to "lean forward, not back" in searching for al-Qaeda and Taliban fighters. In 2003 he was still alleging that apparent "civilian casualties" had resulted from the Taliban moving corpses from hospitals to bombing sites.[30] Military spokesmen denounced most accusations as enemy propaganda, maintaining that extraordinary efforts had been made to minimize civilian casualties.[31] Rear Admiral Craig Quigley was more honest. He conceded it was impossible to check these stories, since "we did not have the people on the ground to check." He added that to date no soldier had been disciplined for breaking the rules of engagement. The Pentagon promised investigations, but no results have been released. There was no contrition, no public review of policies to attempt to reduce casualties. Again, the same cavalier attitude to evidence, with Rumsfeld leading the way.

Much franker was Chief Warrant Officer Dave Diaz, heading the first of the Special Forces A-Teams on the ground directing the bombers onto their targets. He told his men:

> Yes, it is a civilian village, mud hut, like everything else in this country. But don't say that. Say it's a military compound. It's a built-up area, barracks, command and control. Just like with the convoys: If it really was a convoy with civilian vehicles they were using for transport, we would just say hey, military convoy, troop transport.

The pilots came to accept the judgements of men like Diaz, directing fire from the ground. Although Diaz says his men tried to avoid killing civilians, on certain occasions they found women and children intermingled with persons they assumed to be Taliban fighters. He said that since they needed to strike at that moment, "the guidance I gave my team, and the guidance from higher [headquarters] is that they are combatants." Sgt 1st Class Tom Rosenbarger, a 14-year Special Forces veteran, vetted the requests for strikes that Diaz's men called in. But he sat 1,500 miles away in Prince Sultan air base outside Riyadh, Saudi Arabia.[32]

But Rumsfeld's Pentagon systematically conceals the truth. He set up a Pentagon Office of Strategic Influence part of whose stated mission was to generate disinformation and propaganda. After a storm of protest, Rumsfeld assured us that the Pentagon would never lie to Americans. He shut down the office but recreated it in 2002, headed by an undersecretary responsible for "special plans," a euphemism for deception. The Air Force set up a department for "destruction, degradation, denial, disruption, deceit and exploitation"—known as "D5E." As William Arkin concludes, in the new military truth is high on the casualty list.[33]

The Pentagon's ability to control the media by operating a tightly controlled media pool in the war zone has increased through recent wars. The atrocity of 9-11 added some self-censorship by reporters affected by the coercive emotional patriotism sweeping America. Any criticism of the war was widely regarded, not just as unpatriotic, but also as disrespect for our dead. But once the ground war got going, the hacks fanned out. They enjoyed being liberated, roaming around for local color, following rumors of atrocities, paying interpreters for getting striking quotes from photogenic Afghans. This is what reporters are good at and like doing. They reported these incidents frankly and vividly—unlike their avoidance of boring casualty statistics. They showed sympathy and pity for the Afghans. They were not able to do the same in Iraq.

But they are not permitted by their editors to stay long with a story. They move on to the next one. The first rule of the game routinely played by the Pentagon and politicians against the media is never admit mistakes. If you do, they will crucify you. So the Pentagon developed a second rule: stall, avoiding admitting fault and then the incident becomes stale, last week's news. For, as Donald Rumsfeld gleefully noted of journalists, "they've got the attention-span of gnats."[34] Criticism then went from the networks and national newspapers into the minority press and the internet.

Criticism also went abroad. As the last chapter showed, the proliferation of weapons of mass communication shifted ideological power in the world away from the US. Pakistani reporters were in Afghanistan before US ground forces arrived and they detailed numerous American mistakes and atrocities which were reproduced around the Middle East. Once the ground war started, few foreign media could match the resources of US networks or newspapers, or the international wire services. Most Middle Eastern and Asian journalists used these sources to file their own reports from back home in the office. Infuriated by the arrogance and dishonesty of the Pentagon, they wrote commentaries on American atrocities, often using American-provided materials. They did this from Dublin to Da Nang, from Vladivostock to Santiago de Chile. In allied countries, conservative newspapers might support the US line, but liberal ones did not. The British *Guardian, Independent* and *Observer*, and the French *Le Monde* became especially pointed in their reporting. Their articles were reprinted across the world. The contrast between them and the patriotically self-muzzling US media was great.

But Muslim reporters were the most livid. The Qatar-based satellite TV network Al-Jazeera, beaming to 35 million people across the Middle East, was actually in Kabul and Kandahar when the war started. Its Kabul correspondent Tasir Alouni became world famous for his reports showing the devastation caused by US bombing. Al-Jazeera's power was recognized by the Bush administration, which asked the Emir of Qatar to muzzle it. The emir refused, since its activities make him seem liberal, and Al-Jazeera is careful not to attack him. The emir embarrassed the US by publishing its request—which Al-Jazeera publicized with relish across the Middle East. Administration officials then belatedly took the path of democracy. They sought interviews with Al-Jazeera, attempting to get their viewpoint boomed out over the Muslim world. The Bush administration still accuses it of bias, but given the bombings, civilian casualties and Pentagon evasions, Al-Jazeera did not need to doctor its Afghan reporting, or its vivid, horrific photographs of the dead, the dying and the destroyed.[35] Its pictures were genuine, of real civilian corpses, real wounded people. Al-Jazeera has made a specialism of such video sequences in Palestine. In Afghanistan the photos were contrasted with Bush administration denials. This is powerful if perfectly conventional media technique. It is not easy for the viewer to reject the message. Al-Jazeera may have been selective in what it showed, but it invented nothing. Even its tendency to exaggerate the numbers killed only matched American minimizations. They sometimes say 10,000, we say 1,000.

The US exacted brutal revenge, bombing Al-Jazeera's Kabul office just before the Northern Alliance occupied the city. The Pentagon said it had mistaken the building for a Taliban office. Skepticism greeted this, since the bombing ensured that any post-victory massacres and reprisals by Northern Alliance troops were less likely to be reported. Alouni himself was seized and beaten up by Northern Alliance soldiers, and only released after the intervention of Paktia tribal groups. One of his cameramen was arrested and is now in Guantanamo Bay.

These media responses were reflected in different national perceptions of the war. Most Americans approved greatly. Over 60 percent of Americans said afterwards that the war was totally justified, compared to under 10 percent of people in most Muslim countries. Differences with

Europe were smaller but still significant. Fifty-five percent of Americans said that the conduct of the war had been "excellent" or "good," compared with only 35 percent of Europeans.[36] Victory might still outweigh all this, but what did victory achieve? I consider the treatment of the defeated and the consequences for Afghanistan. I leave for the next chapter the war's impact on terrorism.

CONSOLIDATION OF VICTORY: REPRISALS, PRISONERS

The initial consolidation on the ground of the aerial victory depended mostly on the Northern Alliance and warlord forces. They proved as bad as the Taliban's. They ethnically cleansed, and instead of imprisoning women inside the burqa and the home, they raped them. Fifty thousand Pashtuns fled from northern Afghanistan, arriving in a desperate condition at UN refugee camps. Uzbeki warlord Hashim dismissed atrocities with a wave of his hand, saying "They are al-Qaeda." An Uzbek shepherd boy said, "During Taliban times, we would have been beaten for trying to bring our sheep over the hills. The Pashtuns were arrogant, and they were cruel."[37] Now the Uzbeks were on top, driving their sheep wherever they pleased.

Prisoners were maltreated. In an incident confirmed by UN observers General Dostum's soldiers packed several hundred Taliban prisoners into sealed trucks and took them for a long drive. On arrival, said one soldier, "they opened the doors and the dead bodies spilled out like fish." Survivors told of having licked and chewed each other's skins in a desperate attempt to escape dehydration. Reading this reminded me of the appalling descriptions of Nazi cattle-trucks I had read in a previous research project. General Dostum denied it all. When he was not believed, he denied any personal involvement, and promised an investigation—which never materialized. The UN reports that his cronies intimidate and even kill witnesses to the massacre. The Pentagon refused to talk about it.[38] But by now there were still only about 3,000 US and other foreign soldiers in the whole of Afghanistan. They were unable to monitor their allies, let alone the country.

But a few Americans were also involved in atrocities. They were desperate to get intelligence on the al-Qaeda leaders who were the supposed point of the invasion. Reporter Dana Priest described the interrogation techniques used by CIA operatives at a high-security facility inside Bagram air base outside Kabul. There (as in Diego Garcia and other high-security sites) no outsiders are allowed in. Americans present admitted that captives are often "softened up" by MPs and US Army Special Forces troops who beat them up, before they are moved into tiny cells. Then they were interrogated using techniques classified as torture by human rights groups:

> Those who refuse to cooperate inside this secret CIA interrogation center are sometimes kept standing or kneeling for hours, in black hoods or spray-painted goggles, according to intelligence specialists familiar with CIA interrogation methods. At times they are held in awkward, painful positions or deprived of sleep with a 24-hour bombardment of lights—subject to what are known as "stress and duress" techniques.

Some who do not cooperate are turned over to foreign intelligence services whose tortures have been documented by the US government and human rights organizations. One official said "I ... do it with my eyes open." The understanding is, "We don't kick the [expletive] out of them. We send them to other countries so they can kick the [expletive] out of them."

At a September joint hearing of the House and Senate intelligence committees, Cofer Black, then head of the CIA Counterterrorist Center, spoke cryptically about the agency's new forms of "operational flexibility" in dealing with suspected terrorists. "This is a very highly classified area, but I have to say that all you need to know: There was a before 9/11, and there was an after 9/11," Black said. "After 9/11 the gloves come off." Other officials told Priest all this was "just and necessary." One said, "If you don't violate someone's human rights some of the time, you probably aren't doing your job. ... I don't think we want to be promoting a view of zero tolerance on this. That was the whole problem for a long time with the CIA." A second said, "our guys may kick them around a little bit," while a third, referring to decisions made about providing medical treatment to wounded prisoners, said, "pain control is a very subjective thing." Yet it was later revealed as being objective. In March 2003 US officials admitted that the deaths of two prisoners in their custody at Bagram air base had been homicides caused by repeated blunt-force injuries inflicted during interrogation.[39]

All this was clearly worrying some other American soldiers. US Special Forces soldiers probably leaked or facilitated reporters' access to two damaging stories and pictures. From a very secure location inside Kandahar airport came the sickening shots of hooded and chained prisoners, some of them drugged, kneeling before their US captors with hands tied behind their backs. Then they were dragged onto US military aircraft to be taken to Guantanamo Bay. The pictures were shown all over the world. Even more extraordinary was the leaked tape and grainy footage of an encounter at the Mazar al-Sharif fortress where hundreds of Taliban soldiers had just surrendered.[40]

This was the extraordinary meeting between the two young Americans whom the war turned into icons of good and evil. Good was personified by Johnny "Mike" Spann, the 32-year-old CIA officer killed shortly after this encounter, lionized as a national martyr and buried at Arlington National Cemetery. Evil was 20-year-old John Walker Lindh, a loner on a quest for the meaning of life, who had converted to Islam and run away to fight with the Taliban. He had been captured without even firing a shot, demonized and convicted of treason. We did not at first realize they had ever met.

The footage reveals a bright Sunday morning in the compound outside the fortress of Mazar al-Sharif. Dozens of Taliban prisoners are sitting in the compound. Waiting to interrogate them are Mike Spann and a CIA colleague known only as Dave. Spann is wearing blue jeans and a black jumper. A Kalashnikov rifle is strapped across his back. Walker Lindh, known in the prison as Abdul Hamid, is obviously of special interest. He is brought over, his elbows tied behind his back, and pushed down to the ground. He sits cross-legged, head bowed, long hair obscuring his face. He is wearing loose black trousers and a long black tunic.

Spann squats down facing Walker Lindh.

SPANN: Where are you from? Where are you from? You believe in what you're doing here that much, you're willing to be killed here? How were you recruited to come here? Who brought you here? Hey! [*He snaps his fingers in Walker Lindh's face. He does not respond.*]

SPANN [to Walker]: Hey you. Right here with your head down. Look at me. I know you speak English. Look at me. Where did you get the British military sweater? ... How did you get here? ... Put your head up. Don't make me have to get them to hold your head up. Push your hair back. Push your hair back so I can see your face.

An Afghan soldier pulls his hair back, and holds his head up for the picture.

SPANN: You got to talk to me. All I want to do is talk to you and find out what your story is. I know you speak English.

Silence. Spann walks away. Northern Alliance soldiers tighten the ropes tying his elbows behind his back, an officer gives him a kick in the stomach, and his hair is pulled back. Dave walks up.

DAVE: Mike!

SPANN: Yeah, he won't talk to me.

DAVE: OK, all right. We explained what the deal is to him.

SPANN: I was explaining to the guy we just want to talk to him, find out what his story is.

DAVE: [loudly] The problem is he's got to decide if he wants to live or die and die here. We're just going to leave him, and he's going to fucking sit in prison the rest of his fucking short life. It's his decision, man. We can only help the guys who want to talk to us. We can only get the Red Cross to help so many guys.

SPANN: Do you know the people here you're working with are terrorists and killed other Muslims? There were several hundred Muslims killed in the bombing in New York City. Is that what the Koran teaches? I don't think so. Are you going to talk to us?

Walker Lindh does not respond

DAVE [to Spann]: That's all right, man. Gotta give him a chance, he got his chance.

Spann and Dave stand and talk to each other. Both look frustrated.

SPANN [to Dave]: Did you get a chance to look at any of the passports?

DAVE: There's a couple of Saudis and I didn't see the others.

SPANN: I wonder what this guy's got?

Walker Lindh is pulled to his feet by an Afghan guard, and taken away.

Shortly after this footage was shot, prisoners rushed from the fortress and grabbed their captors' rifles. Spann was killed in the early stages of the uprising. The prisoners were isolated inside the fortress and bombed mercilessly. Walker Lindh was captured and taken to the US. He cooperated with prosecutors, admitted he had taken up arms with the Taliban, but denied he had intended fighting against the US or that he had even fired a shot. No contrary evidence to this was produced, but he was sentenced to 20 years' imprisonment.

This had been a "Mutt and Jeff" interrogation routine, with Dave playing the hard man. It violates the Geneva Conventions since Walker Lindh is threatened with speedy death in appalling prison conditions without Red Cross attention, if he does not tell all he knows. The threat was credible, since over a thousand Taliban prisoners did die in Northern Alliance custody.

But all talk of the Geneva Convention, of due process, of evidence openly given and reviewed, remained anathema to the US administration.[41] Around 600 supposedly hard-core prisoners from Afghanistan were taken to a US base at Guantanamo Bay in Cuba and held without trial.[42] They had no access to anyone (including one another). They were outside both the Geneva Conventions and US law. President Bush declared them not prisoners of war but "unlawful combatants." Two grounds were given. Vice-President Cheney said that since the Taliban did not wear uniforms, or "come in as representatives of the army of a state ... they don't satisfy the requirements that are in the Geneva Convention." The second ground was that the prisoners were too bad to be treated well. Bush called them "killers." Cheney said, "They target civilians. That's a violation of the laws of war. ... These are bad people." Ashcroft said they were "uniquely dangerous." Rumsfeld said they were "the hardest of the hard," "the worst of the worst"—"These are among the most dangerous, best-trained, vicious killers on the face of the earth."[43]

Deputy Assistant Attorney-General John Yoo confessed to greater ambition. "What the administration is trying to do is create a new legal regime," he said. Under the Geneva Conventions, Yoo said,

> people are detained usually until the end of the war, and then they are released, they go home. Does that make sense in this kind of a conflict, where the individuals ... who are being detained are members of terrorist organizations?... Does it make sense to ever release them if you think they are going to continue to be dangerous even though you can't convict them of a crime?[44]

Note the word "ever." To hold someone without trial *forever,* without even bringing a charge against him, because you cannot get a conviction, reminds me of totalitarian regimes. Forever is a long time, but 18 months later none of the detainees at Guantanamo Bay had been charged with anything. No one had appeared even in a military kangaroo court, let alone an open one. It is believed that a few prisoners will appear before tribunals before the end of 2003, though these will primarily extract information rather than conduct judicial trials.[45]

The prisoners are held in solitary confinement in a cell sized 6.8 × 8 feet. They are taken out, shackled for interrogation and to shower and exercise in the yard on their own for 15 minutes twice a week. Conditions are not insanitary, there is no evidence of torture, and the Red Cross is visiting (no one else is). Under these conditions, being shackled prior to interrogation must be welcome, signaling a break with solitude and real human contact. My dog loves to be leashed for she knows that means a walk. The Bush administration says the camp regime meets the "spirit" of the Conventions it has rejected. Yet it brooks no outside restraints. The President alone will decide, because of the exigencies of the war against terrorism.

This is complete unilateralism, of a kind not seen since World War II. Any previous breaches of Geneva Conventions by Western states, as for example in British maltreatment of IRA prisoners, have been secretive and shamefaced when exposed—and Britain did submit to the punishment exacted by the European Court of Justice. The US designation of the prisoners as "unlawful enemy combatants" has no standing in international law.[46] The Conventions, signed by the US in 1949, do not allow exceptions for especially "bad" people. They identify only two categories, combatants and civilians. Combatants are the armed forces "of a Party to the conflict as well as members of militias or volunteer corps forming part of such armed forces," or they are "members of other militias and members of other volunteer corps, including those of organized resistance movements" whose main marks are bearing arms and having a "fixed distinctive sign recognizable at a distance" (Article 4.1 and Article 4.2. a, b and c). The Taliban forces fit the first part of the definition and so are (legal) combatants. Al-Qaeda men may partially fit the second part, being volunteers in an organized detachment, and in the war the US military had said they were deployed as a unit alongside Taliban regulars. Full uniforms are probably not required in this definition (and few Afghan fighters on any side had them). The question is whether al-Qaeda fighters were recognizable as combatants at a distance.

In two articles in *Al-Ahram*, Nyier Abdou and Pascale Ghazaleh quoted international legal experts. These disagreed over whether al-Qaeda fighters would qualify as POWs, but they all said that the US could not interpret the laws of war as it pleases. The Conventions state that all prisoners must be given POW status until "competent tribunals" can settle their status. The US had organized one thousand such tribunals after the 1991 Gulf War. But not now. Abdou concluded: "we should guard against extremism, and ensure that the basic values for which we stand are not compromised in the fight against a serious threat. Terrorists believe that anything goes in the name of their cause. The fight against terror should not buy into that logic." Ghazaleh was blunter: "the prisoners have already been condemned ... not to death by a military tribunal—but to subhuman status."[47] This is a fair indication of the range of views among Middle Eastern, and indeed global, elite opinion, except for conservative media in allied countries. This was racial dehumanization of the enemy.

And so the International Red Cross, Amnesty International, Human Rights Watch, lawyers' NGOs and a commission of British judges all challenged the US legal position.[48] Many governments also voiced their disquiet. Some observed that US decisions might come back to haunt them, if US soldiers were captured by some future enemy. Since the Gulf War US soldiers have been the most likely to receive the benefits of the Geneva Conventions. Once again, the US administration confirmed all the world's worst stereotypes of itself. Guantanamo produced yet more global alienation.

All prisoners—not just al-Qaeda—were defined as being as outside a conventional war/state context. The Taliban, despite its planes, tanks, artillery batteries, forts and government infrastructures—which the US took pains to devastate—was considered not a state at all, but a terrorist network of bad individuals. This was absurd. It was the government of Afghanistan. Moreover, the vast majority of the Taliban soldiers, and many of the foreign volunteers as well (most of the Pakistanis, Chechens, Uzbekhs, even some Arabs), had no inkling until they were bombed that they were fighting the United States. They believed their enemies were other Afghan factions. The Chechen, Uzbekh and Kashmiri knowledge of al-Qaeda would be largely confined to gratitude for its help, undercut by its off-putting Wahhabi brand of Islam. In relation to the US they were innocents.

But it was a surprise—it presumably horrified the Bush administration—that this also seemed true of the "worst of the worst." US intelligence officials were disappointed by the information obtained from the detainees, admitting that most were of "little or no education" and almost all were "low- and middle-level" persons. Officials speak of prisoners being classified as "low value" yet sent to Guantanamo just the same. So were all Arabs caught in sweeps on either side of the Afghan/ Pakistan border, and all those denounced to the Americans by someone who bore them a grudge. When the US claims to have captured al-

Qaeda leaders, it holds them elsewhere (location unknown). Guantanamo Bay is merely a holding camp for indefinite detention without trial. It contains small fry. As a Pakistani Embassy official in Washington remarked:

> I personally think ... a lot of them were just cannon fodder. They were people motivated by their village clerics, that Islam was in danger. They went to fight. ... It is very difficult to categorize someone who picked up arms and thought they were fighting for a pristine Islamic movement as someone who really wanted to go like a terrorist and blow up post offices and buses and trains.[49]

After four months, in April 2002, the first detainee was released. This lost soul was so mentally unstable that interrogators called him "Wild Bill." He would eat his own feces and was completely incoherent. After ten months a Pakistani, aged 60, and three Afghans, two in their seventies and a younger man, age 35, were released. Journalists clustered around the three Afghans.

One was Mohammed Hagi Fiz, an illiterate nomad, probably in his seventies, though he himself declared he was 105. He seemed impressed by being met off the plane by President Karzai and the world's press, and was in good spirits. "I had very good food there. Even Mr. Karzai doesn't have as good food here." He proudly showed off new shoes and clothes. He added, "My family has no idea where I am, and I've not had any word from them. I don't even know if they're still alive. All they know is that I went to a doctor for treatment, and disappeared." Karzai said the man was obviously senile. Fiz said he had been initially picked up from an Afghan clinic. Maybe he had also been senile when he went into Guantanamo.

Mohammed Sadiq said he was 90 but seemed in his seventies. He was also frail and used a cane. He had been picked up from his home, he had no idea why. These two said they had played no part in the war, and it is difficult to see how they could have done. The third man was 35-year-old Jan Mohammed, who had fought. He said, "They kept us in cages like animals. We were only allowed out twice per week, for half an hour." He said, "I wasn't Taliban, but the Taliban made me fight with them. I'm innocent. I'm a farmer." All three said they had been treated well by the Americans, though they had been interrogated a dozen times each for upwards of an hour each time. A fourth man, aged 60, was released at the same time into Pakistan.[50]

These were men caught in the wrong place at the wrong time. Again, the Americans were victims of their own lack of intelligence. How many hours of interrogation did it take them to figure out that Fiz was not faking senility? Maybe they thought he was the patriarch of the movement.

Even army sources concede that at least 59 other prisoners are of no intelligence significance. But bureaucratic immobility, and the fear of admitting mistakes or letting go "the twenty-first bomber" stops the Pentagon from releasing them. One senior interrogator was rightly furious. "We're basically condemning these guys to long-term imprisonment. If they weren't terrorists before, they certainly could be now." How ingenious the Pentagon is in creating more terrorists! One consequence of these leaks was the release on March 25, 2003, of 18 more Aghans. They emerged blinking onto the streets of Kabul with no money and no means of getting home after over a year in captivity, still baffled over why they had been kept so long. That left at least 640 still imprisoned in Guantanamo Bay.

The Pentagon seem to have suspected Abdul Ahad Rahim of being the mastermind. He is an Islamic scholar, author of 19 books, formerly with Jamaat-ud-Da'wa, a Wahhabi sect. He is an Afghan but lives in Peshawar, Pakistan, where his library was frequented by Saudis. He had quit Jamaat-ud-Da'wa when it supported the US military operation in Afghanistan, and it is believed the sect leaders were paying back old scores by denouncing him to the Americans. He may have already incurred American wrath for having offered a reward of five million Afghanis for the capture of President Clinton. This was in retaliation against Clinton's offer of five million dollars for the capture of Osama bin Laden. When told that nobody would be tempted to capture Clinton for what amounted to only a few dollars, Abdul Rahim replied that Clinton was only worth that much. It was presumed that this was a joke, but the Americans lacked a sense of humor. Afghans who know him describe him as a scholar who cannot be expected to indulge in acts of terrorism. But Abdul and his brother disappeared—whisked off to Guantanamo Bay. After six months the family received a postcard from the pair saying they were there.[51] Presumably some detainees really were connected to al-Qaeda, but isn't it time for them to be charged with something? If I were Abdul Rahim or his brother, I would now be tempted to become a terrorist mastermind! Meanwhile the discontent of their families is broadcast across the Muslim world. The administration's legal chicanery over Guantanamo was revealed as counter-productive and even comical. There was no need to have alienated almost everyone outside the US. Once again, unilateral militarism plus racism alienated the outside world, for no good reason.

PACIFICATION IMPERFECT

Victory had been assured with only a couple of hundred Americans on the ground. Its consolidation involved several foreign troop contingents, mainly Americans. Pacification after victory has involved about 10,000–12,000, of whom around 8,000 have been Americans. We saw in Chapter 1 that this increase has been normal in imperial conquests, though the killing efficiency of American bombing had exaggerated the contrast. But since the Pentagon was still reluctant to risk American lives, it entrusted the capture of fleeing al-Qaeda groups to Northern Alliance and other warlord fighters. They also preferred to avoid hard fighting and sometimes they accepted bribes from the enemy. Neither Afghans nor Americans were willing to go into dangerous cave complexes. This proved costly at the caves of Tora Bora, where most Taliban and al-Qaeda leaders were believed to be hiding. Most escaped, which is often described as "the biggest mistake of the war," for getting these men had been the main war aim. Eyewitnesses tell of a chapter of errors—of Americans bombing the wrong escape route, of Pakistani troops withdrawn from the border just when the fugitives were headed there, and of warlords accepting bribes to look the other way. The local border population treated them like heroes and helped them escape. So did smugglers claiming religious motives: "Thank God I was able to help the Arabs. I did my duty for my Muslim brothers," said one.[52] But they were also well paid.

Again, the mistakes were part of a pattern. Six months after the new Karzai regime was installed, David Zucchino accompanied soldiers of the 82nd airborne division searching Afghan villages on intelligence tips provided by Special Forces.[53] The soldiers were seeking the many Taliban fighters believed to be in the area. "It is a target-rich environment," said Lt Col. Martin Schweitzer. Zucchino says the local reaction "to the sudden invasion of Americans in body armor was [that] the men and boys were sullen, suspicious and resentful, the women fearful and wary." The GIs told him they often find grenades inside women's clothing. Zucchino notes their high-tech gear: "streamlined M-4 rifles with infrared laser sights that put a red dot on the target. They have NODs, night optical devices, that turn night into day, laser pointers that spotlight targets for attack aircraft, thermal imaging devices that detect body heat and global positioning systems accurate to within a yard." "We own the night," Lt Col. Schweitzer boasted. The Taliban were so outgunned they relied on stealth, roadside bombs and land-mines. When the Americans arrived, they left. When the Americans left, they returned. This was asymmetric warfare, one side poorly armed but fast across familiar terrain, the other heavily armed, but slow amid an alien land. "That's the problem," a sergeant said. "These people won't come out and fight us. They just hang back and blend in." He wanted a "fair fight," like all soldiers confronted by guerrillas!

With help from local informers, the Americans find fixed weapons caches, of which the country is stuffed full. Two of the three 82nd companies found a cache that day, though none found any Taliban. They did find Amar Gul's bin Laden poster. "Hey, sergeant, you gotta see this," said Pfc Andrew Johnson to his squad leader, Sgt Wylie Hutchinson. Gul claimed it was only a lottery poster from Pakistan, belonging to his absent uncle. Hutchinson grabbed the poster down from the wall and crumpled it. "I don't believe you, man," he said, and took him away for interrogation. Schweitzer's summary of the day seemed optimistic: "Damn, we hit 'em hard today." He smacked his fist into his palm. "And we're gonna go back and hit 'em again." They must be quaking at the prospect of losing more posters.

The British love to poke fun (as I have just done) at over-armed, over-protected GIs. The conservative *Sunday Telegraph* of June 30 cited a senior Blair official "closely involved" in the war. He criticized the US search operations as a "march in shooting" strategy, which was "backfiring" and "alienating" the population. He boasted: "We have years of experience in the tribal areas, and we know that using force will just backfire and increase sympathy for al-Qaeda." Brits extol the more rugged virtues of their own special forces—paratroopers, the SAS and the SBS, lightly armed and fast, merging into any surroundings, ready for hand-to-hand action. Some US military experts say that the only foreign troops the US really needs are the British Special Forces. Donald Rumsfeld called them "some of the toughest, smartest troops in the world."

In late April, 1,700 British special forces were looking to clear out al-Qaeda forces from along the Afghan–Pakistan border. They found none. On 10 May, a large arms cache was found and blown up, but an allied warlord protested it belonged to him. Later in May hundreds of British troops rushed to assist Australian special forces in a firefight. The enemy had disappeared by the time British forces arrived. As British troops continued to scour the mountains, UK Defense Secretary Geoff Hoon denied things were going wrong. "This is not war by safari," he said.[54] Indeed, not. On safari you get to *see* the animals.

The small Australian contingent did the best at this type of warfare, if rather unwittingly. Unique in their willingness to take risks, their patrols ranged wider. Thus exposed, they were three times attacked by Taliban forces during May–June 2002. This in turn exposed the Taliban to massive counter-attack from Coalition forces. On one occasion ten Taliban were killed, on another, two. The Australians had to fight hard to avoid casualties, and they deserved their medals for bravery, if not for intelligence.[55]

So the Taliban (a loose collection of factions and warlords anyway) have learned not to concentrate their soldiers. There remains residual counter-insurgency warfare, with thousands of highly equipped troops, backed by multimillion dollar high-tech assets, conducting long, uneventful sweeps for an elusive foe. The enemy occasionally fires at US troops, causing a few casualties. But most have gone home to wait out the US. They have support, most manifest in the frontier areas, though they may be future spoilers rather than rulers. They ambushed and killed two American soldiers at the end of March 2003, and three more in May. Taliban leaders have resurfaced with Mullah Omar declaring that the Americans would be "reduced to rubble." But this will be very low-intensity warfare for a while yet.

In the mass breakout from Tora Bora, dozens of Russian-speaking fighters volunteered to be the al-Qaeda rearguard. They stood out, and had nowhere to go. They stood and died at Tora Bora. There is a memorial to them, with surrounding three-foot wall and pink, green and white flags atop 20-foot poles. The site gets five or six carloads of visitors a day. The local doctor says that at night you can still hear their battle cry, "Allahu akbar," echoing through the valley.[56] Their appeal lives on in myth. They are our terrorists, but to others they are freedom fighters.

No one knows how many enemy fighters are left, either in Afghanistan or Pakistan. Identifying friend and foe is difficult when rival warlords denounce each other as "Taliban" or "al-Qaeda." In the North, Uzbek, Tajik and Hazara warlords squabble; in the capital Tajiks and Pushtuns. They claim loyalty to Karzai, since that brings US aid. Some fights are within ethnic lines, though defections occur across them. One Hazara fighter took his small force over to the Tajiks, saying,

"My leader was a sheep thief. It was a dishonor to be with him." Since the commander was reduced to stealing sheep, allegiance to him was no longer profitable. After fighting in Balkh in the North, one warlord said, "It was not major fighting to become a cause of concern. Only between 30 to 40 men from both sides have been killed."

In Gardez former Governor Padshah Khan Zadran was replaced by Wardak, the appointee of Hamid Karzai, America's client. In retaliation Zadran rained down rockets on the city, killing 30 civilians. A woman said she fled with her six children moments before a mortar round struck. "Now our house is destroyed. We ran away, we were very afraid." Zadran was outnumbered and forced to retreat but vowed to fight on. "I'll send in heavy armor," he fumed, "I'll send in multiple rocket launchers, I'll fire, and fire, and fire, all night and all day, until I bring this to a finish. I'll kill them all, humans and animals." He claimed he was attacked by al-Qaeda and Taliban sympathizers. Wardak's commanders said, "No, no, no. . . . He is a smuggler and a tyrant and a killer. . . . Unless we finish off Padshah Khan people will say the Karzai administration is a failure. There were no Taliban or Al Qaeda. We are going to wipe him out." Zadran still refused to recognize Karzai's government. In September 2002 his forces attacked the city of Khost, whose governorship he claimed. US military officials were anxious to conciliate him, since they needed his assistance against Taliban remnants. The UN envoy to Afghanistan, Lakhdar Brahimi, complained the faction fighting was undermining the Karzai administration. There were also assassinations of foreign aid workers and government ministers, and a near miss on Karzai himself.[57]

Karzai was elected by a national assembly of tribal elders, the *loya jirga*, and so enjoys some legitimacy. But Kabul is secure only because 4,800 international peacekeepers patrol it. Even Karzai's personal bodyguard is all-American. He controls little outside of Kabul. There is no peacekeeping force elsewhere and the US opposes setting one up. He has to divide and rule among the warlords. The foreign troops are insufficient to properly pacify a country this size, and 700,000 Afghans bear arms, only 3,000 of them being in the police force. Crime is rampant and indistinguishable from the tax-extorting road-blocks of warlords. In Herat local warlord Ishmael Khan controls the customs posts on the Iranian border, and so can appropriate $800,000 a year in customs dues. This makes him more powerful in the West than Karzai is in Kabul—a veritable feudal monarch. Fahim Khan controls the Panshir valley with his 18,000 Tajik troops but is also, curiously, defence minister. Opium-poppy production surged in 2002 back up to the highest pre-Taliban levels—they had effectively banned it in 2000. Public order worsened since the days of the Taliban. Its Islamism was oppressive, but it kept down the warlords and the poppies. Foreign aid trickles in. The international community promised $4.5 billion over five years, but remained well behind schedule in delivering it. The World Bank said that $10.2 billion was needed, Karzai himself $20 billion. Afghans are receiving $42 per head from the international community. Bosnians get $326; Kosovans $286 and East Timorese $195. The US fulfilled its initial commitments, but the administration refused an increase proposed by Congress. The war had cost $37 billion by February 2003.[58] American priorities were clear: victory but not pacification, militarism, not nation-building.

Rumsfeld said it "will take time and effort for the government to find its sea-legs," an unfortunate metaphor for a land-locked country. The CIA warned that warlords were bringing "violent chaos." The Pentagon tries to hunt down the Taliban, but can't find them. It alternatively tries to build up an Afghan army, so that the US can soon leave.[59] The army was to reach 10,000 men by the end of 2003, but failed to reach it. Recruitment and training were well behind schedule, and it might in any case break up into its warlord components if the US leaves. In February 2003 Germany said it was considering pulling its peacekeepers out. "Blowback" from the American preparations for war in Iraq was beginning to alienate the Afghan army in training. German peacekeepers were being threatened by them.

But what could we expect, given such a low commitment of resources? In contrast, the international community deployed 60,000 peacekeepers to Bosnia, a much smaller country. Afghanistan was not even "nation-building lite." This would be very disappointing if the US had intended nation-building or imperial pacification. Bush had initially promised "another Marshall Plan." He was lying. The US would not commit such resources to such a peripheral country. There are shorter, less vulnerable routes to bring Central Asian oil to the West. Afghanistan, with its history of failed states and warlordism is difficult to rule. But the US had no vital interest in Afghanistan beyond the removal of terrorism. It used the Northern Alliance and Karzai to force al-Qaeda out of the country, just as in the 1980s it used bin Laden and other Islamists to force out the Soviets. It then abandoned them. It now wants out again. The problem is how to get US troops out without causing too obvious and immediate a collapse so that the world condemns American opportunism.

Only if this happened would the US have done better than the Soviets. In achieving battlefield victory and installing a client regime in Afghanistan, the Soviets took even less time than the US did. In 1979 they airlifted troops straight into Kabul, seized power, brought in 115,000 troops to occupy all the cities, and installed a client regime. Since the US deployed far fewer US troops, it had to wait longer for the Northern Alliance warlords to drive their pick-up trucks into the capital. But having conquered, the Soviets made their big mistake. They did not leave it to their client, but stayed and attempted to impose order. Ten years later, after one million Afghan and 25,000 Soviet casualties, they retreated out of the country, leaving it to civil war. The Soviets had also been too protective of their soldiers—too much armor, not enough light infantry. By the 1980s communism was also reluctant to make sacrifices in imperial ventures.

Has the US done any different? Not yet. Can it do more? Probably not. It lacks the imperial will to consolidate victory and pacify Afghanistan. If this was ever an attempt at Empire, it is ending pitifully. But in reality it was just a punitive expedition. Over a century ago the British lost an expeditionary force in the Khyber Pass, and realized that they could not rule this country. Two decades ago the Soviets came to the same realization after more protracted defeat. The US reached the same conclusion with almost no losses. Al-Qaeda was kicked out of the country, which was the main point. But did Afghanistan benefit? I doubt it.

NOTES

1. *Daily Telegraph*, October 4, 2001.
2. The debate inside the White House is chronicled by Bob Woodward, *Bush at War*, New York: Simon & Schuster, 2002, pp. 176–7, 196.
3. "Why Do They Hate Us?" *Christian Science Monitor*, September 27, 2001.
4. *New York Times*, October 12, 2002.
5. See *www.gallup-international.com/terrorismpoll_figures.htm*; David Miller, "World Opinion Opposes the Attack on Afghanistan," *www.converge.org.nz/pma/rob00311.htm*; *http://europe.cnn.com/2002/US/02/26/gallup.muslims/*; *USA Today*, February 27, 2002.
6. In reality we have not yet done better than the Soviets, as I show later.

7. Woodward, *Bush at War*.

8. Eight reporters in different US newspapers quoted by Carl Conetta, "The 'New Warfare' and the New American Calculus of War," *Project on Defense Alternatives*, Briefing Memo no. 26, September 30, 2002.

9. *Foreign Affairs*, May–June 2002. His flaws are similar to those I identify later.

10. *Los Angeles Times*, January 21, 2002. Actually, Dostum had mostly fought on the Soviet side in the earlier civil wars.

11. Wendell Steavenson, October 23, 2002, *www.opendemocracy.net*.

12. Other estimates failed to meet the most basic standards of research, detailing some incidents, but giving neither sources nor the overall geographic or temporal coverage of their study. This characterized the lengthy report in the *Los Angeles Times*, June 2, 2002, and the apparently uncompleted study by Human Rights Watch to which many journalists referred.

13. Conetta's study occupies 20 pages of summary text and contains no raw data. Herold's is 180 pages, with lots of raw data, available at *http://pubpages.unh.edu/~mwherold*.

14. Quoted by Ian Traynor, *Guardian*, February 12, 2002.

15. So also concludes Kenneth Pollack, *The Threatening Storm: The Case for Invading Iraq*, New York: Random House, 2002, pp. 308–10.

16. MSF Report, February 21, 2002.

17. *Al-Ahram Weekly Online*, issues 566 and 570, December 2001, January 2002.

18. *Associated Press*, April 10, 2002.

19. Ian Traynor, *Guardian*, February 12, 2002.

20. "Ordinary Afghans Hurt by the War," *Time.com*, November 1, 2001.

21. *New York Times*, February 12, 2003.

22. See Stephen Biddle and colleagues, "Skill and Technology in Modern Warfare," *Joint Forces Quarterly*, summer 1999.

23. "Suited Up for Battle," *Los Angeles Times*, October 20, 2001, p. 3.

24. Interviewed by Wendell Steavenson, October 23, 2002, *http://www.opendemocracy.net*.

25. William Arkin, *Los Angeles Times*, October 26–27, 2002.

26. *Independent*, August 5, 2002.

27. Villagers in Lalazha believe that a Hellfire missile fired from a Predator drone killed three of their number because one of them, Darz Khan, known locally as "Tall Man Khan," was assumed from the air to be Osama himself (*New York Times*, February 11, 2002).

28. Rory Carroll, *Guardian*, January 7, 2002; Carlotta Gall, *New York Times*, February 11, 2002; David Zucchino, *Los Angeles Times*, June 2, 2002; Brendan O'Neill "One Wedding, Many Funerals," *www.spiked-online.com/Articles/00000006D95F.htm*; Madeleine Bunting, *Guardian*, May 22, 2002.

29. "Terrorist America Kills Civilians" and "America Commits Massacre in a Village North of Qandahar," two articles in *Al-Sha'b,* October 26, 2001.

30. *Los Angeles Times*, February 22, 2002.

31. Barry Bearak, *New York Times*, February 10, 2002.

32. Quoted by Dana Priest, "In War, Mud Huts and Hard Calls. As U.S. Teams Guided Pilots' Attacks, Civilian Presence Made Task Tougher ," *Washington Post*, February 20, 2002.

33. "The Military's New War of Words," *Los Angeles Times*, November 24, 2002.

34. Quoted by Woodward, *Bush at War*, p. 283.

35. Its photos are available widely, either at *aljazeerah.info/* or at *www.dqc.org/~ben/aljazeera* or *http://rawa.fancymarketing.net/s-photos. htm*.

36. USATODAY/CNN/Gallup Poll, March 1–3, 2002; tables 480/12 and 10f, from *www.worldviews.org/*.

37. Dexter Filkins, "A Tribe Is Prey To Vengeance after Taliban's Fall in the North," *New York Times*, March 7, 2002. *Human Rights Watch Report*, "Stop Abuses in Northern Afghanistan," March 7, 2002.

38. "The War Crimes of Afghanistan," *Newsweek*, August 26, 2002. *Al-Sha'b*, January 3, 2003, referring to a Scottish documentary on the incident, estimated that the number of prisoners killed was 3,000, presumably an exaggeration. See *www.alarbnews.com/alshaab* (in Arabic).

39. Dana Priest and Barton Gellman, "U.S. Decries Abuse but Defends Interrogations and Duress Tactics Used on Terrorism Suspects Held in Secret Overseas Facilities," *Washington Post*, December 26, 2002; *Los Angeles Times*, March 7, 2003.

40. Transcript available from *www.msnbc.com/news/668588.asp?cp1=1*.

41. That is, until during the Iraq invasion, when five American prisoners of war were paraded in uniform in front of television cameras by the Iraqi authorities. Rumsfeld complained of violations of the Geneva Convention. A few days later, American television showed pictures of Iraqi POWs stripped naked, cowering in far more humiliating circumstances. But these were both trivial violations compared to what happened in Afghanistan and Guantanamo Bay.

42. The administration did not release their exact numbers, nationalities or identities, but there were well over 600. Lawyers attempting to represent them said they came from about 34 countries and included about 150 Saudis, 85 Yemenis and under 100 Afghans.

43. *ABCNews.com*, January 27, 2002.

44. Warren Richey, "How Long Can Guantanamo Prisoners Be Held?" *Christian Science Monitor*, April 9, 2002.

45. *New York Times*, April 8, 2003.

46. The phrase came from a US Supreme Court ruling of 1942 dealing with eight Nazi saboteurs in the US. Yet these prisoners had received legal counsel, a speedy trial and appeal to civilian courts. The Guantanamo prisoners have none of these.

47. *Al-Ahram Weekly Online*, February 2002, issue nos 571–2.

48. See, for example, the forthright denunciation of US policies in Human Rights Watch, *World Report 2003*, available at *www.hrw.org*.

49. *Los Angeles Times*, August 18, October 23, and December 22, 2002; Joseph Lelyveld, "In Guantanamo," *New York Review of Books*, November 7, 2002.

50. *Los Angeles Times*, October 30, 2002.

51. The *News International* (Pakistan), internet edition, October 22, 2002; and Associated Press, *www.miraserve.com/pressrev/ENo8july02. htm*.

52. "How Al-Qaida Got Away," *Newsweek*, August 19, 2002.

53. *Los Angeles Times*, October 13, 2002.

54. "Charting the Progress of British Forces Afghanistan," *Observer*, May 19, 2002.

55. Benjamin James Morgan, "The Australian SASR at War in Afghanistan," August 2002. *http://www.efreedomnews.com/*.

56. *Newsweek*, August 19, 2002. It is common to call them "Chechens," but it is not clear from where in the former Soviet Union they came.

57. *Los Angeles Times*, February 19, 2002, *Middle East Times*, 2002, issue 18; *Times of India*, October 26, 2002.

58. Senator Robert Byrd, "Reckless Administration May Reap Disastrous Consequences," Address to US Senate, February 12, 2003, available at *www.CommonDreams.org*. Senator Byrd has been almost a lone voice on Capitol Hill opposing of the new imperialism. Peter Oborne, "On the roads of ruin," *Observer*, May 25, 2003; "Did we make it better?" *Guardian*, May 29, 2003.

59. Michael Gordon, "CIA Sees Threat Afghan Factions May Bring Chaos," *New York Times*, February 21, 2002.

SIX

THE WAR AGAINST (MUSLIM) TERRORISM

THE CRUCIAL DISTINCTION: NATIONAL AND INTERNATIONAL TERRORISTS

I define a "terrorist" as a non-state actor who attacks civilian targets in order to strike terror into the hearts of the enemy community. A "state terrorist" is a state doing the same thing. Obviously, both should be deplored and combated equally. But any war against terrorism must distinguish between two types, national and international. Terrorists all begin as national "freedom fighters," seeking to liberate their own land from what they see as alien oppressive rule. When some of them (usually out of weakness) turn to attack civilians as well as soldiers and officials, they become *national terrorists*, fighting locally, in their own homeland.

National terrorists/freedom fighters have the advantage of being able to fight as "guerrillas," hidden and protected among their own people. They are so well protected that the state seeking to repress them is bound to kill innocent bystanders in the process. Typically, the state's repression discriminates less and less between civilian and terrorist targets. Its forces fire into crowds, bomb or strafe or bulldoze buildings, round up and mistreat large numbers of civilians, etc. Terrorism begets state terrorism, and vice versa. I emphasized in Chapter 4 that freedom fighters, terrorist or not, are usually too deep-rooted to eradicate merely by repression. These national struggles are almost endless—until both sides grow weary and seek to conciliate. Yet there is no reason why any freedom fighters/terrorists should attack anyone except their local enemy. They should not attack the US, since the US rules no foreign lands. They would if the US did, of course.

But a few terrorists shift to become *international terrorists*, attacking groups and states abroad whom they identify as allies of their local enemy. But this is much riskier for them. Then they cannot as easily operate as guerrillas, for if they fight abroad, they fight exposed amid alien communities. Clearly, any American war against terrorism should be directed primarily against those who actually attack Americans—at international not national terrorists. National terrorists should not be the immediate concern of the US, and the US would be hard-pressed to beat them anyway. The fundamental strategy of America's war against terrorism should therefore be to separate international terrorists from any national support base, forcing them to fight in more exposed international conditions and not as genuine guerrillas. If the US strategy does the reverse, driving national and international terrorists together under the protection of sympathetic communities, it will not win the war. It will not "lose" it either, in any final sense, since their military power is insufficient to actually defeat the US. But they can make life extremely unpleasant for Americans for many years to come.

In designing his war against terrorism, Bush the Younger has made three fundamental mistakes. The first is to do exactly what I have just cautioned against, making no distinction between international and national terrorism. The US State Department's annual list of proscribed terrorist organizations gives details of them all, but it does not tell us whether they have recently attacked Americans.[1] The Bush administration has been attacking both indiscriminately, driving them together in self-defense against the US.

The second mistake, as Egyptian writer Ayman El-Amir says, is that Bush has

> blurred the dividing line between terrorism and national resistance. "You are either with us, or with the terrorists," he told nations and governments ... and he made 11 September the litmus test. Under his definition, the decades-long dialogue that sought to curb terrorism, while at the same time safeguard the right to struggle for national liberation, was lost. At times, the dialogue was frustrating and inconclusive, but over the years it produced 12 international conventions against terrorism.

All that progress was now lost, concluded El-Amir.[2]

The third mistake is to conduct a one-sided struggle against terrorists, while forgiving the atrocities of state terrorists. Thus the US condemns the Palestinian authority but not Israel, and it now gives the green light to Russia, China and others to repress their minority national liberation movements as they see fit. Yemen, Uzbekistan, Tajikistan and Pakistan have been showered with aid since the war on terrorism began. When Bush was asked about General Musharraf's arrogation of arbitrary personal and military powers he replied, "My reaction about President Musharraf, he's still tight with us on the war against terror, and that's what I appreciate."[3]

Unfortunately, these three mistakes are deeply rooted in American policy-making circles. A grand vision of future global development was presented by the CIA-led National Intelligence Council in 2000. It was based on expert conferences, in which I participated. The report began by enthusing about high-tech globalization which would bring renewed economic growth to the world. However, it observed that not everyone would benefit.

> Regions, countries, and groups feeling left behind will face deepening economic stagnation, political instability, and cultural extremism, along with the violence that often accompanies it. They will force the United States and other developed countries to remain focused on "old-world" challenges while concentrating on the implications of "new-world" technologies at the same time.

The main "new-world challenge" identified was the proliferation of WMDs. The "old-world" challenges were increased ethnic and religious strife and terrorism, whose underlying cause was seen as economic failure leading to state failure or state repression, both of which only increased ethnic and religious strife. Focusing on "transnational terrorism," it declared:

> States with poor governance; ethnic, cultural, or religious tensions, weak economies; and porous borders will be prime breeding grounds for terrorism. ... Much of the terrorism ... will be directed at the United States and its overseas interests. Most anti-US terrorism will be based on perceived ethnic, religious, or cultural grievances.[4]

This differs markedly from the explanation of ethnic/religious strife and terrorism which I gave in Chapter 3. The CIA-sponsored report saw ethno-nationalism not as modern but as "old world," and blamed it on economic failure, seen as exclusion from the process of American-led globalization, and on political failure—failed states. But politics suddenly disappeared when the report tried to explain why they attack the United States: their grievances against the US were entirely ethnic, religious and cultural. But why should this turn them against the US?

Only by adding a familiar American ethnocentrism: Americans are the "new-world" moderns; whereas unstable parts of the world are the "old world" carrying deep cultural resentments of us. This is the message American bestsellers carry in their titles as well as their texts: *The Lexus and the Olive Tree* and *Jihad versus McWorld*.[5] They resent us because we are modern. It is a simplistic, ethnocentric way of dismissing any grievances caused by our aggression. But we will find that international terrorists are largely unconcerned with our culture. They do not hate our culture or our democracy or our wealth, simply our foreign policy. Obviously, no document authorized by the head of the CIA (as this one was) would blame US foreign policy. In fact George Tenet has declared that the difficulty of eradicating terrorism arises from its "fundamental causes," which are "poverty, alienation, disaffection, and ethnic hatreds deeply rooted in history."[6] The preferred American story is that their own history, backwardness, poverty and cultural resentment causes terrorism—so we do not even have to listen to what they say are their actual grievances. Of course, the consequences of this misperception are appalling. Obviously, unlike our present foreign policy, we cannot possibly abandon our overall culture, democracy or wealth. All we can do, if we think these are the sources of their hatred, is to repress and kill them. This is supposed to be an *intelligence* document!

The NIC Report did mention state oppression, specifically by Russia, China and Middle Eastern states. It also implicitly made a distinction between "transnational" and other kinds of terrorism, though it did not pursue this. But any exploration of these issues is blocked by the overall stress on economic and state failure in Southern countries. Indeed, the NIC Report is much more sophisticated than the National Commission on Terrorism's Report, also published in 2000. This offered no explanation at all for terrorism. It identified "religiously motivated terrorist groups" operating alongside other terrorist groups "driven by visions of a post-apocalyptic future or by ethnic hatred. Such groups may lack a concrete political goal other than to punish their enemies by killing as many of them as possible."[7] What nonsense! They are as goal-orientated as any other political movement.

Unfortunately, after 9-11 it became almost impossible for Americans to raise issues of state oppression or to distinguish between different types of terrorism. After a short period of self-questioning, motives and causes were forgotten. Terrorism was evil, period. So Anthony Cordesman's major book on counter-terrorism quotes the NIC Report at length, for three pages, but with all the references to state oppression and distinctions between types of terrorist removed. Everything is now attributed simply to economic and state failure, without any discussion of rational motivations or causes.[8]

This perspective might make some sense of those truly desperate sub-Saharan "black holes" I identified in Chapter 3, which are failed economies and failed states. But this region's terrorists do not attack the US and the US does not attack them. The perspective makes very little sense when applied to the targets of the current US war against terrorism. Present Muslim terrorists come from a variety of countries, including the rather strong states of Israel, Saudi Arabia, India and Russia—and all except Russia have been rather successful in the global economy. As we see later, international terrorists have also been professionally successful people. They are, of course, attacking their local enemy, and sometimes Americans too, for *political* reasons.

Almost everyone ought to be able to agree on the desirable technical counter-terrorist measures. They must be rigorous, multilateral and applied with due regard for civil liberties. "Rigorous" means with enhanced security and vigilance measures and more resources for intelligence agencies. "Multilateral" means it must be fought in cooperation with other countries. Unilateralism—everyone agrees—would be a recipe for disaster. Since the nation state is responsible for security over its own territories, only cooperation between governments brings results. Luckily, it is easy to accomplish, since they all want to do it. Finally, since the US says it fights for freedom, it must do this with regard for civil liberties, demonstrating that democracy can subject violence to the rule of law. I will not discuss such technical measures further, but they could easily win the war against *existing* international terrorists, who are very exposed to attack.

But all the security measures in the world will achieve nothing if the US and others fail to staunch the flow of *future* terrorists. This flow will continue if international terrorism remains nourished by national liberation struggles. Only if the two forms of terrorism are separated can counter-terrorism measures work. The rest of this chapter is concerned with understanding how they are joined at present and how they might be separated. I look first at existing international terrorists. Who are they, where do they come from, whom do they hate, why does that include us, who are their sympathizers, and can they recruit future sympathizers? But first I must make one obvious point about *this* war on terrorism.

THE WAR AGAINST MUSLIM TERRORISM

The war against terrorism is directed almost entirely against Muslims. Twenty-four of the 36 currently proscribed organizations on the State Department list are Muslim. The remaining ones are almost all leftists, mostly in Colombia and Peru. The only non-Muslim ethnic or religious groups are the Basque ETA and the Northern Irish paramilitaries. The US does not proscribe or attack Hindu terrorists in India or Sri Lanka, nor Christian terrorists. It attacks Muslims.

The State Department also lists 26 countries whose nationals are said to present an elevated security risk within the United States. All male immigrants aged 16 or over from these countries who are not US citizens or resident aliens must report to the INS to be registered, fingerprinted and photographed. If they do not report, they are deported. If they do report and have in any way violated their visas, they are immediately taken into secret, indefinite detention. Of the 26 countries, all but North Korea are Muslim. The US made one embarrassing mistake. In December 2002, Armenia was added to the list. There was an immediate outcry. The Armenian ambassador protested simply and to the point, "We are a Christian country." Armenia was promptly removed from the list.

Twenty-five thousand men had reported by January 2003, and over 10 percent of them will be deported. A coalition of nine civil liberties groups called it a "flawed and misguided" scheme which has "damaged America's global image." As they observed, a real terrorist would be hardly likely to show up for registration. As is typical of the administration of Bush the Younger, the numbers of detainees, their names, and the location of their detention remain classified information. But they are virtually all Muslims. The immigration authorities do not detain South Koreans, who share the same ethnicity, language and historic religion with the "evil" North; while they privilege Cubans (from a "rogue state" country) who can arrive illegally and stay. So they can distinguish political differences among Koreans and Cubans, but not among Muslims. They are *all* suspects. What could be clearer to Muslims? This is a religious war.

Indeed, five days after 9-11 Bush the Younger referred to "this crusade, this war on terrorism." In private, he added, "They hate Christianity. They hate Judaism. They hate everything that is not them." White House councils of war routinely began with Christian prayers, and a former Bush speech-writer (whose phrase "axis of hatred" was then turned into "axis of evil") described the White House as pervaded by "the culture of modern Evangelicalism."[9] The administration quickly went into damage control to assure us that its war was not against Muslims or Islam. True, it was not directed against all Muslims, but it was *only* directed against Muslims. The Muslim world could hardly fail to notice, and its reporters did not fail to remind them.

The leaders of the two largest Muslim movements in Indonesia (and in the world) were invited to an annual congressional inter-religious prayer breakfast in Washington in February 2003. Both they and their organizations are moderate, but they declined, citing the detention of Indonesian citizens and the coming war on Iraq. One of them, Dr Ahmad Sjaffii Maarif (with a doctorate from the University of Chicago), said on Indonesian television that "only idiotic people" would attend the prayer session. As he said, "people could be praying for world peace at the same time as there was an attack on Iraq."[10] He was out by only three weeks.

The administration's bias must unfortunately be reflected in this chapter. I write almost entirely about Muslim terrorists, very little about other terrorists and not at all about state terrorists. *Mea culpa*. I start with the obvious terrorist.

OSAMA BIN LADEN

Osama bin Laden was born in Saudi Arabia in 1957. His mother was Syrian, his father a Yemeni who moved to Saudi Arabia around 1930, working as a dock laborer. He was a success story, starting a construction company which grew to be the biggest in the kingdom. Grown wealthy and well connected, he died when Osama was only 13. Four years later Osama married the first of his four wives, the maximum permitted under Islamic law. He has many children and appeared to enjoy a normal family life, insofar as his unusual career permitted.

He was well educated and received a Saudi university degree in economics and public administration. Then he ran some of the family businesses, amassing a personal fortune of around $300 million. He traveled extensively in the Middle East but probably never visited the West. Like his father, he embraced the austere Wahhabi version of Sunni Islam dominant among the Saudi elite. As a student he joined the Muslim Brotherhood, but was not politically active. He is soft-spoken and unassertive in person, possessing not personal but media charisma, for he is very photogenic—Saladdin with a Kalashnikov to Muslims, disturbingly Christ-like to us. But from his Saudi years, no one would have expected the notoriety that followed.

This originated in the 1979 Soviet invasion of Afghanistan. For Islamists, the Soviet Union was a bigger threat than the US, for it imposed godless communism throughout its Empire. The poorly armed Afghan mujahedeen fighters confronting Soviet troops needed all the help they could get. It came mainly in the form of CIA and Saudi financing and Pakistani training, but secondarily from an "international brigade" of radical Islamist volunteers drawn from over 30 countries, come to free a Muslim land from atheism. Bin Laden was the man the Saudis chose to channel money and men to the Afghan jihad. The Afghans and the Pakistani secret service (the ISI) had supposedly requested a royal to head the Saudi mission, but none was willing to endure the hardships. Bin Laden, wealthy, well connected, who already knew Afghanistan, was the closest they could get.

He began by donating construction equipment and fund-raising, and in 1984 established a hostel in Pakistan for incoming fighters. This turned into a military training camp spawning more in Afghanistan. Between 10,000 and 25,000 foreign Muslims volunteered for the jihad, comprising a useful 10 percent of all the Afghan fighters. Some went by way of his camps. It is unlikely he or his camps received CIA funds (which were channeled through the Pakistanis), though clearly the US was his ally at this time. Bin Laden also fought at the front, apparently bravely. In 1988, near the end of the war, he renamed his organization *al-Qaeda*, the base. So far, he was an international freedom fighter, attacking only military targets.

Next year he returned to Saudi and used al-Qaeda to organize welfare for disabled veterans and to channel healthy veterans into the liberation struggle in Kashmir. He also suggested to the Saudi government that he start a jihad in South Yemen, then under a leftist government. He was turned down. He made himself a nuisance by repeatedly warning of an impending invasion by Saddam Hussein. In 1990 Saddam did invade Kuwait and threaten Saudi Arabia. Bin Laden offered to form an Islamic international brigade to fight him. Instead, the Saudis turned to the more powerful Americans, who brought 400,000 foreign troops into Saudi Arabia. The US bases stayed, causing consternation among Arabs. The Prophet's dying edict had been "Let there be no two religions in Arabia," and many Muslims believe that the land of Mecca and Medina, Islam's two most sacred places, should not be defiled by infidel troops.

Bin Laden now began to denounce the royal family as US puppets.

He could not now stay a free man in Saudi Arabia, yet he wanted to live with his family under Sunni Islamic laws. He had few options. He returned to Afghanistan, trying to mediate in the civil wars erupting after the Soviets left. Failing abjectly, he took his family to the Sudan. He was deprived of his Saudi citizenship in 1994, and the Saudis tried to assassinate him on more than one occasion. He was now an exile, banned from his native land and from most other countries.

He was Sudan's biggest businessman, but while there also made the decisive turn to international terrorism. He was probably unconnected to a Yemeni bombing in 1992 targeted at US soldiers, and to the 1993 bombing of the World Trade Center in New York.[11] He may have had a hand in 1995 bombings in Saudi Arabia aimed at US soldiers. He had links to an Egyptian organization which failed in an attempt to assassinate President Mubarak. He probably trained Somalis who opposed US forces during their ill-starred foray into their country in 1993, perhaps training the men who shot down the Black Hawk helicopters. So he was already attacking American soldiers but not civilians. Remember that many saw the Somali incident as legitimate resistance to a US invasion. But he must have also begun plotting the 1998 embassy bombings in East Africa, which took him clearly into international terrorism against civilians.

In 1996 US and Saudi pressure forced the Sudanese government to ask him to leave. Only Afghanistan would take him, and the Americans and Saudis thought he could do little harm there. How wrong they were! There he began training a second generation of jihadis, mainly to fight the US. Shortly after his arrival, he issued his first "Declaration of War," calling for expelling American forces from the Arabian Peninsula. In February 1998 he founded "The International Front for Jihad on the Jews and Crusaders," succeeded the next year by "The International Front of Islamic Movements." Their names were probably grander than their powers, but he was beginning to make a stir through the network of radical mosques and madrassas (Islamic schools) which fed in the young jihadis.

The US military was his target, but it was well protected. So, like other weak "freedom fighters," he was drawn toward easier enemy civilian targets. The East African embassy bombings were the first terrible escalation into international terrorism. Though the US staff were the main targets, almost all the 200+ dead were ordinary Africans working in or around the embassies. The bomb in Tanzania mostly killed Muslims. There were further unsuccessful plots against US embassies and military installations, before the successful attack on the destroyer USS Cole in Yemen in 2000, which killed 17 US sailors.

His career culminated in 9-11. That day his targets were overwhelmingly civilian, though the Pentagon, the World Trade Center and either the White House or Congress (targeted by the plane which the passengers brought down) are the symbols of American Empire. Many Middle Easterners distinguish clearly between the Pentagon, which they regard as a legitimate military target, and the twin towers, which they agree was a terrorist attack. But all three targeted the citizens of the new imperialism. Like many terrorist acts, they were designed to bring forth a terrible reaction from the oppressor. They certainly succeeded.

We see in his trajectory the move from national to international liberation struggle, and from military to civilian targets. The major external influences were the first Afghan War and the forcible experience of exile. These interacted with the one unwavering thread through his career: defense of Islam against foreign imperialism, first the Soviet Union in Afghanistan, then the United States in Arabia. All seven speeches made between 1996 and 2000 threatened US military personnel (in one he added British and French troops). In 1997 he first broadened the threat to civilians:

> This war will not only be between the people of the two holy mosques and the Americans, but it will also be between the Islamic world and the Americans and their allies because this war is a new crusade led by America against the Islamic nations.

In 1998 he uttered the chilling words, "all those who believe in Allah and his prophet Muhammad must kill Americans wherever they find them," saying that the US had never distinguished between soldiers and civilians, from Hiroshima to Palestine and Iraq. He exulted over 9-11:

> There is America, hit by God in one of its softest spots. Its greatest buildings were destroyed, thank God for that. There is America, full of fear from its north to its south, from its west to its east. Thank God for that.

From 1996 onward, he consistently gave three reasons for attacking the US: the US military occupation of Saudi Arabia (sometimes the whole Arabian peninsula); US support for Israel/Zionists/Jews; and the 1991 US invasion of Iraq and the subsequent bombing and starving of its children. Later he added the US invasion of Afghanistan and the invasion of Iraq. These all concern US imperial interventions in the national struggles of Muslims. So bin Laden's motives are simple: he is an anti-imperial Islamist. It is not true (as Presidents Mubarak and Musharraf and others say) that only after 9-11 did he pick up the Palestinian issue. In 1996 he had denounced "American support of Jews in Palestine, and the massacre of Muslims in Palestine and Lebanon." Anti-Zionism dominated the 1998 interview with John Miller, in which he denounced "Jewish and Zionist plans for expansion," Palestinians "slaughtered and assaulted and robbed of their honor and of their property," "Jewish Zionist blackmail," the "despicable and disgraceful" American role in Palestine, and Jews using America "to further their plans for the world."[12]

These were *political* grievances. He barely said a word about Western culture. He did not denounce materialism or consumerism or Christian dogma or liberated women. Apparently he cared nothing about McDonald's or MTV.[13] As an austere intellectual, he probably never came into contact with them. He has said that the West is "debauched," but by blood, not sex. Feminism was of no interest. Women appeared in his statements only as victims of imperialism, alongside children. American journalists harp on a cultural clash between the West and Islam. So do authors Benjamin Barber, Thomas Friedman and Samuel Huntington. But this is all an ethnocentric blind to avoid having to discuss the things that Muslim opponents of the US actually care about. Bin Laden did denounce economic exploitation, but not by capitalists (he is one), rather by imperialists brutally seizing land and property by force of arms. He attacked American military imperialism. So if the new imperialism takes wing, there will probably be more bin Ladens.

Though the message is explicitly Islamist, it is implicitly somewhat narrower. He attacked the US and pro-Western "apostate" Arab regimes for repressing Arabs. He said nothing about Africa, and almost nothing about Chechnya or Asia. For all his time elsewhere, bin Laden was rooted in the Arabian peninsula, obsessed by US policy in the Arab Middle East. He is in reality a pan-Arabist.

Obviously, the US *could* satisfy his grievances. If it did not support Israel, if its troops left the Arabian peninsula, if it made up with Saddam, bin Laden would stop attacking. It is unlikely the US would do all of these things (it would seem like capitulation). But despite the religious rhetoric and the bloody means, bin Laden is a rational man. There is a simple *reason* why he attacked the US: American imperialism. As long as America seeks to control the Middle East, he and people like him will be its enemy.

Abu Qatada is a Palestinian/Jordanian firebrand cleric in London. Asked his view of 9-11, his response poured out:

> America did not ask itself, "Why is this happening to us?" Do you think that by what the US is doing now, it can stop what will happen to it in the future? Not only from Muslims, but there are lots of people in the world who hate the US. Is this going to end? Why doesn't the US reconsider itself to find out the reason behind all this? ... So far there are more than 7,000 people killed in Afghanistan and thousands of children killed in Iraq. I don't think our people will forget what happened to them. Bin Laden did not descend from the sky full of hatred for the Americans, but reality is what made bin Laden who he is. As long as this reality exists, the production of his like will be there. ... The US did not reconsider or change its policies against other nations and this fact will create someone who will hate the US as much.[14]

Though Abu Qatada is not a man I often agree with, here he is right. Bin Laden did not fall from the sky. He was created by the foreign policies of the Soviet Union and then the United States.

AL-QAEDA: THE AFGHAN/PAKISTANI BASE

Al-Qaeda means "the base." The base first settled in Northern Pakistan, then crossed the border into Afghanistan, and was then forced back again, probably into Northern Pakistan. Al-Qaeda is inconceivable without the international brigades formed for the Afghan War. They gave the motivation, the networks, the armed solutions, the training. Virtually all al-Qaeda terrorist suspects trained in these camps and fought in these brigades. Their rigorous military training distinguishes al-Qaeda from other organizations.[15] So US foreign policy should *never* create another war in which an international Islamic brigade might form to aid a national liberation struggle. This prospect clearly looms in Iraq.

All these jihadis were Sunni Muslim males—no Shiites. Almost all were young, aged between 17 and 30. The largest group came from nearby Pakistan and Kashmir. Then came the Arabs, led by Saudis, Algerians and Egyptians, followed by Yemenis, with much smaller numbers from other Arab countries. Chechens and other Soviet Muslims formed a substantial bloc, with a scattering of others from all over the Muslim world. Ironically, the only language common to some in all the groups would have been English. Few of the Arabs were engaged in their own liberation struggles. But the Pakistanis/Kashmiris had been fighting India; the Caucasians and Central Asians had been fighting the Soviets, and the few Uighurs had been fighting China. *None* of these were fighting against the United States. Though many were to express resentment against the US for "abandoning" them once the Soviets were ousted, such sour grapes would not cause them to kill Americans.

When the Afghan war ended, there was further two-way traffic between Afghanistan and areas where Islamists were involved in national terrorism/liberation struggles. The 1990s then saw two contradictory trends. On the one hand, the network of radical mosques and madrassa schools was expanding outside of its original Arab and Pakistani/Indian home, aided by Saudi money. But, on the other hand, the Islamist surge of the 1980s was now stalling. In only two minor Muslim states, Afghanistan and Sudan, were Islamists close to seizing power. In this second period of Afghan training camps, bin Laden's influence grew among the Arabs, but was much less among Pakistanis and Russian speakers. Two to three thousand fought in 2001 in Afghanistan in al-Qaeda units, but only about a quarter of these had taken the oath of allegiance to bin Laden.[16] He deliberately kept his organization small and Arabic-speaking to preserve tightness. All the jihadis shared a diffuse sense that their own local struggles were connected (or they would not be in Afghanistan). But few were closely linked to bin Laden or al-Qaeda because these remained essentially pan-Arabist.

About one-quarter of these 800 or so core fighters died under the US assault. Perhaps 400 of them escaped from Tora Bora into Pakistan, with maybe another 200 escaping by different routes (though other jihadis are hard to tell apart from al-Qaeda). Many of the fleeing fighters were captured and turned over to the Americans, some were demoralized by rapid defeat and slunk back to their homes, others lay low in remoter regions of Pakistan, Iran and Northern Iraq. A few might now have joined the al-Qaeda international network. But the American invasion of Afghanistan gave them all much greater reason to hate the US.

AL-QAEDA: THE INTERNATIONAL NETWORK

The network is dispersed and decentralized—no central committee, no command-and-control center, perhaps not even local "cells" except when plotting specific attacks. Reliable information is hard to come by, but those receiving "orders" from senior al-Qaeda figures may number only 100–300.[17] Like the Afghan jihadis they are all Sunni Muslim males, almost all were aged 17–30 when they first entered the network (some are by now older). Most were Arabs, though they had succeeded in spreading wider. Almost all had been in stable employment. They tended to be well educated and they could have been materially comfortable had they pursued their professions full-time. Most were educated in technical subjects, not the humanities, though in their leisure time they took Islamic theology courses.

So, for example, most of the Jemaah Islamiah detainees in Singapore had technical backgrounds, at the lower end in metal machining or maintenance fitting and then ranging through computer information technology and electrical engineering. Former Indonesian President Abdurrahman Wahid (also a leading Islamic intellectual) identified a connection between training in the sciences and engineering and a literalistic interpretation of Islam. He said young Muslims from the developing world apply the "modeling and formulistic thinking" associated with engineering or other applied sciences to their "reflection on their faith." Martin Marty and Scott Appleby suggested that fundamentalists in all religions share backgrounds in applied sciences, technical and bureaucratic fields that predispose them to "read scriptures like engineers read blueprints—as a prosaic set of instructions and specifications."[18]

Again the Saudis were the most numerous, followed by Egyptians, Yemenis and Algerians. The Egyptians are mainly there because of collaboration between al-Qaeda and the al-Jihad faction of the Egyptian Islamic Group. The Algerians are there because of collaboration with the GIA, an Algerian faction of the FIS. Then comes a sprinkling from almost all other Arab countries. There were at least two each from Jordan, Syria, the Lebanon and Iraq, though some of these had Palestinian refugee origins. Palestinian refugees in Lebanon formed a small faction called Asbat el-Ansar. No one seems to have been recruited in Palestine itself. African Muslims were recruited specifically for the US embassy bombings. There are several Pakistanis, plus larger numbers in allied Kashmiri outfits, and some Malays and Indonesians. There have been a few Western converts, like Richard Reid, and rather more French citizens of Algerian and Moroccan extraction. There are no Turks or Iranians or Indian Muslims (apart from Kashmiris), and probably no Chechens. Well over 90 percent speak Arabic and there are no Shiites.

These men are almost all exiles from their homeland. Almost all had fled from Arab regimes that were repressive, religious, but hostile to radical Islamists and pro-Western. They fled to the West simply because its organizing freedoms were greater. Apart from Afghanistan and Pakistan, al-Qaeda may have had most adherents in the US or the UK. Bin Laden is said to have made more satellite phone calls to Britain than any other country. The next biggest "cells" may have been in places like Hamburg, Frankfurt, Milan, Madrid, New Jersey and Florida. The West dominated the experience of most of them—they lived in the West, and the West propped up the regimes that exiled them.

Muslim countries are stuffed with terrorists/freedom fighters, and we in the West have been stuffed full of fear of Islam. So it may come as a surprise that during the 1990s, these small al-Qaeda connected networks were virtually the *only* ones attacking Westerners. The Lebanese Hezbollah had stopped attacking Westerners in the mid-1980s when the West stopped interfering in the Lebanon. The Palestinian Fatah may have murdered the CIA station chief in Beirut in 1983. The Palestinian Abu Nidal had killed Westerners in the 1980s but disappeared in the early 1990s. The tiny Palestinian splinter group, the PLF, hijacked the Achille Lauro in 1985, killing one American. No Palestinian organization has targeted Westerners since. Nor have the Chechens or other Caucasian or Central Asian or North African groups—except where ransom ventures go wrong and kidnapped Westerners end up dead.

The other internationalist groups associated with bin Laden are small splinter groups from much larger national movements in their homelands which have either renounced terrorism or target it against local enemies, not foreigners. The Algerians in the network split off from the large FIS, the Egyptians from the large Al-Gama'a Al-Islamiya (as did the New Jersey network led by the "blind sheikh" which perpetrated the 1993 World Trade Center bombing). The Muslim Brotherhood is probably the largest political organization across the Middle East. Though many terrorists, like bin Laden, started there, the Brotherhood has not supported them for over 20 years. So whatever the broader ideological resonance of bin Laden's calls to arms, his main recent activity—killing Westerners—does not attract many Muslims. They complain about the US but they don't try to kill Americans. Maybe we should respond in kind.

NATIONAL AND INTERNATIONAL TERRORISTS

1. Chechnya

I now review the links between national and international terrorists in the Muslim world. Chechnya is the oldest Muslim liberation struggle. It evokes strong hatreds and both sides have committed many atrocities against civilians. Of course, Russia exaggerates the links between Chechen rebels and al-Qaeda to get American blessing for state terrorism against the Chechen resistance movement. Traditional Chechen nationalism was secular, clan-based and locally orientated. But the first Afghan War began to change that. Chechens were moving between the two theaters of war, and Saudi money for religious schools came into the region. In the mid-1990s the Chechen leader Dudayev used Islamist rhetoric and created a council of religious elders to help bolster his support (he was soon killed, however). Yet secular elements were responsible for negotiating the 1996 truce with Russia, under which Chechnya received considerable autonomy within the Russian Federation. The truce held, more or less, for two years.

But in 1998 Arab fighters arrived, some with Afghan experience. Their leader Khattab was born in 1969 in Saudi Arabia. He abandoned a high-flying school career age 17 to fight first in Afghanistan, then Tajikistan, and finally Chechnya. In 1999 his Arabs led a Chechen attack on Russian Dagestan, breaking the truce. Lacking local support, they were driven back, and the enraged Russians renewed the war with greater ferocity. This caused a rift between the mainstream Chechen fighters and the Arabs who had brought this disaster on them. The secular Chechens took the brunt of the Russian attack which culminated in their defeat in Grozny in January 2000. The Arabs were supposed to have secured the mountains for fallback positions, but Chechen fighters complained that, after having suffered terrible losses fighting their way out of Grozny, they got no help from the Arabs. There has only been sporadic fighting since then, mostly by Khattab and his local ally Basayev. The mainstream Chechen fighters have been licking their wounds to fight another day. The Russian government is still repressing, though it also engineered a referendum on Chechnya's future in March 2003 which achieved the desired pro-Russian result. All is not bleak there. Both sides are weary of war.

Khattab spoke warmly of bin Laden, though he seems to have had few links with him. Communications with the Middle East were logistically very difficult and his money came mainly from Chechens and Russians (the Russian army valued him as a provocateur to destroy the Chechen cause—he was good at that). He himself referred to an Islamic struggle involving only the Caucasus region. In an interview of February 2001, he said Chechnya was "just a tiny territory" but part of a larger, religious war. "I'm a soldier of Islam and ... I will fight the infidels no matter where I am." A year later he was dead, probably poisoned by Russian agents. His brother's eulogy claimed he had been seeking martyrdom for 14 years. He had failed to achieve it in Afghanistan or Tajikistan, but Allah finally granted it to him in Chechnya.[19]

Khattab's career shows that internationalist terrorists can harm a national liberation struggle. The Chechens would have been better off without him and his Arabs. There are still Arabs in the Chechen and neighboring Georgian hills, but they are now marginalized, and Chechen fighters do not seem to have moved to the Middle East or the West. Bin Laden occasionally refers to the Chechens' struggles. But they have no interest in his main goal, attacking Americans, which would bring down the wrath of a second Great Power on their heads. After 9-11 this possibility came nearer. Some Chechen fighters, including Arabs, were using lawless parts of neighboring Georgia as rest areas to shelter from the Russian offensive. US military advisors were sent to help the Georgian government cope with them, and the danger loomed of US/Chechen clashes there. These should be avoided by the US like the plague. Americans do not need Chechen enmity. Yet in February 2003, the US State Department yielded to Russian requests to add three Chechen Islamic groups to its list of proscribed terrorist organizations.

2. The Balkans

In the Wars of the Yugoslav Succession, Muslim rebels were fighting in Bosnia, Kosovo and Macedonia. Islamic volunteers turned up to help, and some may have had connections with bin Laden. The Serb and Macedonian governments tried to finger all the rebels as "fundamentalists" and "al-Qaeda," but their motives were transparent. These are very secular Muslim communities, and though the West was slow to act in Yugoslavia, it eventually sided with them in Bosnia and Kosovo. The Bosnian Muslims were grateful for the foreign fighters who came to aid them, but after the Dayton Peace Accords they pressured them to leave. The US bombed Serb soldiers and allowed the Albanian Muslim rebels free rein in the province. Indeed, the US initially allowed them to raid over the border in Macedonia. Now, alongside the Europeans, the US is trying to conciliate the dispute. These Muslim rebels have reason to thank the US, not bomb it. US policy makes a difference to these national liberation movements. If it helps them, they give thanks and expel jihadis. If bin Laden did attempt to expand here, he failed miserably.

3. The Middle East

This is the crucible of terrorism. It contains both nationalist struggles against non-Muslim states and rebellions against oppressive Muslim states. Because of the strategic importance of the region and US interventions, there are greater possibilities of links with international terrorism. Many "freedom fighters" in the region have made the switch to terrorism, being too weak to take on only military targets. All the Palestinian militias attack Israeli civilians, especially settlers in former Arab lands.

Most Middle Eastern states back some of the national terrorists. Israel has backed Lebanese Christian falangists. Hezbollah in the Lebanon and Hamas and Islamic Jihad in Palestine are extensively funded by Iran, while poorer Syria also gives them a little. Saudi Arabia bankrolls Hamas and Islamic Jihad. Iraq paid pensions to the families of Palestinian suicide-bombers. That is because all these countries support the Palestinian struggle against Israel, while not wanting to go to war with Israel themselves. None of them nowadays support organizations which attack Westerners. Al-Qaeda is not linked to the Palestinian movements, and the PLO and its offshoots are considered faithless by radical Islamists.

The Bush and Sharon administrations allege that there have been al-Qaeda contacts with Shiite governments and terrorist movements—that is with Iran, Syria and the Lebanese Hezbollah.[20] Their evidence is thin, it confuses national with international terrorism, and it minimizes the conflicts between Shiites and Sunni. The Sunni/Shiite divide is hard to bridge. For most of the 1980s, Shiite Iran and the Sunni regime of Saddam Hussein fought a terrible war in which over a million were killed. In the mid-1980s the Shiite (Alawite) Syrian regime butchered 30,000 Sunni dissidents. In the 1990s Pakistani and Taliban Islamists murdered many Shiites. In the Lebanon the reverse happened when Hezbollah helped the Lebanese army dispose of an al-Qaeda group near Tripoli in December 1999.[21] As Olivier Roy notes, the radical Sunnis attacking the West combine terrorism with ideological conservatism. They simply want the Sharia, Islamic law, in the especially reactionary form of a "Sharia emirate." Unlike the Khomeini Shiite revolution in

Iran, they have no leveling goals, no "Islamic leftism," and this limits their popularity. Al-Qaeda regards Shiites as heretics.

Cheney, Rumsfeld and Wolfowitz all claimed falsely that 9-11 was sponsored by Iraq. CIA director Tenet is just as persistent about Iran. John Bolton named Iran, Iraq and North Korea, followed by Libya and Syria, as states which are both "uniformly hostile to the United States" and "state sponsors of terrorism." He said Iran is "one of the most egregious state sponsors of terrorism" and (quoting his President) Iraq "has long-standing and continuing ties to terrorist organizations." During the invasion of Iraq, Colin Powell finally got into the act, accusing Iran and Syria of aiding terrorists, and threatening them with serious consequences if they did not desist.[22] Iran, Syria and Iraq do help terrorists. Libya and North Korea used to. But none of them aid *international* terrorists, those who attack Americans. They support Palestinian terrorists attacking Israel. Indeed Libya has long had a warrant out for bin Laden, accusing him of complicity in the 1994 murder in Libya of two Germans. These new imperialists are perversely pursuing a war against terrorists who do not attack us, but who may do so if they carry on. Since these are guerrilla wars, deeply rooted among local populations, the US is pursuing a war it cannot win.

Hezbollah, the Lebanese Party of God, is fighting what it sees as a liberation struggle for the Lebanon against Israeli incursions—and in past decades against Christian falangist militias. Its program says, "Israel is an aggressive entity that practices terrorism; occupation is one of the forms of terrorism. Hizbullah of Lebanon is a popular resisting trend against occupation and terrorism." Israelis see things differently. Hezbollah, they point out, still intervenes in the Palestinian intifada. A Hezbollah "offensive" in May 2002 was only restrained by Iran, they say. But even at its most aggressive and expansive, Hezbollah only attacks Israel, not the United States. It has disclaimed any aggressive intentions against the West for over 15 years.

Sheik Muhammad Hussain Fadlallah, Hezbollah's spiritual leader, has repeatedly condemned al-Qaeda attacks as "not compatible with Shariah law" and the "true Islamic jihad." Its bombers were not martyrs but "merely suicides," because they killed innocent civilians, and in a distant land, America. Hezbollah is a national not an international terrorist group. It would be a dangerous enemy, being deeply entrenched in the Southern Lebanon, with parliamentary deputies in the national assembly, and with about 5,000 well-armed fighters. Better not to convert them into our enemies.[23]

After Saddam's defeat in the Gulf War, some Sudanese Islamists tried to rally radical Islamists behind Saddam. There were a few conferences (it is likely al-Qaeda representatives took part[24]), but nothing emerged except a tacit agreement among enemies sharing a more menacing enemy (the US), not to attack each other. The Saudis alone have financed him—so that he will go abroad and not bother them. The links between Islamic regimes and al-Qaeda are otherwise only indirect, through the financing of the madrassa/ulema infrastructures which nourish its sympathizers. The only two states that ever offered bin Laden home bases were Sudan and Afghanistan, two of the poorest and weakest regimes in the world. They do so no longer.

Of course, Muslims fighting in many places may think of themselves as engaged in a similar struggle. Many radical Islamists share an eventual goal of universal armed jihad. They may even offer each other technical assistance, as did other terrorist groups who otherwise shared nothing in common—like the IRA, the Basque ETA and (perhaps) the Colombian FARC. Similarly, the US sometimes shares intelligence information with Iran. But Islam is in reality riven by sects, nation states and language barriers. Most militants are embroiled inside their own version of Islam and inside their own national or regional struggles. Most large movements, like Hezbollah, the Palestinian militias, the Kashmiris and the Chechens, are in reality much more national than international in their aspirations.[25]

Nor does al-Qaeda offer policies which could unite these disparate movements. The Iranian ayatollahs came to power with a social and economic, as well as a religious program. Even some Sunnis were influenced by them. Yet the ayatollahs failed, and most Iranians would like to be rid of them. The Sunni radicals of al-Qaeda have almost nothing to say about the economy or politics, besides a simple call for "the Sharia." Imagine letting the Rev. Jerry Falwell run the US or the Rev. Ian Paisley rule the UK! We saw the Taliban in action in Afghanistan. They had policies on burqas and videos, but not on the economy, health or education. Al-Qaeda and its allies offer zero prospects of social and economic development for Muslims. All they offer is anti-Americanism.

But the more Americans denounce and attack other Middle Eastern governments and movements as part of a single, undifferentiated war on terrorism, the more likely these are to link up with each other and with al-Qaeda. This is the perfect way to convert national into international terrorists. US policy, if sufficiently stupid, might end one thousand years of Muslim disunity. It is exactly what bin Laden is kneeling towards Mecca and praying for.

But bin Laden has a lot to worry about. Radical Islamists reached their peak five years ago, and then lost ground. They had risen with the failure of Arab socialism and secular nationalism, and then fell as Islamist solutions also proved incapable of solving the problems of the Middle East. Gilles Kepel demonstrates that radical Islamism and international terrorism declined during the mid-1990s.[26] The Algerian radical movements destroyed themselves in a paroxysm of violence which spiraled out of control during 1994–96. By the end of 1997 the sole al-Qaeda-linked Algerian splinter group, the GIA, had virtually disappeared from inside the country, while the main nationalist terrorist organization, the AIS, declared a truce. The Algerian government won the battle, though local murderous banditry remains.

The collapse was even greater in Egypt. In 1997 Al-Gama'a Al-Islamiya, the largest group of Islamist radicals, called off its six-year campaign of violence. Over 1,200 people had been killed, mostly militants and police, but including some Coptic Christians and foreign tourists. The terrorists bailed out because they were losing. Khaled Dawoud, of *Al-Ahram*, quotes one of the leaders: "Before the violence started, we had our own mosques and were able to move freely to spread our ideas and principles. After six years of violence, thousands are in prison or on the run, and we are not able to express our views." Kepel adds that the regime had much public support for its crack-down, especially from middle-class Islamists. It helped that Mubarak got paid for his moderate stance on Israel and his help in the Gulf War. The US wrote off much of Egypt's foreign debt, and the middle class stopped moving its savings abroad. Investment increased and the economy expanded. This was also the period in which Clinton seemed to be trying to conciliate the Israeli/Palestinian dispute. American policy can be constructive.

A few Egyptian hardliners refused to accept the cease-fire and per-petrated the Luxor massacre in November 1997, killing 58 foreign tourists and four Egyptians. The attack appalled Egyptians, not least because it wrecked tourism, one of their main industries. It also enabled Mubarak to persuade other governments to crack down on Egyptian political exiles. Terrorism seemed finished in Egypt. Even the exiled hardliners linked to bin Laden said they would stop attacking the Mubarak regime. They said, "We will fight the bigger evil, which is supporting all the tyrannical regimes in the Arab world: the United

States." They really meant they were too weak to strike any targets within Egypt.

Radical Islamists also declined in Africa, in the Sudan and Somalia. In Somalia in the early 1990s the Islamist group Al-Ittihad al-Islamia thought its time had come. The failure of the Somali state and the rise of warlordism enabled it to seize control of some towns and set up its own training camps. It seemed quite powerful, though it had a purely domestic agenda and did not attack foreigners. Yet its seizures of territory alienated local warlords and the Ethiopian government. They soon drove it out. By the time bin Laden arrived in the Sudan—and by the time Al-Ittihad made it onto the State Department's list of terrorist organizations—it was almost finished.[27] Since 9-11 rival Somali warlords, just as in Afghanistan, have tried to tar their enemies as al-Qaeda, but the US is not that stupid. Islamism seems finished here, for the present.

So by the late 1990s these exiled international terrorists could only operate fairly freely among sympathetic populations in three Muslim countries, Afghanistan, Pakistan and the Yemen. Retribution came savagely in Afghanistan. In the Yemen it came in 2002 through US–Yemeni cooperation. But Pakistan remained a special case.

4. Pakistan

Few Pakistanis are adherents of al-Qaeda. But the indirect links are stronger, through shared fighting experience in Afghanistan and Kashmir, and through the madrassa schools. This is where Pakistani, Afghan, Kashmiri (and perhaps even a handful of Bangladeshi) terrorists/freedom fighters first imbibed radical Islamism, where today bin Laden is idolized as a holy warrior, and where international terrorism directed at Westerners has recently begun.

Anar Khan is a well-paid Pakistani bank executive. At age 42, with four young sons, he felt too old to fight when 9-11 erupted. As a younger man he had fought in Afghanistan, alongside many Arabs. Bathed in the fiery televised glow of the burning twin towers, he turned to his four sons and exulted: "See? Evil brings evil upon itself. This is Allah's punishment for the wrong that America has done to Muslims."[28] The Pakistani pharmacist Ijaz Khan Hussein did fight in 2001, as a volunteer medical orderly for the Taliban. He had been assigned the grisly task of picking up body-parts from the bombing. By February 2002 he and one other man were the only survivors from a truckload of

Pakistani volunteers who had arrived in Afghanistan four months earlier. But this experience of bloody defeat had not deterred him.

> We went to the jihad filled with joy, and I would go again tomorrow. If Allah had chosen me to die, I would have been in paradise, eating honey and watermelons and grapes, and resting with beautiful virgins, just as it is promised in the Koran. Instead my fate was to remain amid the unhappiness here on earth.

A nearby seminary sported a signboard with the names of 140 Pakistani "holy warriors" who had died in Afghanistan. A young man shouted out, "Jihad will continue until doomsday, or until America is defeated, either way."[29]

The wars across the Afghan/Pakistani borders were the great incubator of jihad in the 1990s, and they retain this role on a regional scale. Local and international jihadis influenced one another, and many Islamists who had no prior feelings of hostility toward the US had just been bombed by it. Pakistanis training in bin Laden's Afghan camps were mostly members of small groups involved in the Kashmir war—Harkat-ul-Mujahideen (HuM), Harkat-ul-Jehad-e-Islami (HUJI), Al Badar, Lashkar-e-Taiba (LeT) and Jaish-e-Mohammed (JeM). These and other smaller groups are very loosely coordinated by the umbrella United Jihad Council.[30]

The HuM began in 1985 as an organization of Pakistani volunteers fighting against the Soviets. Then it shifted its jihad to Kashmir. In 2002 its splinter group HUJI was credited with the suicide bombing which killed 11 French naval engineers, a car bombing at the US Consulate in Karachi, killing 11 Pakistanis, and a bus bombing which wounded but did not kill foreign tourists. HuM boasted it ferried "thousands" of fighters from Afghanistan into Kashmir—hundreds, more likely. Banned in Pakistan, it operates openly in Pakistani-controlled parts of Kashmir. Shabir Ahmed Madani, a HuM militant told reporter Philip Smucker: "We have sent all of our Afghan friends to Kashmir. . . . The army won't dare come across this valley and try to close us down. We have guns and we won't let his forces across this ravine." He gave Smucker a bank account number and name for anyone interested in donating to his group's holy war!

The Pakistani authorities turn a blind eye or sympathize. Mohammad Muslim is the regional chief of the government's ISI security force. He denies that al-Qaeda cells operate inside Kashmir, but then calmly says, "the US government destroyed the World Trade Center so that it would have an excuse to destroy Afghanistan." The regional police chief sagely nods agreement. "After that, the US military killed tens of thousands of women and children in Afghanistan."[31]

These organizations are not al-Qaeda "cells." They have their own national liberation struggle in Kashmir. Bombing of foreigners only began after the US bombed them in Afghanistan. Most Pakistanis view Kashmir as a legitimate national liberation struggle, and most Pakistani assistance to the Kashmiri movements is channeled through radical Islamist groups. What had been a secular-dominated autonomy movement in Kashmir became more Islamist in the mid-1990s. The more secular Jammu-Kashmir Liberation Front (the JKLF) began to decline under pressure from Pakistanis and other foreign jihadis. India (like Russia in Chechnya) became enraged at the infiltration, and both governments now spurn local attempts at compromise. However, as in Chechnya, a rift between national and internationalist elements appeared. In May 2002 the United Jihad Council expelled the four groups with the closest ties to bin Laden.

President Musharraf cannot crack down on all his radical Islamists. He cannot carry public opinion, nor even his own security agencies. His support for the US in Afghanistan created an electoral backlash in November 2002, when Islamist parties secured a majority in the two most northern provinces. In May 2003 they announced their intention of introducing Sharia law into the provinces. Even police raids which find Kalashnikovs and incriminating documents do not necessarily lead to prosecution, for these might be for "legitimate" purposes in Kashmir. The most that can be achieved is separation between the Kashmiri struggle and international terrorism. Visible US pressure on Musharraf to crack down on Kashmiri-aimed terrorism would increase anti-US feelings, and he would probably resist. The Bush administration does seem to be aware of his difficulties, and of its own power limitations in the region.

5. South-East Asia

I skip across India whose very large Muslim population remains uninvolved in terrorism (except in Kashmir itself), to South-East Asia. Almost unknown before the year 2000, international terrorism then surfaced and grew in the region, culminating in the terrible Bali bombing of November 2002 in which an estimated 191 persons were killed, most of them Australian tourists. A jihadi network called Jemaah Islamiah (JI), sometimes connected to smaller local groups, was probably behind this and other smaller incidents. Its adherents came from Malaysia, Singapore, the Philippines and Indonesia—almost invariably by way of Afghanistan where they received military training and encountered al-Qaeda.

The region's security services gave details of three main regional leaders. Omar al-Faruq is a 31-year-old from Kuwait who fought in Afghanistan and was then sent by al-Qaeda to lead operations first in Malaysia and then Indonesia. There he married, lived quietly and gave classes in the Koran. Unfortunately, this mastermind forgot to get himself an Indonesian passport and was picked up by the Indonesian police. Singaporean and Indonesian authorities have added two Indonesian citizens, Riduan Isamuddin, alias "Hambali," and Abdul Azis, alias "Samudra."[32]

Hambali was born in West Java, Indonesia, in 1966, one of 13 children in a poor family. Female relatives helped him study at Islamic schools. Samudra, 35, is a trained computer engineer, born in the Sudan and then living in West Java. As young men both were involved in radical Islamist groups resisting President Suharto's secular Indonesian government. But they did not get much support. Suharto's repression worked, and these two fled to Malaysia, where they worked for three years. Then they went to Afghanistan. They returned to Malaysia in the early 1990s, married Malaysian citizens, had children and ran Islamist classes. There they may have recruited young Muslims to fight in Afghanistan. They may have helped the 1993 World Trade Center bombers to escape through the region and planted a bomb in a Philippine airliner which killed one Japanese businessman.

After Suharto's fall in 1998, they returned to Indonesia where democratization produced an upsurge in ethnic and religious violence. The two were active in Muslim rioting against Christians in the Maluku Islands, in the Christmas Eve 2000 bombing of churches in nine Indonesian cities and later bombings in Manila, the Philippine capital. Hambali is said to have met with some of the 9-11 bombers and other al-Qaeda men in Malaysia in 2000, and to have connections with the USS Cole attackers. Next year he was supposedly behind a foiled plot to blow up the US embassy and other targets in Singapore. Since Omar al-Faruq also claims responsibility for most of these incidents, all three must have been hyperactive. Their overall career seems typical of international Islamist terrorists: local radicalization, then exile and the Afghan brigades, then al-Qaeda. All three men are cosmopolitans. One was born in the Middle East, one in Africa, and all three are fluent in Arabic.

But how could such cosmopolitans exploit local struggles in the region? In Singapore and Malaysia radical Islamists are persecuted, but there are no border grievances they can mobilize. But the far south of the Philippines is fertile ground. The majority of the Muslim population is discriminated against in this overwhelmingly Christian country, and the government is a loyal US ally. Thus the main Muslim autonomy movement, the Moro Liberation Front, became somewhat anti-American. Yet it was rather secular and did not attack foreigners, unlike the small radical Islamist terrorist splinter group, Abu Sayyaf. In the 1990s Abu Sayyaf descended toward mere banditry, losing its Islamist credentials, but the MLF splintered, generating an Islamist faction (the MILF) as activists returned from fighting in Afghanistan.

Bush the Younger's first step in widening the war against terrorism was to commit 650 US soldiers to help the Philippine government hunt down Abu Sayyaf. This helped Abu Sayyaf recover some Islamist legitimacy, and it encouraged the MILF to make stronger anti-American statements. This resulted in the killing of two of the American soldiers in October 2002. The Afghan/US war, reinforced by local US intervention, probably turned some of these national fighters into international terrorists. But other MILF leaders are unhappy about this. A government negotiatior with the MILF said it had "promised to help us arrest the suspected links of al-Qaeda and Jemaah Islamiah in the South." The MILF, he said, "is more than willing to provide concrete proof that it's not a terrorist group by helping us root out terrorists in the country." He said about 100 of them had infiltrated the MILF. But in February 2003 the Bush administration announced that more American troops, 3,000 of them, would be sent to the Southern Philippines. A Pentagon official said the objective was to "wipe out the Abu Sayyaf guys." Three thousand American soldiers, equipped with their usual fire-power, might be able to cope with 250–400 lightly armed guerrillas, but local experts said that a revived Abu Sayyaf now had considerable support among the local population. This is American folly, with a high risk of converting a national into an international struggle.[33]

Indonesia is easily the world's biggest Muslim nation. Though Islam is politically well organized in Indonesia, it is overwhelmingly moderate and few favor an Islamic state or Sharia law.[34] After 9-11 the Indonesian government at first resisted suggestions that international terrorists had infiltrated the country, since it did not wish to compromise recent progress toward democracy by giving more powers to the army and security forces, with their poor human rights record. Things are not always what they seem in Indonesia. In 2000 a bomb had exploded underneath the Jakarta Stock Exchange, killing 15 people. The bombers proved to be members of the notorious Kopassus, the special forces unit of the Indonesian military trying to destabilize the government. Some suspect that they were also behind some church bombings. The specter of bin Laden under the bed suits the hard right everywhere.

Nonetheless, Muslim/Christian communal violence periodically erupts in the Muluka Islands and parts of Central Sulawesi. Small but violent Islamist paramilitaries from Java and Sumatra, especially Laskar Jihad, had helped foment this. But Laskar does not seem to have been connected to the Afghan veterans. The rioting and church bombings seem overwhelmingly local affairs, rooted in local politics.[35] In 2000 only two of the many bombings and killings in Indonesia were aimed at foreigners—at the Philippine and Malaysian embassies. The rebel movement on the Aceh peninsula is also Islamist, but in its own traditional way. It did target ExxonMobil oil installations, but these were part of the Indonesian exploitation of their homeland. There has been no jihadi presence in the national liberation struggles within Indonesia of Aceh, East Timor or West Papua, nor in the intermittently murderous ethnic struggles of West Kalimantan.

The Bali bombing shocked the Indonesian authorities. It killed 60 Indonesians and badly hurt the tourist industry. They quickly agreed that internationalist terrorists were responsible, and began to hunt down JI. They quickly caught Samudra and over 20 other suspects, including the Islamist cleric Nakar Bashir, who formally heads JI. Some detainees have confessed to further projected attacks on Western targets, including American embassies, banks and social clubs. They said their goal was to create a single Islamic state out of the various Muslim population concentrations in the region. But they have an awful long way to go! There were said to be 520 Afghan war veterans in Indonesia, but where would other recruits come from unless the US further alienates the region's Muslims? International terrorism should have peaked here.

CONCLUSION

1. Existing terrorists

Al-Qaeda is actually rather weak. The call for all Muslims to unite against the US came from a small group of conservative Arabian Sunni exiles, with little connection to either the regimes or the mass movements of the Muslim world, even the violent ones. Few of these wish to fight against the US. Some in "the Arab street" hurl rocks and even occasional Molotov cocktails at US embassies; Arab intellectuals write diatribes against US policy; Arab states dissemble to simultaneously placate the US, the street and the intellectuals. But no large organizations or regimes are channeling discontent into killing foreigners.

Few Muslims applaud the killing of civilians. There was revulsion against the African embassy and Bali bombings, as there had earlier been revulsion against civilian death-tolls in Algeria and Egypt. The response to 9-11 was more ambiguous. Many thought the US had it coming, but they did not approve (except perhaps for the attack on the Pentagon, a military target) and they did not think that Muslims could have done it.

Al-Qaeda became influential because of a war directed against godless communism. Then came a surge in radical Islamism across the Middle East, spreading further afield later. By the new millennium, that surge was ended. But both Afghan Wars linked the jihadis with deeply rooted liberation struggles in Kashmir and Chechnya. These are still ongoing, as are much smaller struggles in the Philippines and Indonesia. It no longer links them to struggles in South Yemen, the Horn of Africa, Bosnia and Kosovo. They acquire more general sympathy from the struggle of the Palestinians. But there is no reason for any of these movements to identify al-Qaeda's enemy as theirs. Most know this would be a mistake. Al-Qaeda's resonance *should* therefore be in decline, as should all internationalist terrorism directed at the US.

Al-Qaeda consists of Arab exiles too weak to take on their own states. None of them can rely on a supportive base community in their homelands. They are *not* like the Chechen, Kashmiri, Achenese, Palestinian or Hezbollah movements. Comparisons should not be made with the IRA, the PLO or the Colombian FARC. Al-Qaeda are not guerrilla "fish in the sea," hiding among a broad sympathetic population. They are isolated extremist splinter groups, living in alien lands. They had begun by attacking their own Muslim governments, from bases located within a few cities, with little public support. They were easily targeted by governments ignoring the niceties of civil liberties. In defeat, they fled to the West. But their safety there was destroyed by 9-11. A concerted international counter-terrorist effort began. After all, ordinary civilians of the US, the UK, France, Germany, Egypt, Algeria, Kenya, Tanzania, Afghnistan, India, Malaysia, the Philippines, Indonesia, Australia and other places have been killed by al-Qaeda and its associates. Almost all governments are now cracking down on them, killing, interrogating, eavesdropping, infiltrating. What Somali or Yemeni warlord will risk protecting al-Qaeda now? The Indonesian archipelago is now closing. Iran is an unreliable ally. No wonder al-Qaeda adherents fled to the further recesses of Kurdish Iraq. Pakistan alone remains quite supportive. The base remains more or less where it began, but the international network is weakening.

Loose networks like al-Qaeda are not easy to track down, and they retain sympathizers. A few perpetrators, given skill and luck, can pull off occasional atrocities. I doubt they can repeat a coup on the scale of 9-11. The perpetrators had expected much less. That three American planes would be on time and hit their targets was (for them) very good luck. They are trying to acquire simple chemical and biological weapons, though whether they can actually deploy them is another matter. They are now targeting weaker civilian targets, a sign of weakness. They have managed no attacks in the US since 9-11, and very few elsewhere. Present networks are being hard-hit. Al-Qaeda is on the run. *Left to themselves*, there is little future for present internationalist terrorist networks. Every new terrorist act makes life more dangerous for them, and converts another government into support for the war on terrorism. For present perpetrators, time is not on their side. They would be finished in three years.

2. Future terrorists

"Left to themselves" would mean that they can no longer make the two connections forged in Afghanistan in the 1980s and 1990s—with Muslim national liberation struggles, and with a resonant anti-American struggle comparable to the anti-Soviet struggle. If all other conflicts involving Muslim countries were avoided by the US, then al-Qaeda and other international terrorists could be defeated within a few years.

Yet the US is doing the reverse. Consider first the puzzlingly pessimistic estimates of terrorist strength given by the Bush administration and some counter-terrorist experts. The Pentagon claims al-Qaeda is active in "up to 60 countries," Katzman's says "cells have been identified or suspected" in about 40 countries. Conetta identifies "affiliations or operational cells in more than 40 countries." "Cells" sound rather organized, but how many were "identified" versus "suspected," and what does "affiliation" mean—that bin Laden knew one Nigerian, one Philippino etc.?[37] The President and Vice-President go higher. In January 2002 Vice-President Cheney said there was now "a worldwide terrorist network. ... In the al Qaeda organization alone, it may be in some 65 to 70 countries. We had upwards of 100,000 terrorists trained in those camps in Afghanistan, and they're out there now."[37] The number 100,000 was repeated several times in White House press briefings. But in his 2002 State of the Union address Bush came down a little:

> most of the 19 men who hijacked planes on September 11 were trained in Afghanistan's camps, and so were tens of thousands of others. Thousands of dangerous killers, schooled in the methods of murder, often supported by outlaw regimes, are now spread throughout the world like ticking time bombs, set to go off without warning ... tens of thousands of trained terrorists are still at large. These enemies view the entire world as the battlefield, and we must pursue them wherever they are.

But "tens of thousands" would still leave an army of terrorists, striking terror into our hearts. I stifle the thought that our leaders lie for electoral purposes (since fear of terrorists does stiffen the Republican vote). Assuming they are sincere, how do they arrive at such large numbers?

The answer is that they must be adding together al-Qaeda and other international terrorists with many national terrorists. Adding all the Chechen, Kashmiri, Pakistani, Indonesian and Palestinian militants would reach up to "tens of thousands" of persons, and 40–50 organizations. And indeed, the State Department and CIA lists of terrorist organizations do add together national and international terrorists, Hamas and Hezbollah alongside al-Qaeda. So did Bush the Younger in his 2002 State of the Union speech and so have counter-terrorism experts. Explicit confirmation came from President Bush on October 18, 2001: "So long as anybody's terrorizing established governments, there needs to be a war."[38]

Such numbers figure only in bin Laden's own wildest dreams! This would be a war the US could not win, since some of these nationalist liberation movements are deeply rooted in modernity. Much greater repression has been tried than US imperialists could muster. Stalin deported *all* the Chechens. Sharon drives tanks over houses and uses Palestinians as human shields for his soldiers. Indian soldiers do much worse in Kashmir than Americans do in Afghanistan. Despite the repression, these terrorists keep on coming back. Righteous rage fuels their resolve; death is accepted as martyrdom, either for God or the nation. Let Putin, Sharon and Vajpayee take the brunt of their enmity. They and their predecessors created it.

Why should any of these national terrorists consider themselves enemies of the US? Bin Laden himself worries that the connection might not be obvious to them. In his 1998 interview he urged all Muslims to "pool all their resources and their energy to fight the Americans and the Zionists and those with them. They should, however, avoid side fronts and rise over the small problems for these are less detrimental. ... It is far better for anyone to kill a single American soldier than to squander his efforts on other activities." For him Chechnya, Kashmir and Palestine were only "side fronts." He saw the greatest threat to his jihad as coming not from the US but from men like Movsar Barayev, the Chechen leader. The day before he died in the storming of the Moscow theater in October 2002, Barayev told the London *Sunday Times* correspondent Mark Franchetti: "We aren't terrorists. ... All we ask for is to pull out the troops from Chechnya." Shariff Jullabi, a Moro Liberation Front commander, says: "We are not connected to the terrorist activities in the other parts of the world. Our objective is the regaining of our homeland."[39] If all Muslim insurgents said, just pull back the Indian, Israeli, Indonesian, Philippino, etc. troops, there would be no universal jihad, no role for al-Qaeda. This is what terrifies bin Laden.

It is easy to stem the flow of future terrorists. The US should leave alone conflicts involving national liberation fighters—Chechens and other ex-Soviet republic and autonomous region fighters, Uighurs in China, Kashmiris and numerous other smaller fighters around the north-eastern borders of India, Moros in the Philippines, the various fighters of the Indonesian achipelago, Tamil Tigers in Sri Lanka, Palestinian and Lebanese fighters, and all others active in the Muslim/Christian border zone running across Africa and Asia. Nor should the US side with secular against Islamist sides in Muslim civil wars. The same logic should apply to divided countries approaching "failed state" chaos, like Somalia, the Congo or Afghanistan. Stay away from these quagmires! The logic might also apply to class or land wars. Steer clear of Colombia, Bolivia, Venezuela, Nepal and West Kalimantan and other peripheral regions of Indonesia. Of course, if any of these do attack Americans, this logic does not apply.

But the US should not merely stand aside. It should denounce terrorism and state terrorism equally, and accompany this with its best conciliation services, backed by material incentives for those willing to compromise. In the case of Palestine, the US could wield considerable influence on both sides, since they are both its clients. But in most cases US pressure can be more effectively applied on state terrorists, simply because it grants aid and trade privileges to states and not to resistance movements. The US government does in principle require states receiving aid or trade to have good human rights records. But the war on terrorism has eased the requirement. It should have *toughened* restrictions on state terrorists, for they generate terrorism.

The Middle East is the crucial region for the war on terrorism. The Pew Research Center's 2002 survey of public opinion in 44 countries found that most people in most countries across the world approved of the war against terrorism. But it is not being directed against most of these countries. It is targeted against Muslim countries. Six Muslim countries were included in the survey. Only one approved of the war, Uzbekistan, suddenly receiving large quantities of American aid for helping in the war. In the other five—Jordan, Pakistan, Egypt, Turkey (all supposedly US allies) and the Lebanon—far more opposed the war than supported it. In Jordan 85 percent opposed the war, in Egypt 79 percent. These are, behind Israel, the largest recipients of US foreign aid. But they see the war as an attack against Muslims, and they are right. Everywhere the US confuses Muslim national liberation movements with international terrorists, and attacks them both together. What else can Muslims think? Present international terrorists are being killed, but future ones are being created at a faster rate. What a disastrous war!

NOTES

1. US State Department, Fact Sheet, Office of Counterterrorism, October 23, 2002.
2. In "The Mutation of Terrorism," *Al-Ahram Weekly*, November 21–27, 2002, no. 613.
3. US policy is roundly denounced by Human Rights Watch in the Introduction to its *World Report, 2003*, available at *www.hrw.org*, from where the Bush quote is taken. It adds "To fight terrorism, you need the support of people in countries where the terrorists live. Cozying up to repressive governments is hardly the way to build those alliances."
4. National Intelligence Council, "Global Trends 2015: A Dialogue about the Future With Nongovernment Experts," *www.cia.gov/nic/*.
5. Thomas Friedman, *The Lexus and the Olive Tree*, New York: Farrar, Straus & Giraud, 2000; Benjamin Barber, *Jihad versus McWorld*, New York: Times Books, 1995.

6. George Tenet, CIA Director, statement before the Senate Foreign Relations Committee, March 21, 2000.

7. National Commission on Terrorism, *Countering the Changing Threat of International Terrorism*, part 1, p. 3, *www.access.gpo.gov/nct/*.

8. Anthony Cordesman, *Terrorism, Asymmetric Warfare, and Weapons of Mass Destruction*, Westport, Ct: Praeger, 2002, pp. 2–6.

9. Bob Woodward, *Bush at War*, New York: Simon & Schuster, 2000, pp. 45 and 94; David Frum, *The Right Man*, New York: Random House, 2003.

10. *New York Times,* January 29, 2003.

11. Rohan Gunaratna sees his hand in more plots: *Inside Al Qaeda*, New York: Columbia University Press, 2002.

12. His biography is in Gunaratna, *Inside Al Qaeda*, ch. 1; Peter L. Bergen, *Holy War, Inc.*, New York: The Free Press, 2001, pp. 44–52; Paul Williams, *Al Qaeda: Brotherhood of Terror*, London: Alpha Books, 2002, pp. 91–104, 128–142; Gilles Kepel, *Jihad. The Trail of Political Islam*, Cambridge: MA, Harvard University Press, pp. 314–23. For his speeches, see *www.pbs.org/wgbh/pages/frontline/shows/binladen/*; *www.september11news.com/OsamaBinLaden.htm*; *www.abcnews.go.com/sections/world/DailyNews/miller*; *www.pbs.org/wgbh/pages/front line/shows/binladen/*. His anti-Jewish statements are listed at *www.adl.org/terrorism_america/bin_1.asp*.

13. Peter Bergen also noted this omission, in his book *Holy War Inc.*, p. 222.

14. Canadian Broadcasting Corporation, June 2002, ''The Recruiters'' (interviews with terrorist suspects), *www.cbc.ca/national/news/recruiters/index.html*.

15. As Gunaratna emphasizes: *Inside Al Qaeda*, p. 70.

16. All figures are guesswork, mutually inconsistent and distorted by the special interests of intelligence services. They appear in: *Reuters*, Islamabad, September 27, 2001; Carl Conetta, ''Dislocating Alcyoneus: How to Combat al-Qaeda and the New Terrorism,'' Project on Defense Alternatives, Briefing Memo, no. 23, June 25, 2002; Ahmed Rashid, *Taliban*, New Haven, CT: Yale Nota Bene Press, 2000, ch 10; and Gunaratna, *Inside Al Qaeda*, pp. 58–60.

17. My main sources on them were Gunaratna, *Inside Al Qaeda*, chs 3 and 4; Paul Williams, *Al Qaeda*, pp. 2–5, 105–125; Bergen, *Holy War Inc.*, pp. 29, 106–12; *New York Times*, February 13, 2002; *Los Angeles Times*, September 23, 2002; *Guardian*, September 4 , 5 and 9, 2002.

18. Kumar Ramakrishna, "Jemaah Islamiah: Aims, Motivations and Possible Counter-Strategies," *www.ntu.edu.sg/idss/Perspective/research_050221.htm*; Marty and Appleby, "Introduction" in their *Fundamentalisms Comprehended*, Chicago: University of Chicago Press, 1995.

19. See Anatole Lieven, "Nightmare in Caucasus," *Washington Quarterly*, winter 2002, and his *Chechnya: Tombstone of Russian Power*, New Haven, CT: Yale University Press, 1998; Mowaffaq Al-Nowaiser, *www.Arabia.com*, May 4, 2002; *www.ict.org.il/articles/articledet.cfm?articleid=94*.

20. Gunaratna reproduces these allegations, *Inside Al Qaeda*, pp. 45, 146–9.

21. Gilles Kepel, *Jihad: The Trail of Political Islam*, Cambridge, MA: Harvard University Press, 2002, p. 224; *Le Monde diplomatique*, October 4, 1998; Marc Sirois, *www.yellowtimes.org*, October 6, 2002.

22. See Woodward, *Bush at War*, pp. 48–9, 60–1, 317–18; John Bolton, "The International Aspects of Terrorism and Weapons of Mass Destruction," *Remarks to the Second Global Conference on Nuclear, Biological and Chemical Terrorism: Mitigation and Response*, November 1, 2002; *Los Angeles Times*, March 31, 2003.

23. See *www.almashriq.hiof.no/lebanon/300/320/324/324.2/hizballah/*; *New York Times*, January 27, 2002; Eyal Zisser, "The Return of Hizbullah," *The Middle East Quarterly*, fall 2002.

24. Colin Powell suggested so in the flimsy terrorist part of his case to the UN Security Council for invading Iraq, presented in January 2003.

25. Olivier Roy, *The Failure of Political Islam*, Cambridge, MA: Harvard University Press, 1994; and Mark Jurgensmeyer, *Terror in the Mind of God: The Global Rise of Religious Violence*, Berkeley and Los Angeles: University of California Press, 2000.

26. Kepel, *Jihad*. So does Anthony Shadid, *Legacy of the Prophet: Despots, Democrats and the New Politics of Islam*, Boulder, CO: Westview, 2001, who adds the cases of Iran and Jordan.

27. CDI Terrorism Project, *www.cdi.org/terrorism/somalia-pr.cfm*.

28. Tim McGirk, *www.time.com*, September 24, 2001.

29. *New York Times*, January 27, 2002. Some scholars believe the "beautiful" or "fair virgins" so often repeated in jihad; circles is a mistranslation of the ancient Arabic for "white raisins," a great delicacy in early Islamic times!

30. Gunaratna, *Inside Al Qaeda*, pp. 205–19; *www.fas.org/irp/world/para/*.

31. Philip Smucker, "Al Qaeda thriving in Pakistani Kashmir," *Christian Science Monitor*, July 2, 2002.

32. Gunaratna, *Inside Al Qaeda*, ch. 4; "Confessions of an Al-Qaeda Terrorist," *Time Magazine*, September 15, 2002; US Department of State, "Patterns of Terrorism, 2000" and "Background Information on Foreign Terrorist Organizations," *www.state.gov/www/global/terrorism*; The *Australian* and the *Sydney Morning Herald*, both November 18, 2002; and *www.emergency.com/2002/hambali.htm*.

33. Carlito Pablo, "Moro Rebels to Hunt Jemaah Islamiah Agents," *Philippine Daily Inquirer*, November 5, 2002; Greg Miller, "US Troops to Fight in the Philippines," *Los Angeles Times*, February 21, 2003; see also Gunaratna, *Inside Al Qaeda*, pp. 181–5.

34. Robert Hefner, *Civil Islam. Muslims and Democratization in Indonesia*, Princeton: Princeton University Press, 2000.

35. Harold Crouch, "Qaida in Indonesia? The Evidence Doesn't Support Worries," *International Crisis Group*, October 23, 2001; Robert Hefner, "Muslim Politics in Indonesia after September 11," *www.house.gov/international_relations/hefn1212.htm*.

36. Kenneth Katzman, "Terrorism: Near Eastern Groups and State Sponsors, 2001," Congressional Research Group, Washington; Conetta, "Dislocating Alcyoneus"; Judith Miller in *New York Times*, January 15 and 16, 2001. The State Department has been more modest, linking al-Qaeda to only to 7 of the 36 terrorist organizations on its proscribed list: "2002 Report on Foreign Terrorist Organizations," *www.state.gov*.

37. See *www.ABCNEWS.com*, January 27, 2002.

38. Cordesman, *Terrorism*, pp. 51–76, who also quotes Louis Freeh, head of the FBI, making the same connections.

39. *Los Angeles Times*, October 26 and November 15, 2002.

SEVEN

THE WAR AGAINST ROGUE STATES AND NORTH KOREA

ROGUE STATES

Rogue states are conventionally defined in American foreign-policy circles as "nations exhibiting a chronic inability to engage constructively with the outside world"—that is, they challenge global norms and global order.[1] A state is officially considered rogue-like if it (1) develops weapons of mass destruction, (2) supports terrorism, and (3) abuses the human rights of its citizens. For Americans Iran, Iraq, Libya, North Korea and Cuba have formed the usual rogues' gallery, though Syria and the Taliban have been sometimes added. These are all small, poor and not very powerful states in the South of the world. Most are also Muslim. It is bizarre that the new imperialism should focus all its energies on such puny enemies.

Cuba does not really fit. Cuba adheres to international norms, has no weapons of mass destruction, does not support terrorists, and abuses its own citizens no more than do about a third of the world's states. Cuba even wants to be a friend of the US and likes American culture—it is the only baseball-playing rogue state.[2] It earns the "rogue" title only because the US hates Cuba's liking for socialism and because Cuban-Americans want revenge. There are also missing cases, states that should be considered rogues but aren't. Israel and Pakistan have weapons of mass destruction, have supplied other states with nuclear technology, and abuse their populations' human rights. Pakistan also supports terrorists. But the US calls them allies, not rogues. The US also avoids bad-mouthing bigger states. No China or Russia or—when the term first appeared—Indonesia, most of whose massive human rights abuses of the

1990s were condoned by the US. The US only hurls abuse at weaker, unfriendly states. Finally, some American behavior is obviously rogue-like in different ways, ignoring international norms of conduct, making war freely across the world.

How would we decide if a state truly was a rogue? Being condemned by UN resolutions might be a measure of deviance from international norms. Since 1970 most resolutions have been aimed at Israel. Iraq is a distant second, though matching it in the 1990s, and with most of its violations of resolutions called "flagrant." Israel escapes this label mainly because the US vetoes such resolutions. So these two have stood out in recent years. Others violated in specific, usually older circumstances— Turkey over Cyprus, South Africa during apartheid, Morocco over the Western Sahara, Croatia and Serbia during the wars of the Yugoslav succession, Indonesia over East Timor. Cuba, Iran and North Korea were not in violation during this period. On the other hand, the US was a deviant in the sense that since 1970 it vetoed resolutions no less than 73 times (35 of them to defend Israel), far more than all other permanent members of the Security Council combined. Its last veto, in December 2002, was of a resolution criticizing the killing by Israeli soldiers of several UN employees and the Israeli destruction of a World Food Program warehouse in the West Bank. We might also consider non-conformity to WMD treaties. North Korea withdrew from the Nuclear Non-Proliferation Treaty in 1992 and 2003, while Israel, Pakistan and India never signed up to it. The US withdrew from the chemical and biological weapons conventions, while Russia, China and Iraq signed conventions but did not fully comply with them.

No measure is ideal. The American list does seem to contain some genuine rogues, and North Korea and Iraq were probably the worst of them. But on the whole the most fundamental criteria of a rogue state are that the US does not like it, and that it is not too powerful.

But "rogues" are not simply people pursuing interests that happen to conflict with ours. They are bad guys—"evil-doers," insist Bush the Younger and other neo-conservatives. Normally, there is only one way to deal with such people: we punish them, hard and vigorously. In international relations this means at a minimum "containment" through isolating them from the world, and at a maximum invading them to effect regime change. Only aggression is considered acceptable against rogues. We do not offer them inducements to change their behavior, except from weakness. A special term of abuse has emerged to describe a policy of inducement—"appeasement," invoking the greatest rogue of them all, Hitler. Yet to conduct US foreign policy by deploying abusive language brings problems.[3]

It reduces strategic flexibility. It is a "one size fits all" label, ignoring the fact that each case is unique, requiring flexibility from both sides. We deal most effectively with those who oppose our will—like our own children—with a carrot-and-stick mixture, punishing bad behavior, while offering rewards for good behavior. Completely irredeemable states (like children) are very rare. Otherwise we work on what they want as well as what they fear. If we only punish them, we drive them into a corner and give them no incentive to come out. We should not then take their hostile response to punishment as evidence that they cannot be redeemed. This may create a self-fulfilling prophecy. If the US names a state as a rogue, its incentive to acquire WMDs secretively increases, for they are a deterrent against American force. This actually encourages more proliferation.

It personifies foreign policy, demonizing the single leader—Castro, Gadafi, Saddam, the Ayatollah, the two Kims. Yet dictators emerge out of real structural conditions which their mere removal may not solve. Nor do dictators run their regimes single-handedly. Indeed, they are rarely the extreme hardliners of their administrations. They lead by steering between contending factions. But demonizing them forces them into hardline defiance in order to stay alive. It gives them the Churchillian war-leadership option, protecting his small, embattled country from the Great Satan. Demanding regime change rather than behavior change gives the leader no incentive to change; while changing the leader may solve nothing.

It damages US relations with allies who do not view such states as evil. Unilateral American sanctions on Iran, Libya and Cuba produced strong negative reactions from allies. The relentless pursuit of Cuba alienated almost everyone. Bush's Axis of Evil speech produced general alarm. Europeans were disturbed at the term "axis," which sought to tie in today's tinpot dictators to the global, genocidal menace of Hitler. The South Korean and Japanese governments expressed alarm at the likely alienation of North Korea. Everyone condemned the abuse directed at a deeply split Iranian regime, whose moderates needed encouragement, not abuse. The speech could only help drive Iranian moderates into the arms of the extremists.

It loses a sense of proportion, inviting ridicule. In 2002 Bush the Younger addressed a historic meeting ratifying the enlargement of NATO over Eastern Europe. He declaimed:

Great evil is stirring in the world. . . . We face perils we've never thought about, perils we've never seen before. But they're dangerous. They're just as dangerous as those perils that your fathers and mothers and grandfathers and grandmothers faced.[4]

His European audience treated this with incredulity. To compare Saddam or bin Laden to Hitler as a threat to the world is patently ludicrous. Hitler's regime had killed over 20 million people! Foreigners also see the rhetoric of evil as hypocritical. They might agree that in certain respects Saddam has pursued evil policies. But why in that case were we actually helping him at his very worst, when he was gassing his own people?

Treating states as rogues hasn't worked. The US has applied the stick more than the carrot for over a decade. It has isolated and punished all of them with economic sanctions. Against Iran, Libya and Cuba, the US also legislated "secondary sanctions" against foreign companies trading with them. US intelligence agencies sought to destabilize and overthrow them, arming their neighbors and domestic opponents (like the Kurds and Shiites in Iraq). The US used military force against Libya and Iraq, including bombing Gadafi and Saddam in the hope of killing them. Bush the Younger offered even fewer carrots than his predecessors. Yet this did not change their behavior or induce regime change. It did reduce their resources, making their people suffer much more than their leaders. They remained "rogue states" and alienated peoples, hating us even more, though able to actively defy us less. Of course, actually invading and conquering such countries might work in the limited sense of removing the leading rogue. But whether that would improve the underlying situation of the country is another matter.

Most importantly, it is unclear what is cause and what is effect in a stick-driven policy against "rogues." Driven into a corner, do they pursue weapons of mass destruction even more, because they feel it is the only way they can counter the might of a hostile US? Or is it simply their pursuit of these weapons which incurs punishment? This and the next chapter examine the level of threat and the methods of countering it in the two cases which seem the most "rogue-like," North Korea and Iraq.

NORTH KOREA—THE RHETORIC OF EVIL AND THE REALITY
OF RETREAT TO DETERRENCE

North Korea might qualify as a rogue state, whatever our reservations about the term. It is highly repressive, has actively pursued WMDs, and it used to sponsor terrorists—though this ceased some years back. But the regime is also very threatened. As the last, unreformed communist state in Asia, it is defined by the US as a deadly enemy. The US has repeatedly tried to finish it off by economic strangulation and has threatened preemptive military, including nuclear, strikes. That its economy is a basket-case is also its own doing. All this means it is in deep trouble. How long can it survive, especially given a militarism which absorbs one-quarter of total GDP? It will fall, sooner or later, and be absorbed into an economically stronger South, backed by the US. Pragmatically, the best policy would have been for the US to do nothing except unconditionally guarantee the security of South Korea. Let North Korea collapse under the weight of its own incompetence and repression. However, cold-war ideology, followed by rogue-state rhetoric, prevented such a pragmatic solution. This zone of American policy embodied good against evil way before the neo-conservatives arrived in power.

So American policy has long been to precipitate North Korea's fall as fast as possible, driving this remnant of communist failure into the ground, alongside Cuba. Understandably, North Korea was and is fearful, and this has been its main motive for acquiring WMDs. It cannot use them for aggression, for this would invite total destruction. The regime sees them as a cheaper deterrent against outside threats than its present million-strong army, and it can also profit from selling nuclear and ballistic technology abroad to generate scarce hard currency. These motives lie behind its continued nuclear brinkmanship. Since the potential benefits are high, it is willing to take risks.

Since the peninsular was the frontline of the cold war, diplomacy tended to involve the Great Powers of the region more than the UN. In 1985 the Soviet Union made a constructive move, persuading its ally to sign the Nuclear Non-Proliferation Treaty and abandon its nascent nuclear program. In return the Soviets would supply North Korea with energy. Unfortunately, this was very bad timing, since the collapsing Soviet Union could not deliver on the deal. So in 1992 North Korea denied access to its nuclear facilities to the international inspectors, contrary to its obligations under the NNPT. Next year, amid suspicions that it had reprocessed enough plutonium for one or two nuclear weapons, the North said it might withdraw from the treaty: give us enough aid—especially fuel—to prosper, or we will develop nuclear weapons. Since North Korea already had formidable conventional military power, it was not clear that threats could deter it. A buy-out seemed a sensible policy, pragmatically reasoned President Clinton.

THE CLINTON DEAL

In 1994, after difficult negotiations, Clinton accepted the offer. In return for North Korea eliminating its nuclear program, the US would begin to normalize relations and ease trade sanctions. Activity in North Korea's nuclear weapons production site at Yongbyon was suspended. At its five-megawatt plutonium production reactor, US personnel helped ship spent fuel rods out of the country, and construction was suspended on two larger reactors. In return, an International Consortium (South Korea, Japan and the United States) delivered heavy fuel oil to the North to offset its immediate energy loss, and would construct two light water nuclear energy reactors to provide for Korea's additional fuel needs. This type of reactor is less easily convertible into weapons production. Humanitarian food aid was added later. "A soft landing for North Korea is in our national interests," declared the State Department. But the US also believed the regime was on its last legs. Clinton did not expect it to survive until the light water reactors came onstream in 2003. Beneath an apparent policy of behavior change, lay the expectation of regime change. But this did not happen.[5]

North Korea retained the technology and expertise to restart its effort, should it decide to do so, and its existing chemical weapons and ballistic missiles remained outside the agreement. During the 1990s North Korean missile tests and a suspicious underground facility severely strained relations. But the agreement got back on track in 1999 when North Korea suspended missile tests and the underground facility was inspected and declared safe by US officials. In return Clinton announced some easing of trade sanctions. Secretary of State Albright said that if the Koreans broke the agreement the US would return to aggressive containment. Clinton told the North that it would be "pointless" to develop nuclear weapons. If they ever used them, "It will be the end of their country."[6] The US was offering carrots while waving sticks.

We don't know whether the North Koreans ever intended to keep their side of the bargain. There has to be doubt about this. But the US certainly failed to honor its commitments. There were long delays in beginning the construction of the light water reactors, and by 2000 they were at least six years behind schedule. Were the delays part of pressure to force regime change? The North Koreans began to perceive the agreement as a trick, to starve them of energy. They asked to renegotiate. In July 2000 they offered a further deal, though as usual they expressed it as a threat. They would continue to develop their missile program and to export missile technology unless the United States paid it $1 billion per year. Clinton, under conservative pressure in Congress, did not respond. In early 2001 the CIA Deputy Director summed up the North's stance.

> It has so far held to its missile launch moratorium and it has signaled its interest in negotiating a missile deal with us. At the same time, the North's proliferation activities remain robust—for a profit and for a purpose: To keep our attention, to underline their greatest source of leverage, and to remind us of what it is they are willing to haggle over.

THE BUSH BLUFF

But House and Senate Republicans were now denouncing US policy as appeasement, and the Korean "offer" enraged them. A House Committee wrote a blistering attack on the Clinton policy, claiming that the North Korean nuclear program had only been strengthened by the 1994 agreement. This was not correct. The Clinton agreement had not been a waste of time, even though the Koreans had not complied with all of it. The nuclear weapons program had been capped at an early stage, before it had acquired much plutonium. Without the agreement, by now North Korea would have 50 nuclear weapons instead of one or two. Missile flight tests also remained suspended.[7] Nonetheless, Republican hawks urged the new Bush administration to shift policy toward the stick.

Bush mollified them with aggressive rhetoric. He told South Korea's President Kim Dae Jung, visiting Washington in March 2001, that his "sunshine policy" of conciliating the North wouldn't work since North Korea would never conciliate. In June he demanded new terms from Pyongyang, asking for more stringent verification of Korean compliance, an acceleration of inspections, and reductions in its conventional forces. A Bush official said, "North Korea's conventional forces are very destabilizing and potentially as dangerous as its missile exports." This was a serious escalation of demands by the US, but unless threats worked (and they never had in the past), the US would have to offer something in return—perhaps electricity from South Korea. But the administration did not offer specific carrots or sticks—what North Korea might expect if it complied, and what if it did not.[8] The Bush administration was talking loudly but carrying neither stick nor carrots. So the North denounced the proposal:

> The US side, while proposing to resume negotiations without precondi-tions, unilaterally set out and opened to the public topics of discussion ... before both sides sat together. [North Korea] cannot but interpret the US administration's proposal for resuming dialogue as unilateral and conditional in its nature and hostile in its intention.

Bush then escalated with his Axis of Evil speech, reinforced by threats of preemptive strikes. US Undersecretary of State, John Bolton, said North Korea must "get out of the missile-proliferation business" or face iso-lation and collapse. Bush added that he "loathed" the North Korean leader, Kim Jong Il, whom he said was a "pygmy." This was extra-ordinary rhetoric. When it became obvious that Bush intended to invade Iraq, Kim Jong Il quite reasonably thought he would be next. Asked who was responsible for deteriorating relations between North Korea and the US, 38 percent of South Koreans blamed the US and 31 percent North Korea—a reasonable response to their mutual bluster over the previous year.[9] The US was launching a preemptive invasion of Iraq because Saddam Hussein did not fully cooperate with UN weapons inspectors. How much more likely was a mere airstrike on the North Korean nuclear plants, especially since Korean weapons development was much more advanced than Iraq's? But it was obvious that the US would not attempt this while absorbed with Iraq. So in October a senior Northern official looked a US State Department official in the eye and said, "Your president called us a member of the axis of evil. ... Your troops are deployed on the Korean peninsula. ... Of course, we have a nuclear program."[10]

He seemed to be admitting violating the 1994 agreement, though only in uranium, not plutonium enrichment. US intelligence confirmed that North Korea had already begun a project for a bomb based on highly enriched uranium, a slow process but easier to hide. North Korea had three motives for admitting its transgression now—retaliation against new American demands, upping the ante for another buy-out, and seizing the opportunity presented by the US preoccupation with Iraq. Kim had joked the previous month to the Japanese Prime Minister that he might now "try nuclear exchanges" with the United States.

Bush's bluff had been called. He used some of what few cards he had, refusing to talk to the North Koreans and suspending fuel shipments, in conjunction with a somewhat reluctant Japan and South Korea. But this merely persuaded North Korea to resume its nuclear program on a much greater scale. It immediately expelled the UN weapons inspectors from the Yongbyon nuclear complex and withdrew from the NNPT. Since Bush still refused to negotiate, the reactor at Yongbyon was restarted "for peaceful purposes" only, a claim greeted with some skepticism. If reprocessing plutonium began there, North Korea could arm 6–12 nuclear weapons by the end of 2003—and many more if the two larger reactors were finished. North Korea declared that "if the United States is willing to abandon its hostile policy toward the North ... everything is negotiable." But presumably it now wanted a bigger buy-out.

The Bush administration still had no real policy. It said it favored "dialogue" but not "negotiations," unless the North Koreans first agreed to go back to the previous agreement. Rumsfeld blustered, "We are capable of fighting two major regional conflicts. ... We're capable of winning decisively in one and swiftly defeating in the case of the other, and let there be no doubt about it." This was bad bluffing. A Bush official confessed to the *New York Times*: "I'm not saying we don't have military options, I'm just saying we don't have good ones." Powell said the US "could not reward bad behavior" by the North Koreans, yet the alternative was to have the weapons program resumed in full. In January 2003 Powell changed his tune and said there would be negotiations. Perhaps the US would resume Clinton's "carrot and stick" strategy: more aid for North Korea if it cooperated, sanctions if it did not. At the same time North Korea formally withdrew from the NNPT. At the end of February Powell announced that US food shipments to North Korea would resume but at a level of around half the previous year's. Next day US officials said that the North Koreans had restarted the Yongbyon nuclear reactor. It remained unclear what either side intended. At first America's regional allies urged the US to resume bilateral talks with North Korea. They wanted the two of them to talk sense to each other before starting multilateral talks. But the main point was to get them both to talk at all, so they then also tried to persuade North Korea to join in multilateral talks. We awaited results.

North Korea does not at present rely on nuclear weapons for deterrence, nor even on its very large army, since its military technology is mostly outdated. Instead, it has a unique geographic asset. It has 10,000 artillery pieces dug in within range of Seoul, the South Korean capital, which lies very close to the border. Though American air power could presumably take them out in time, in the meantime, it warned the US, it would retaliate to any American aggression by engulfing Seoul— including the large US base at Yongsan—in "a sea of fire." The US had banked on Kim to fall by now, yet he seemed firmly in power. Economic sanctions hurt, but Kim did not seem to care what suffering this might inflict on his people. Some Republican hawks were urging tougher military threats, but would the US risk a major war in the peninsular against the wishes of South Korea? In any case, the US was fully occupied with Iraq. By the end of the Iraq crisis, Kim Jong Il might have achieved a credible nuclear deterrent. He had every incentive to defy the US and get there quickly, since it might protect him or give him a bigger eventual buy-out. "In Kim Jong Il's view, what's the difference between North Korea and Iraq?" asked one US official, "Saddam doesn't have one, and look what's happening to him."

The new imperialists may be just stalling until they have finished with Iraq. Then they might increase military pressure, including striking at the nuclear plants. That way lies serious risk of the nightmare scenario of devastating war on the peninsular and is deeply opposed by South Korea. The new president Roh Moo Hyun has declared, "It is better to struggle than to suffer deaths in a war. Koreans should stand together, although things will get difficult when the United States bosses us around."[11] After the Iraq invasion and further threats to Iran and Syria, all committed against the wishes of America's regional allies, the new imperialists seem capable of risking a Korean war, mad as it would be. Nonetheless, they probably do retain some reason, in which case they know that they failed their first test against rogue states. Within nine months of declaring a war against three rogue states, the US had its bluff called against one of them. Either the North Koreans are offered bigger bribes to desist or they will quickly acquire a credible nuclear deterrent. Even if they took the bribes, they might still not comply, and join the nuclear club anyway. The US and the world probably has to accept this as a fact of life, and fall back to the deterrence option of coping with WMDs which I outlined in Chapter 1.

Luckily, despite the "rogue-state" rhetoric, this seems a rational regime of a familiar communist type. The US might dust off its old

Soviet policies: credible nuclear and conventional deterrence, abandoning the policy of preemptive strikes, allowing US and South Korean military deployment to be transparent to the North, establishing a hotline phone link with Pyongyang, and supporting South Korean economic engagement with the North. The significant concession it might require in return would be an end to WMD and ballistic missile exports. If Pyongyang refused or evaded this, the US might try to interdict such exports on the high seas. This might lead to crises, but with negotiations as the outcome, as in the cold war.

At a Washington dinner for a visiting South Korean delegation in February 2003, American mouths dropped open when a top Korean envoy said that his incoming government would prefer that North Korea had nuclear weapons to seeing it collapse. One American said: "I sense major trouble ahead in [our] relationship. The impression I got is that for Roh [the new South Korean president] and his generation, the ultimate goal is to reunite their country and get us off the peninsula."[12] That would leave a united Korea with nuclear weapons, which the South Koreans were hinting was a nice bonus for them. Seoul would then be a member of the nuclear club.

Japan might respond to this potential threat by joining the club too. Nonetheless, that would be less threatening for the region than to increase the paranoia of the peninsular's present nuclear power. North Korea should not remain a "rogue" outside the community of nations. Let us forget good against evil, introduce a little pragmatism, and play baseball with them. This might be a bitter pill for the new imperialists to swallow. But, unlike their incoherent position of aggressive rhetoric and no real stick, it is realism. They were much more confident about overcoming Iraq.

NOTES

1. Taken from former National Security Advisor Anthony Lake's much cited article "Confronting Backlash States," *Foreign Affairs*, March/April 1994. Lake actually used the term "backlash state."

2. In North Korea baseball was banned as an imperialist game in 1945. After 1992 it began to creep back into the country, influenced by Cuba!

3. Most of these are noted by Robert Litwak, *Rogue States and U.S. Foreign Policy*, Baltimore, HD: Johns Hopkins University Press, 2000.

4. *Los Angeles Times*, November 21, 2002.

5. For the various agreements and negotiations, see Litwak, *Rogue States and US Foreign Policy*, ch. 6; and Joseph Cirincione et al., *Deadly Arsenals: Tracking Weapons of Mass Destruction*, New York: Carnegie Endowment for International Peace, 2002, ch. 14.

6. *Washington Post*, July 12, 1993.

7. David Albright and Kevin O'Neill, *Solving the North Korean Nuclear Puzzle*, Washington, DC: ISIS Press, 2000.

8. David Albright and Holly Higgins, "North Korea: It's Taking Too Long," *Bulletin of the Atomic Scientists*, January/February 2002. Construction of the two reactors did not even start until late 2002.

9. *Los Angeles Times*, February 18, 2002.

10. All official statements from *www.usinfo.state.gov/regional/ea/easec/nkoreapg.htm*. North Korean statements from *www.CNN.com*, October 17, 2002; *New York Times*, February 14, 2002; and *www.cdi.org/weekly/2002/issue31.html*. Some South Koreans disputed that this was said. They requested a transcript or tape from the State Department, but this was not forthcoming.

11. Quotes from *New York Times*, December 30 and November 24, 2002, and February 24, 2003.

12. *New York Times*, February 11, 2003

EIGHT

IRAQ ATTACK

Iraq differed in three crucial respects. It was much weaker than North Korea, it has oil, and it had defied the US more openly. These were the reasons it had always been the leading candidate for attack. Of course, it was Saddam Hussein's invasion of Kuwait that led to the US-commanded, UN-approved attack by 29 nations in 1991. This kicked him out of Kuwait, but went no further. Bush the Elder and his national security advisor Brent Scowcroft recall that they stopped short of trying to overthrow him because this would have lost all their Arab colleagues from the coalition.[1] The UN then demanded Saddam renounce his WMDs and imposed harsh economic sanctions and stringent weapons inspections to enforce this. The Americans and British added inter-mittent bombing of their own. This greatly weakened the Iraqi economy and killed many Iraqis, as well as degrading his military capacity.

But the US wanted more, and in 2003 the administration of Bush the Younger launched a second invasion, this time without UN support and with only one significant ally, Britain. Most of the world opposed this, was deeply suspicious of American motives, feared the aftermath of victory, and strongly preferred an alternative policy of "smart sanctions" which had been recently emerging. All this threatened to destabilize the Middle East, the UN and the whole US alliance system. I shall deal with these broader issues in my final chapter. Here I examine Iraq itself, starting with the more suspect American motivations for invasion.

SUSPECT AMERICAN MOTIVES—OIL AND REVENGE

One powerful motive was oil, absent from North Korea. Arabs like to say that oil is God's blessing to them. No, it is their curse. Water would be more useful. Iraq has the second largest proven oil reserves in the world, at least 11 percent of the world's total. Its oil is also of high quality and is easy and cheap to extract. At present, sanctions prevent much of its oil from being extracted. Replacing Saddam by a loyal client state would obviously give the US and its oil industry greater control of global oil supplies. The Bush administration is also permeated by oil interests. The President's own family has substantial oil interests, but suspicions centered on Vice-President Cheney, formerly head of Halliburton, the biggest manufacturer of oil equipment. In 1998, while he was its CEO, a Halliburton subsidiary did $22 million of business with Saddam. Cheney at first denied this, then retracted his denial, then invoked the presidential prerogative to stall judicial investigations into his role in national energy policy. Luckily for him, the new Republican majority in Congress halted the investigations in 2001. There are also close links between the US oil industry and the Republican Party, conservative think-tanks and the Iraqi exiles in alliance with the Bush administration. All benefit from oil money.

These links make the administration more sensitive to oil-industry needs. The interests of the industry and the US economy are not the same—the industry wants high oil prices, the US economy low ones—but they would willingly compromise on medium but stable prices. The US government was also alienated by Saddam's switch in 2000 from dollars to euros in payments received for the oil it sells under the UN-administered oil-for-food program. He was seeking to play off France and Russia against the US, and this also boosted Iraqi trade with the whole euro zone. After a successful US invasion the Iraqi oil industry would likely be rebuilt by US firms, denominate its sales in dollars, and invest profits in the US. The bonanza for the Anglo-American oil industry would be securing privileged contracts to extract the oil—and perhaps even to grab Iraqi oil assets through privatization of the state-owned oil industry. This was being advocated by conservative US think-tanks, ostensibly for the neo-liberal "free-market" reasons discussed in Chapter 2, and their views were reproduced on the US State Department website. Ahmed Chalabi, the US-backed leader of the opposition Iraqi National Congress, promised "American companies will have a big shot at Iraqi oil."

All this lends considerable credence to the view that the Bush administration wanted to invade in order to get its hands on Iraqi oil. It would also send a warning to Iran (with 9 percent of the world's oil reserves), then considering switching its large oil sales to euros. The dollar's reign as the hegemonic currency would continue. And it would be a rebuff to France and Russia, whose companies' lucrative oil contracts in Iraq would be threatened. This was one reason they looked less favorably on invasion, for suspect motives cut both ways.[2] Obviously, oil did matter, enormously. If Iraq lacked oil, it would probably not be a candidate for invasion.

The evidence is also very clear that US policy-makers were extremely worried by Saddam's oil policies. The "Cheney Report" of April 2001, on US energy needs, predicted that American consumption of foreign oil would have to rise by 50 percent over the next few decades. It recommended that the main goal of US policy should be to protect what it called "free oil markets." But "freedom" might be achieved by force. It clearly identified Saddam as the main enemy:

> Iraq has effectively become a swing producer, turning its taps on and off when it has felt such action was in its strategic interest. ... Iraq remains a destabilizing influence to US allies in the Middle East, as well as to regional and global order, and to the flow of oil to international markets from the Middle East. Saddam Hussein has also demonstrated a willingness to threaten to use the oil weapon and to use his own export program to manipulate oil markets.

The report called for policy to counter Saddam's malign influence, including a potential "need for military intervention."[3] What could be more premeditated—or less like free markets?

Yet nothing in Saddam's oil strategy contravened international norms. It is entirely legitimate for a nation state to seek to get the largest profit out of its own natural resources, if this is done peacefully (Saddam had breached this when he invaded Kuwait in 1990). In the 1970s Saddam had interfered very productively in "free markets," i.e. controlled by a few giant foreign oil corporations. He had negotiated deals with Soviet and French oil companies to break the power of the Iraqi Petroleum Co., an Anglo-American cartel which had organized a boycott of the Iraqi nationalized oil company. His success enabled Iraqis to benefit from their own oil, and this was probably his biggest contribution to his country. The switch from dollars to euros was consistent with this policy of playing off the rich countries against each other. This is how poor countries *should* try to play the markets for their exports. It is the best way they can develop. Of course, most of Saddam's other policies only frustrated Iraqi development.

But did the US oil industry believe its interests required an invasion? This would risk the stability of the Gulf states which provide over 20 percent of the world's supply of oil and over 40 percent of its proven reserves. Nor might the aftermath of military victory be an Iraqi regime pumping more oil at prices suitable to the US. It might also put at risk other US interests in the region—balancing Iran, and protecting Israel, Jordan and Egypt. It might increase the attractions of Islamic jihadis, destabilizing friendly Muslim regimes, inviting terrorism directed against oil installations. None of this might be good for the supply and price stability of oil, which had been quite satisfactory for the West over the previous decades. No one can accurately calculate all these risks. But the oil industry trade press tended to argue that they made an invasion irrational. Adel Beshai, Professor of Economics at the American University in Cairo, was typical in saying: "From the point of view of the price of oil, the best thing would be not to attack Iraq at all. ... An attack could lead to a host of unpredictable events. ... Attack Iraq and you open a Pandora's box."[4]

Of course, oil companies are not military or political experts. If the Bush administration assured them that regime change could be effected without any of this blowback, they would probably be reassured. This seems the likeliest explanation. The war *is* about oil, but filtered through the overconfidence of the new imperialists. But if oil was *all* that mattered, the US would have a different Middle East policy, seeking to be friends not only with Saudi Arabia and the Gulf States, but also with Iraq and Iran. Instead, they are two-thirds of the Axis of Evil. The more rational policy is surely to cut out risky war and just befriend them. Then they will also denominate their sales in dollars. More must be swilling around the brains of Bush the Younger than just oil.

The world suspects a second liquid is the adrenalin rush of revenge. Saddam Hussein humiliated Bush the father, and Bush the son wants vengeance. After the 1991 war Saddam did not fall, as Bush had expected. He remained in power, massacring Bush's Kurdish and Shiite allies, surviving sanctions and bombing raids, switching his oil sales to euros, defiantly bad-mouthing the US all the while. He even supposedly tried to assassinate Bush the Elder in 1993. In 2002 Bush the Younger began telling audiences, "This is the guy that tried to kill my dad."

The cry for vengeance also derived from Saddam's effrontery in challenging American imperialism. He was only a tinpot dictator. How dare he! He was also such a repressive ruler that "regime change" really *ought* to be popular. Yet somehow Saddam managed to make himself an inspirational figure across the Middle East—the little guy who can defy the superpower. He is popular among millions who should really hate *him*, not the US! He repressed leftists and Islamists, but they denounced the US, not him. Kim Jong Il does not inspire such feelings, nor do the ayatollahs. Castro in his younger days, when Latin America was full of Marxists, might be the closest. He defied the US and so was persecuted beyond all reason. So too Saddam.

Some of the White House team had personally shared the sense of humiliation during the 1990s. In 1998 Cheney, Rumsfeld, Bolton, Perle, Abrams, Armitage, Wolfowitz and the administration's token Muslim, the oilman Khalilzad—all prominent decision-makers now— had urged Clinton to depose Saddam. When Bush the Younger reached office, the last Clinton policy option, "smart sanctions," was still being explored by the State Department. But the Pentagon set to work on an invasion plan. The balance of power between them was changed by 9-11. Cheney immediately urged the President to attack Iraq as well as Afghanistan. Rumsfeld and Wolfowitz supported him, but Powell and others convinced the President that this was not the best time.[5] But as the Aghan war began to wind down in September 2002, the war-drums resumed and power shifted toward the chicken-hawks. White House Chief of Staff Andrew Card added a dose of electoral cynicism, "From a marketing point of view you don't introduce new products in August"—meaning congressional elections were coming at the beginning of November and war was the tried and tested product. Indeed, war-fever helped the Republicans win control of both Houses, a tremendous asset to Bush. But though the White House did engage in electoral manipulation, it was in pursuit of sincere goals. Bush truly saw Saddam as an affront to the *pax americana* and believed the American electorate would too.

The desire for revenge has been a common imperial motivation. Think of the British response to the Indian Mutiny of 1857, or the response of the German Empire to the revolt of the Hereros in South West Africa in 1907. In all cases, the natives had dared defy (and even kill a few representatives of) "civilization." They must pay—and they certainly did pay, in their thousands. Imperialists easily feel humiliated because they normally feel so invulnerable. The emotional power of the desire for revenge, the willingness to take risks, and the sense of exhi-

laration coming as revenge is prepared and accomplished were all evident in the Bush policy toward Iraq, as they had been among the British
in India and the Germans in South West Africa. Chicken-hawks like
Wolfowitz, Perle and Feith could hardly wait for the next confrontations with defiant states—Iran, Syria and even Saudi Arabia. During the
war Rumsfeld and Powell both warned Syria and Iran that they should
behave, or else.[6]

That revenge plus oil were not entirely rational motives did not
reduce their power, though obviously the US could not expect international support for them. But the Bush administration preferred a
different interpretation of its motives: invasion was the best response to a
rogue state abusing the human rights of its citizens, sponsoring terrorists
and developing weapons of mass destruction. A preemptive invasion
could therefore secure peace and order in the world.

On the first point, few would argue, and the discovery of mass graves
after the war only confirmed it. The only quibble concerns the past. A
member of Egypt's state Shura Council comments:

> the state terrorism practiced by Saddam's regime inside Iraq has surpassed in
> brutality and bloodshed that perpetrated by any other despotic regime in the
> world. Given this reality, no one is about to quibble with Washington's
> contention that the Iraqi regime systematically violates human rights.
> However, the bitter irony is that the Americans only brought up this issue
> recently, having conveniently overlooked it during the many years in which
> Saddam served US interests.[7]

Yet Saddam's oppression was not a central part of the US case against
Iraq until after the invasion began. This was because if expressed earlier,
this argument would seem to invite action through the United Nations.
The UN could declare that Saddam had a case to answer under international law for committing crimes against humanity or even, against
the Kurds in 1988, genocide. But this would be to go through UN
judicial procedures that the US rejects. So the US kept quiet until the
invasion was underway, and I proceed to the two grounds advanced
beforehand by the Bush administration.

HIGHER AMERICAN MOTIVES

1. Saddam's sponsorship of terrorism

The case linking Saddam to terrorists was fervent but flimsy. Bob
Woodward says that Vice-President Cheney, Defense Secretary

Rumsfeld and his assistant Wolfowitz all immediately argued in White House meetings that the 9-11 terrorists were sponsored by Iraq, and so the US should attack Iraq as well as Afghanistan. Officials also kept repeating the story that Czech intelligence had unearthed a meeting between the hijacker Mohamed Atta and an Iraqi agent in Prague. This was despite repeated Czech denials, confirmed by British leaks that the rumor had started as part of an obscure intelligence feud between the British and the Czechs.

Rumsfeld ploughed on regardless, claiming "bulletproof evidence" of al-Qaeda agents trained in Iraq in chemical and biological warfare. Pressed, he conceded that this came from one detainee of dubious veracity. Responding to a congressman who asked him what was different now that compelled invasion, he barked, "What's different? What's different is 3,000 people were killed." Asked about evidence that Iraqis had helped kill the 3,000, he replied amid laughter, "That happens to be a piece of intelligence that either we don't have or we don't want to talk about."

Bush had opposed Rumsfeld's early pressing for war against Iraq only on tactical grounds, saying, "public opinion has to be prepared before a move against Iraq is possible." So he began to repeatedly use the post-9-11 climate of fear of terrorism to press the case. He declared, "you can't distinguish between Al-Qaeda and Saddam when you talk about the war on terror" and "the regime has long-standing and continuing ties to terrorist organizations. And there are Al-Qaeda terrorists inside Iraq." Taliban remnants had indeed regrouped in Northern Iraq, but in Kurdish-controlled areas outside of Saddam's control. Nonetheless, they figured in Bush's request (and Congress's authorization) for military powers against Iraq.

When pressed, the administration retreated from the present to the future: Saddam *might* supply WMDs to terrorists. Bush said: "Iraq could decide on any given day to provide a biological or chemical weapon to a terrorist group." Saddam would be very unlikely to do this, since he and bin Laden are enemies and the terrorists might use them against him. Bin Laden has said that Saddam wanted Kuwaiti oil for his own aggrandizement, and was not "a true Muslim" but an "apostate". Other Islamists routinely call Saddam "socialist," a term of abuse which Americans should be able to easily understand. CIA Director Tenet testified that a handover might only happen "under extreme circumstances, when he believes he is likely to be toppled." This would be a reason *against* attacking him, of course.

General Brent Scowcroft, National Security Advisor during the Gulf War said, "Saddam is a problem, but he's not a problem because of terrorism." French judge Jean-Louis Bruguère has spent decades investigating terrorism. He said: "We have found no evidence of links between Iraq and al-Qaeda. And we are working on 50 cases involving al-Qaeda or radical Islamic cells. I think if there were such links, we would have found them. But we have found no serious connections whatsoever." Baltasar Garzon, his Spanish equivalent (famous for having even-handedly hounded General Pinochet and corrupt Spanish Socialist ministers) said the same. Even Kenneth Pollack, who presents the fullest case for invading Iraq, does not include sponsorship of terrorism in it.[8] Blair's official dossier of September 2002 against Iraq focused only on Iraqi weapons of mass destruction, with no mention of terrorist connections. British Foreign Secretary Jack Straw was diplomatic but damning: "It could well be the case that there were links, active links, between al-Qaeda and the Iraqi regime before September 11. What I'm asked is if I've seen any evidence of that. And the answer is: I haven't." Even Bush seemed to abandon the allegation. Canadian Prime Minister Chrétien says he asked Bush about the alleged links. Bush replied: "That is not the angle they're exploring now. The angle they're exploring is the production of weapons of mass destruction."[9]

But Bush resurrected the allegations in his 2003 State of the Union speech, asserting that Saddam "aids and protects terrorists. Secretly, and without fingerprints, he could provide one of his hidden weapons to terrorists, or help them develop their own." Note again the hypothetical "could." So could anyone. The evidence was presented a week later by Colin Powell to the UN Security Council. It proved extremely thin. It added the name of Al-Zarqawi to the al-Qaeda man who had undergone a medical operation in Baghdad and then joined the jihadi group Al-Ansar in Kurdish-held territory. But Ansar's leader, Mullah Krekar, is a longtime enemy of Saddam and vehemently denies any connection. Zarqawi seemed to be a nobody, not on any FBI wanted list, his name supplied by suspects tortured in Jordan. Powell also produced more testimony from the man in custody whom Rumsfeld had previously admitted was unreliable, and he said that Iraq had infiltrated an agent into the higher levels of Al-Ansar. This could be disinformation to destabilize Al-Ansar, though it would not be surprising that Saddam would want to get inside intelligence on these hostile fighters. Never mind a court of law—I doubt this evidence even satisfied CIA scrutiny.[10] It did not satisfy British intelligence according to its report of early February 2003. This said flatly that there were no links between the Iraqi regime and al-Qaeda.[11] Nonetheless, throughout the invasion of Iraq Bush, Rumsfeld and others continued to assert the link as if it were established fact, and few Americans challenged them.

Just before the invasion bin Laden appeared on Al-Jazeera, denouncing the "Crusaders's preparations to occupy the former capital of Islam (Baghdad), loot the fortunes of the Muslims and install a puppet regime." He urged Iraqis to fight for God and not for "nationalism," "pagan regimes" or "infidel socialism"—all references to Saddam, whose name he cannot bear to mention.[12] Colin Powell bizarrely claimed this proved that bin Laden and Saddam were linked! Bin Laden was assuming that the attack on Iraq would turn more Muslims into jihadis. It obviously sent some jihadis into Iraq to fight for Saddam. Bin Laden and Bush thrive off each other, each helping the other's prophecies to be self-fulfilling. Bin Laden wants the ensuing chaos, and so does the Likud right in Israel. But Bush seems to march only half-wittingly into it.

2. Saddam's weapons of mass destruction

The case against Iraqi WMDs had more substance. Saddam used chemical weapons during the 1980s, killing about 20,000 Iranian soldiers and perhaps as many as 100,000 Kurds.[13] After the Gulf War the UN inspectors unearthed a sizeable Iraqi arsenal. Sixteen thousand free-fall bombs, 110,000 artillery rockets and shells and 75 Scud-type ballistic missiles could deliver either chemical or biological materials on the enemy, though with doubtful accuracy. So the UN banned Iraq from possessing chemical, biological and nuclear weapons, and ballistic missiles with a range of over 150 kilometers. Saddam still tried concealment, but by 1998 the UNSCOM inspectors had destroyed almost all his chemical weapons and ballistic missiles, plus their production facilities and his half-formed nuclear weapons program. Iraq probably retained some Scud-type missiles of dubious accuracy, some chemical precursors and biological seed stock, plus the skilled personnel and know-how. Development work probably continued in small, covert establishments.

In 2002 the British government and CIA reports said that Iraq still possessed useable chemical and biological weapons, though much reduced from 1991, and that Iraq had about 20 Al-Hussein missiles with a range of up to 650km. Any such weapons would breach UN Security Council Resolution 687. They admitted Iraq did not have nuclear weapons since it lacked fissile material, but the British report contained the most alarming claim that Iraq could launch "chemical and biological weapons within 45 minutes of an order to do so." Both reports documented lies from the Iraqi government, and concluded that Saddam still sought to develop all these weapons. At this time US intelligence officers were leaking their unhappiness at political interference with their reports. Only much later, in May and June 2003, did similar British leaks occur, alongside reports that both Colin Powell and Jack Straw had also been unhappy with the quality of intelligence reports. Not only the Iraqis were practicing deception.

Renewed UN inspections found some missiles slightly exceeding the range limit, plus a very few signs of more weapons. They were reasonably sure Iraq had no nuclear weapons, but said the Iraqis had failed to explain what had happened to some past missiles and biological and chemical weapons. Colin Powell's report to the UN Security Council added no significant new evidence. Most experts believed that Saddam was concealing some WMDs and missiles and that if left alone he would try to develop more, since Iraq remained weaker than Iran in conventional forces, and could not counter Israel's nuclear and missile superiority.[14] WMDs were also Saddam's sole potential deterrent against a hostile US. He believed they had saved him in the 1980s from defeat by Iran, and in 1991 from final defeat by the US. Being defined as a rogue state, fit only for regime change, increased his desire to acquire WMDs. Of course, his record against his neighbors and his own citizens did not invite trust either.

Nonetheless, constrained by bombing and UN inspections, he could not develop the production facilities necessary for serious WMD production. The draconian international regime had not reformed him but it had largely disarmed him. US security experts agreed he had only a few weapons and was much weaker than in 1991.[15] That is why the US was not at all deterred from invading Iraq. When it did, it encountered only inaccurate Scud-type missiles which hit open spaces. None were loaded with chemical or biological materials. During the invasion US forces uncovered no WMDs, only defensive protective clothing and gas masks. No steps to load such weapons had been taken. If US and British forces find no weapons of mass destruction at all, this renders this whole argument specious. Even if they find a few containers of mustard or sarin gas, it would seem that this so-called preventive war was preventing nothing.

Saddam still presented a conventional weapons threat to Kuwait, a small country with a long record of territorial disputes with Iraq (though they had just signed a peace treaty supposedly settling these). Kuwait and perhaps the small Emirates and Saudi Arabia might need protection from him. But they had this already. Saddam represented no threat whatsoever to the territory of the United States. Neither the CIA nor the British had suggested this. Yet Bush and Congress both did. Bush had asked Congress to authorize an invasion of Iraq because of "a high risk that the current Iraqi regime will ... employ these weapons to launch a surprise attack against the United States or its armed forces." Congress duly endorsed this, overwhelmingly. In his 2003 State of the Union speech Bush again compared Saddam to Hitler in terms of his threat to the world, and called his threat imminent.[16] He and other officials continued to assert this all the way through the invasion.

This was an insult to our intelligence. Saddam could mount no such attack. For him to have attacked US forces abroad, say in Kuwait, would have invited instant obliteration. Even as a preemptive strike against a possible future threat, invasion was unnecessary. Only if he were a madman would he ever attack the US even if he had many more WMDs. This would mean wipe-out. He had possessed many more WMDs in 1991, but had not used them then because he feared US retaliation. He saw them only as a deterrent against the US, and he believed they had already worked in this role. Charles Duelfer, deputy chairman of UNSCOM, has given the details of his private talk with high-ranking Iraqi officials in 1995. They revealed that Saddam

> thought that if Iraq used chemical or biological weapons against the coalition, retaliation would end his regime and probably him personally. He was successfully deterred. However, my interlocutors went on to describe how they had loaded BW and CW agent into various missile warheads and bombs before hostilities began in 1991. Moreover they dispersed these weapons and pre-delegated the authority to use them if the Americans moved on to Baghdad. The Iraqis stated that these actions apparently deterred the United States from going to Baghdad.[17]

Nor did Saddam pose much risk to Israel, Iran or Turkey. His armed forces had been devastated in 1991 and were now quite ramshackle. Israel had a nuclear deterrent, Iran had stronger, and Turkey much stronger, conventional forces—and they both have much larger populations. Syria was weaker but had friendly relations with Saddam. It is difficult to see how he might present a serious threat to any country except Kuwait, the tiny Emirates and perhaps Saudi Arabia, all of which were well protected by the US. As the war itself finally proved, the Iraqi forces were even minimally effective against the US only in low-intensity, half-guerrilla combat in the cities. In all other contexts they were rolled over by enormous aerial and artillery bombardment—and then by superior hand-guns—before they could even get into range to fire their own weapons. This was asymmetric warfare indeed. Iraq posed no military threat whatsoever to the world or to the US.

But the American whipping-up of "threats" produced a further serious consequence. If Saddam was asserted to be an imminent threat to the United States, this might legitimize a nuclear strike by the US against Iraq. Since the US had declared the threat was imminent, it instructed its regional military chiefs (STRATCOM) to evaluate the possibility of using nuclear weapons to attack deep Iraqi bunkers and chemical and biological facilities. This is a bigger threat to the peace of the world than any of Saddam's present actions or capabilities, for it breaks the 50-year firewall erected against first-strike use of theater nuclear weapons. If the US used nuclear weapons for such purposes, it would clearly be the biggest rogue state in the world. Predictably, however, Saddam had no such hardened underground resources, so nuclear weapons were not needed this time.

True, if Saddam ever had managed to build up his conventional and WMD forces again, his threat to the region (though not to the US) would increase. He had also shown a tendency toward overconfident aggression, matching that of the new imperialists. He attacked Iran in 1981 when he saw its armies had been weakened by the Iranian Revolution, but the Iranians had fought back tenaciously. He invaded Kuwait in 1990, misled by a ghastly mistake by the US ambassador into thinking that the US would not intervene (the kind of mistake which would fit Scott Sagan's argument, discussed in Chapter 1, that deterrence sometimes fails). After the US assembled a massive army to retake Kuwait, Saddam wrongly believed he could negotiate his way out. When the US aerial bombardment actually started, he immediately backed down and offered to withdraw his troops. When he did move his troops out of Kuwait, the US bombed them as they moved. As with Iran, he had underestimated the venom of his enemy. But he would surely not make the same mistake twice with the Bushes. Indeed, when in brinkmanship he moved his troops toward the Kuwaiti border in 1994 and the US responded with its own troop movements, he quickly backed down.[18] Saddam required regional vigilance, but he was rational. That is why he stayed in power so long, against all odds.

If, as the new imperialists said, Saddam was acquiring WMDs to use them, despite certain and massive US retaliation, then they were saying he would cut his own throat if provoked. Since they were now provoking him, making his overthrowal and death probable, from their perspective he would certainly strike out with everything he had—including, they said, giving WMDs to terrorists. But I do not believe they thought this. Instead, they were lying. This is certainly what chief UN weapons inspector Hans Blix believes. In a scathing attack on Britain and the US, Mr Blix accused them of planning the war "well in advance" and of "fabricating" evidence against Iraq to justify their campaign. He said: "There is evidence that this war was planned well in advance. Sometimes this raises doubts about their attitude to the [weapons] inspections." He said Iraq was paying a "a very high price in terms of human lives and the destruction of a country" when the threat of banned weapons could have been contained by UN inspections.[19]

So the reasons given for the invasion of Iraq were mostly false. In reality the invasion was fueled by a mixture of motives to which the new imperialists would not openly admit. Some of them might be considered as suspect motives—oil, revenge and a belief that it could dominate the Middle East by military force. The desire to dominate also had mixed motives—oil again, defense of Israel, but it also contained a genuine desire to bring freedom and democracy to the region. Saddam was seen as an evil tyrant, whom the US could usefully remove, while the UN could not. So underlying all these reasons was a supreme confidence that American military power could bring them all to pass. In fact, the new imperialists must have welcomed Saddam's stupid obstinacy, since it strengthened their case. But Iraq was not the whole story. There were bigger ends in view. Said Raghda Dirgham, Washington bureau chief of *Al-Hayat* (a joint London/Beirut paper sometimes described as the *New York Times* of the Arab world), "The war on Iraq is not a war for the sake of Iraq but rather it is for the sake of American greatness via the window of Iraq which has provided a golden opportunity found by the hawks of the American administration."[20] She was correct.

THE NEIGHBORS

The neighbors were the only ones facing any threat from Saddam but apart from Kuwait they said they opposed invasion. The Arab League urged Iraq to comply with UN resolutions and helped persuade Saddam to agree to inspections in 2002. But the League declared "absolute rejection" of invasion. The Saudi Foreign Minister, Prince Saud al Faisal, said war would be a "catastrophe" for the region. Bulent Ecevit, then Prime Minister of Turkey, said, "We have used every opportunity to tell our friends in the US administration we are opposed to military action against Iraq." President Mubarak of Egypt repeatedly opposed war and advised the US to focus on Israel instead. King Abdullah of Jordan told Bush at his Texas ranch that war would bring virtual "Armageddon" to his neighborhood. Syria opposed it. So even did the tiny Gulf sheikdoms. In the entire Middle East, only Israel (loudly) and Kuwait (quietly) supported an American-led invasion. A Kuwaiti official admitted: "It is Kuwait, not Iraq, that is isolated." Ironically, Iran, an "Axis of Evil" country, was not strongly opposed. Though the regime officially opposed a US invasion, most Iranians and reformist politicians would rejoice at the fall of their old enemy. Yet this was undercut by the fear that they might be next. Given Iran's hatred of Iraq, the US could have secured Iran's help for the invasion, and this would have strengthened the Iranian reformists against the Islamists. Instead Iran was alienated.

The neighbors' words might be taken with a pinch of salt. None would shed a tear if Saddam disappeared, and some privately expressed different views. Syria, Jordan and Egypt remained unequivocally opposed. They felt trapped between Saddam Hussein and George Bush, both rushing headlong to a war that would harm them too—just as many of their subjects felt trapped between their hatred for their own state and their hatred for the US. But Pollack says most of the Saudi elite privately favored an invasion with maximum force, provided it would quickly overthrow Saddam and replace him with another stable regime. "Get it over quick," he says they urged the US. In the end most of the neighbors agreed with this when they believed invasion was inevitable anyway. But they would also have preferred any US forces operating from their own territories to be invisible! Ninety percent of Turks opposed America's war, yet in the end the Turkish government saw that its effects—major economic dislocations, refugee flows and increased threat from the Kurds—would be worse if they stayed out than if they joined in. When push finally came to shove, most local states minimally and usually covertly cooperated. But not the most democratic neighbor. In a free vote the Turkish parliament rejected the realpolitik arguments of its government. It refused bribes to allow US troops to operate from Turkish territory.

The US described this as an alliance of the willing, but the few neighborhood helpers were heavily bribed. The US showered aid and military equipment on them. Bahrain got radar and advanced missiles, Kuwait 400 Hellfire missiles and 16 Apache Longbow helicopters, the United Arab Emirates got 80 F-16 fighters, Oman got 12 F-16s, laser-guided bombs, missiles and JDAMs. Turkey's bribe had to be upped from $4 billion to $14 billion to $26 billion to a real value of over $30 billion—though without success.[21] The neighbors only provided base rights, and only Kuwait and Qatar provided them without restrictions. The price of this "alliance of the billing" was the proliferation of conventional weapons of mass destruction in the neighborhood.

The weapons were also useful additions to the repressive powers of the neighbors, necessary to suppress their peoples' opposition to American policy. This completely negated US claims that it would bring democracy to the Middle East. Condoleezza Rice blithely predicted a "march to democracy" if Saddam was removed. Colin Powell announced a $29 million program to encourage democratic reforms in the region. "Hope," he said, "begins with a pay-check." But the pay-checks to repressive rulers dwarfed this one a hundredfold. As an Islamist writing in a Muslim Brotherhood newspaper commented, Powell was "buying our subjugation for 9.5 cents a person."[22] Though the US might in some idealized way want to bring democracy to the Middle East, it actually brought militarism.

Two writers in *Al-Ahram* summed up Arab reactions to Powell's plans for democracy. Salama A Salama wrote: "America cannot act to upgrade governance in the Arab world when it is simultaneously crushing underfoot the rights of the Palestinian people, bracing itself for war against Iraq and positioning its forces in the region regardless of the intolerable political pressures this places on Arab governments." Omayma Abdel-Latif added: "The US is not genuine about promoting democracy in this region because they wholly realise that establishing democracy may give power to anti-American forces like Islamists or nationalists." He said the US would not allow forces that might undermine their interests in the region to come to power, even if this happened via democratic means.[23] He was right, of course.

THE NEIGHBORS AND SANCTIONS/INSPECTIONS

The neighborhood states were uncooperative not because they liked Saddam but because they preferred another policy option and feared the aftermath of war. They said containment through economic sanctions and military pressure had worked. Saddam was not a present danger to anyone. Anti-war sentiment across the world said the same thing. Why invade now, they all asked? The neighbors wanted a different sanctions policy, with clearer specification of both carrots and sticks, and with some benefits for themselves. They favored "smart sanctions," targeted more precisely on military imports into Iraq, coupled with step-by-step easing of sanctions in response to acts of cooperation from the Iraqis.[24]

The US countered that sanctions had already weakened and were being flouted. It said that for much of the 1990s "sanctions fatigue" had set in, Iraqi evasion grew, and the UNSCOM inspectors were being held back by Security Council inaction. The sudden 1995 revelations about Saddam's WMDs made by Iraqi defectors had briefly toughened up inspections, but then fatigue returned. By 1999 the economies of Jordan, Syria and Turkey had become so entwined with Iraq's that they were massively evading the sanctions with smuggling. Iraqi oil was openly coming through the Syrian pipeline. France, Russia and others were also intermittently infringing sanctions. In 2000 it was discovered that China was constructing a national fiber-optic communications system for Iraq, of benefit to the Iraqi military. The UN turned a blind eye, not wanting to destroy the neighbors' economies, unable to restrain Security Council Powers.

Yet if the UN was weakening containment through inaction, the US was undermining it through action. The US never accepted the UN policy of behavior rather than regime change. When Saddam slowly and imperfectly began to comply, the US refused to begin lifting some of the sanctions. In 1991 Bush the Elder had declared a preference for regime, not behavior, change. Robert Gates, his deputy national security advisor, said sanctions would remain as long as Saddam ruled Iraq. In 1994 Secretary of State Warren Christopher was asked whether US support for general sanctions was aimed at deposing Saddam. He replied: "We want compliance with all the UN resolutions. And I don't believe he can do that and stay in office." Madeleine Albright, in her notorious TV interview of 1996, was asked about the cost of sanctions in Iraqi children's lives. She replied: "We think the price is worth it." She later added: "We do not agree with the nations who argue that if Iraq complies with its obligations concerning weapons of mass destruction, sanctions should be lifted." In 1998 Congress voted for funds to support Iraqi exiles overthrow Saddam (the CIA was already doing this). The US believed that economic sanctions, including ones on consumption goods, would hurt the Iraqi people so badly that they would rise up and overthrow Saddam. Debates raged over how many Iraqi children died in the 1990s as a result of the sanctions. It is certainly over 200,000, though it is probably not the 500,000 often asserted by critics of sanctions.

The main culprit was, or course, Saddam, but the US was also culpable, since it deliberately inflicted hurt to achieve regime change. The result in practice was a policy nobody wanted—neither behavior nor regime change, but containment, making it impossible for Saddam to acquire many weapons, denying life sustenance to Iraqis, but changing nothing.[25] It gave Saddam no incentive to fully comply. What was the point, since the US would overthrow him anyway? As a senior Egyptian official put it, the Iraqis reasoned, "If the game is to topple us, then we'd be crazy to cooperate any further." The inspectors were now faced with increased Iraqi non-cooperation. The US finally told the inspectors to get out of Iraq 48 hours before it began the massive bombing operation Desert Fox. This actually used information on targets gathered by American spies who had infiltrated UNSCOM, thus giving Saddam further reasons for resisting inspections. For the next two years there were no inspectors.

The lack of UN/US agreement undermined both multilateral and unilateral policy options. Offering Saddam a combination of sanctions and incentives to accept tight weapons inspections would not have been a farfetched policy. It had just never been tried. "Smart sanctions" would be such a policy. Its components would be: lift sanctions on consumption goods and target them at military goods; impose secondary sanctions on companies and governments caught evading them; bring Iraqi oil outlets under UN control and permit some of the neighbors' trade outlets; offer incentives to the neighbors to comply; increase monitoring of Iraqi trade and military activity; pass UN resolutions authorizing force in case of serious defined breaches. Pollack believes the US could not achieve this unilaterally, nor could the UN achieve it multilaterally—since some Security Council Powers would not enforce it.[26] Saddam might not accept any agreement, since he seemed set on Iraq becoming a "Great Power" in the region. For a country of only 23 million, half of them children, even with oil, that might require WMDs. So enforcement would remain imperfect, sanctions fatigue and evasions would recur, Saddam might get some weapons. But politics is the art of the possible. As in the 1990s, Saddam would be contained by what the UN and the US could agree to and enforce, and the Iraqi people would suffer less.

"Smart sanctions" became a serious option in 2001, and Colin Powell became actively involved in diplomacy involving them. In May 2002 UN Resolution 1409 laid out a framework for applying smart sanctions for a six-month trial period. However, the US retained through its veto the ability to ban any specific goods entering Iraq. It was expected to use it to block apparently innocuous items like computers and medical equipment which it argued had some dual-use potentiality. It appeared to many at the UN that the US was again undermining any targeted sanctions policy.[27] But US administrations were also becoming divided. In 1999 Pollack says he was brought into the Clinton National Security Council to develop options for overthrowing Saddam; and Bush the Younger's mantra of regime change began in early 2001.[28] Then came 9-11 and the Bush administration soon escalated from a stringent interpretation of smart sanctions to regime change by force. The next year it was reasoning that the UN weapons inspectors would confirm the case for invasion, whether they found serious "material breaches" of UN resolutions or not. If they did, the breach was clear; if they did not, this proved Saddam was concealing a breach. Saddam my have been concealing the few WMDs he had, since they remained his only credible deterrent against invasion, which he correctly believed was now virtually inevitable, whatever he did. In truth, UN *and* US policy toward Saddam had been incoherent for a decade.

THE NEIGHBORS' FEAR OF BLOWBACK

Despite quite widespread fear of Saddam, the imperfect record of sanctions/inspections, and the near certainty that invasion would overthrow Saddam and eradicate WMDs, the neighbors still did not back it. This was because they feared the aftermath of invasion more than they feared Saddam and his WMDs. They worried firstly that shaking up the ethnic balance in Iraq would spill over their own borders. Saddam's main virtue in their eyes was that he managed to hold a conflict-ridden multi-ethnic country together. Like them, he did this repressively: Saddam and his Sunni elite oppressed the Shiite majority and the Kurdish and Turcoman minorities. If control over the Kurds weakened, this would stir up Kurds in Turkey, Iran and Syria. There might be Turkish, Iranian and Syrian incursions into Iraq. The Al-Badr Corps, an army of Iraqi Shiites living in Iran and trained by the Iranian army, might again enter the country. The Sunni majority suffering under Alawite minority rule in Syria, the oppressed Shiites of the oil-rich eastern province of Saudi Arabia, the Jordanian Palestinian majority under Hashemite rule, the Bahraini Shiite majority under a Sunni monarch—all might be awakened by power changes in Iraq.[29]

As I noted in Chapter 4, the worst cases of ethnic or religious conflict and cleansing occur where the weaker group is emboldened to resistance and revenge by help from co-ethnics or co-religionists living in neighboring states. Iraq was now a tinderbox in which these inflammatory materials were present, but had been damped down by Saddam's repression. Introduce a conquering American army aiding the oppressed, with Turkish and Iranian forces and proxy forces lurking over the borders and there was a significant risk of an ethnic/religious conflagration.

But the neighbors also feared more general political disturbances among Arabs. Massive bombing, large Iraqi civilian casualties and Rumsfeldian imperial arrogance would be shown daily on their television screens, alongside Palestinian suffering. The neighbors took special umbrage at the timing of the invasion. Saudi Arabia, Egypt and Jordan constantly told the Americans to get the Israel/Palestine peace process going *before* any attack was launched against Iraq. Forget the bias the US had shown toward Israel, they said—just be the honest broker now! But how strong would be the blowback from the "street"? Anti-American demonstrations and riots would occur. Perhaps no regime would actually fall, since they were good at repression. They would prefer to lighten their rule, but knew that cooperation with the Americans would provoke opposition. Islamists and nationalists were poised. Since these are not democracies, opposition is expressed by riots, bombings and coups, not by polite parliamentary resolutions.

The House of Saud suppresses riots every year. Many Saudis believed a war would increase the influence of Prince Sultan over the more pro-American Crown Prince Abdullah. Sentiment was increasing to remove the American forces from Saudi soil. The Hashemite monarchy of Jordan seemed not as wobbly as formerly. Riots in the Beduin city of Maan in November 2002 were worrying, since the Beduin provide the monarchy's main power base. The Islamist opposition was strengthened by Jordan's cooperation with the US, though they did not yet espouse violence. Except for the killing of USAid worker Larry Foley, assassinations and bombings in Jordan seemed amateurish. The conspirators were quickly rounded up and liquidated. But among the Palestinian two-thirds of the population radicals were poised to exploit the unpopularity of Hashemite support for the pro-Israeli Americans. The Egyptian regime seemed more stable. But President Mubarak spoke of his fears during a question-and-answer session with Egyptian university students. If the United States hit Iraq, no Arab ruler would be "able to curb popular sentiments. There might be repercussions and we fear a state of disorder and chaos."[30] What they feared was not revolution from below (which is rare in the Middle East) but military coups with populist rhetoric—new versions of "Arab socialist" or Ba'athist-type regimes, though this time with Islamist overtones.

But the biggest fear across Muslim countries was that an American client regime in Iraq, giving the US privileged access to oil, would remain a propaganda bonanza for al-Qaeda and other radical jihadis, confirming their crudest stereotypes of American imperialism subjugating Muslims. Mahathir Mohamad, Prime Minister of Malaysia, pro-Western, with a 20-year record of suppressing Islamist tendencies in his country, said of a war on Iraq:

> It will lengthen the anti-terrorist campaign, it will undermine the world economy, it will create a sense of uncertainty and fear throughout the world. If America persists in removing Saddam Hussein by military means it will only anger the Muslim world. The Muslim world is already angry enough for them to produce terrorists who carry out suicide attacks. If the attack on Saddam Hussein is mounted there will be more willing recruits to the terrorist ranks.[31]

No one could accurately calculate the likelihood of such repercussions. Yet, overall, no Muslim regime doubted that instability and violence would grow if the US invaded Iraq, especially while still favoring the Israelis in Palestine. Mubarak said this repeatedly for over a year, but told his aides that Washington wasn't listening.

Washington did listen but believed that it had the power to invade Iraq, topple Saddam, and create a stable, controlled aftermath in the country. The US would develop a more prosperous and democratic Iraq and lead the Middle East toward a better future. The new imperialists had been abandoning containment, which was working albeit imperfectly, because of blithe confidence that they *could* invade, conquer and reorder Iraq. But could they?

THE INVASION: A MILITARY SUCCESS

The most powerful military in the world worked out its strategy for defeating a third-rate military power. There were disputes. Rumsfeld wanted a war relying more on hi-tech RMA plus Special Forces, with a force total of somewhere around 100,000; some generals preferred heavy infantry and tank assaults, and a force of over 200,000. So far as I know, their debate only concerned the invasion itself. Nobody seemed to pay serious attention to the force size needed for pacification afterwards. For the invasion, Rumsfeld was right—the disparity between US and Iraqi forces was such as to require only around 100,000 for a campaign of (as he said) "weeks rather than months." Hasty revisions were made when the Turkish parliament vetoed plans for 62,000 US troops to invade from Turkey, but they were not needed.

The main attack was as planned, aerial. Over 15,000 supposedly precision-guided bombs and missiles, including over 750 deadly cruise missiles, plus numerous cluster and other "dumb" bombs were blasted on Iraq in the first 18 days of war. The targets were largely military and government centers. The Afghan War had taught the Pentagon to give out less information about its bombings yet display more concern to avoid killing civilians. Rumsfeld called the bombing his "shock and awe" campaign because the shocked Iraqis would immediately realize that resistance to such awesome power would be futile. When the ground offensive followed, it was expected the Iraqis would quickly lay down their arms, with little fighting. There would be risings against Saddam, especially by Kurds and Shiites, and the invaders would be greeted as liberators.

American military superiority did make for a swift victory. The bombing took out the Iraqi command and control centers and demoralized Iraqi troops at the receiving end who received few orders after the first days. No coordinated defense was possible. Most Iraqi soldiers fled home, but a few reacted with tactics geared to the American preferences for devastating fire-power, low civilian casualties and even lower American casualties. Iraqi forces could put up little resistance in open spaces where they were sitting ducks to superior American fire-power. But some retreated to fight in dispersed small groups in urban settings. Thousands fought with determination, though often showing more bravery than sense. Only some adopted true urban guerrilla tactics; others rushed at tanks in pick-up trucks or at the run, rather than lurking in buildings and cellars, popping out at short-range of US and British troops (as Chechen fighters did). There were a few suicide bombings and some combatants dressed as civilians suddenly revealing weapons, tactics denounced by the Pentagon as "terrorism." But how else could they kill American soldiers, all of whose weapons could greatly out-range theirs?

The major setback was that no risings against Saddam occurred. Shiites did not rise up, and the only Kurdish fighters were those advancing with US assistance from areas which were already Kurdish-held. No generals defected, and pro-American Iraqi units could not be formed from the POWs. Many Iraqis did seem happy to see the invaders, though many were hostile. Most seemed to be waiting to see who won before displaying any emotions. The Pentagon said the reason was that Iraqis were being coerced by Ba'athist loyalists and that the Shiites did not trust the US after having been betrayed in 1991. It said the Saddam loyalists were executing soldiers or civilians who tried to flee, while civilians were coerced into being human shields for the soldiers. Some of these allegations were correct, for the Iraqis fell back to a guerrilla campaign. But there were perhaps more regime loyalists than expected, and more of an Iraqi or Arab nationalism, which predictably made them dislike the infidel invader whatever their feelings about Saddam. Above all, liberation by long-range aerial, artillery and tank bombardment is not popular for those at its receiving-end, whether they are soldiers or civilians.

With final military victory almost achieved after 25 days of the invasion, US/British military casualties were about 150, half of them the result of accidents or "friendly fire." Iraqi military casualties remained unclear, but most estimates were in the 5,000–10,000 range. There were only about 8,000 prisoners. These low figures resulted from a short war and widespread Iraqi flight.

Civilian casualties resulted from the same three types of systematic "mistake" I noted in the Afghan War: some US weapons are not "smart," even smart ones go wrong, and humans (especially frightened ones) are not as smart as their weapons. A few errant cruise missiles are known to have landed far away from their targets in Turkey, Syria and Iran, while many more can be presumed to have just missed their targets, killing and maiming civilians. The US and British eventually admitted, in response to NGO allegations, that they were using "dumb" cluster bombs again. But the overall level of civilian casualties remains unclear.

We know most about Baghdad, where most of the foreign journalists reporting from the Iraqi side of the war were based. Elsewhere behind Iraqi lines would have been very dangerous for reporters, and the US and British militaries gave out much less information on bombing locations than they had in Afghanistan. Nonetheless an independent research group (Iraqbodycount.org) has estimated minimum and maximum civilian casualties in war incidents reported by at least two independent foreign correspondents. They are very rough figures and they must be underestimates. Reporters could not be present everywhere and Muslims bury their dead quickly. By June 4, a month after the war ended, their minimum casualty estimate was 5,400 and their maximum just over 7,000. The real total may have been closer to 10,000. So the total Iraqi casualties from the war itself were probably 15–20,000.

Then we must add whatever humanitarian disaster might ensue from the disruption of food, electricity and clean-water supplies and the collapse of civilian authority. In the 1991 Gulf War such deaths contributed about three-quarters of the estimated 200,000 total Iraqi dead. Perhaps the US and Britain, plus the UN and NGOs, could between them produce stop-gap solutions quickly enough to avert massive disaster. Yet enough would probably die to make total civilian casualties outweigh military ones. In this sense it would be a fairly typical modern war. But the RMA did reduce the total (military plus civilian) number of those directly killed in the war. If the US really could bring peace, freedom and democracy to Iraq, and then to the region, this might not seem too high a price to pay.

But once again the Pentagon tried to deflate the price of victory by being economical with the truth. General Franks declared again, "We do not do body-counts," while Pentagon spokespersons denied almost all alleged incidents. This time, sensitive to bad publicity, they accompanied the usual denials by repeated assurances that "we are taking the greatest possible steps to minimize any civilian casualties." The American media also kept repeating this, and (unlike Afghanistan) I failed to find *any* estimates of total Iraqi civilian casualties in mainstream American media outlets. But where the incidents were too egregious to be brushed aside, we were told that "an investigation is underway"—until the journalists' attention span was exhausted. Even eyewitness reports were dismissed or ignored, as we see in these three tragic examples.

The first example is of dumb bombs, cluster bombs which killed at least 33 civilians in the town of Hillah. Roland Huguenin-Benjamin, of the Red Cross, described it as "a horror, dozens of severed bodies and scattered limbs." Arab cameramen working for Reuters and Associated Press filmed "babies cut in half, amputated limbs, kids with their faces a web of deep cuts caused by American shellfire and cluster bombs." The West will not see these images because they were censored by editors in Baghdad. Western reporters later visited the city morgue, full with over 60 bodies, which they described as "a butcher's shop of chopped-up corpses." The Red Cross is adamant that all the victims were "farmers, women and children." Dr Hussein Ghazay, from Hillah hospital, confirmed that "all the injuries were either from cluster bombing or from bomblets that exploded afterwards when people stepped on them or children picked them up by mistake." The Pentagon replied by saying that it was investigating but that at present there were "no indications" that the US dropped cluster bombs there.[32]

The second example is of smart bombs. The bombing of Shu'ale (or Al-Naser) market in Baghdad on March 28 killed somewhere between 34 and 62 Iraqis. Eyewitnesses reported seeing a plane and its white missile line in the sky moments before the blast threw them to the ground. Yet both the US and British governments suggested it resulted from errant Iraqi anti-aircraft missiles. Then an elderly local showed the *Independent*'s Robert Fisk a piece of the missile's fuselage. It contained serial numbers which the *Independent* tracked down as belonging to either a Harm or Paveway missile manufactured by Ratheon Corporation in McKinney, Texas, and supplied to the US Naval Air Systems Command. The navy confirmed that its Prowler jets had been over Baghdad that evening. A reporter on the USS carrier *Kittyhawk* was told by a Lieutenant Fluck that his crew had fired a Harm missile at an air-defense unit but had not seen where it had landed. Harm missiles tend to be inaccurate when faced by an enemy repeatedly turning its radar on and off, as the Iraqis were doing.[33] When the US and British drop 8,000 missiles and bombs on Iraq in ten days, *of course* some smart ones went off-course. That is what missile "circular error probability" estimates are all about. And *of course* some of the bombs were not smart but designed to clear whole areas of anything living.

The third example concerns the mistakes of US soldiers on the ground. We have vivid interlocking accounts of a tragic incident involving Bakhat Hassan and his large family. Some reporters interviewed Bakhat and other badly wounded survivors in hospital afterwards. Bakhat had managed to pack his family group of 17 people in a Land Rover to flee from missile and rocket attacks from US helicopter gunships. He said US soldiers at the first checkpoint had waved them through. As they approached a second checkpoint, they waved again at American soldiers in Bradley Fighting Vehicles. The soldiers didn't wave back. They fired. "I saw the heads of my two little girls come off," Hassan's heavily pregnant wife, Lamea, 36, said numbly. She repeated herself in a flat, even voice: "My girls—I watched their heads come off their bodies. My son is dead." The final family death-toll was 11—Bakhat's daughters, aged two and five, his three-year-old son, his parents, two older brothers, their wives, and two nieces aged 12 and 15. On March 16, Hassan and his family had begun to harvest their tomatoes, cucumbers, scallions and eggplants. It was a healthy crop, and they expected a good year. "We had hope," he said. "But then you Americans came to bring us democracy and our hope ended." Lamea is nine months pregnant. "It would be better not to have the baby," she said. "Our lives are over." Surviving family members spoke on Al-Jazeera television of how the soldiers had fired repeated volleys at their car. The pictures of the riddled Land Rover confirmed this—as did the fact that all of the 17 persons in the car were killed or badly wounded.[34]

Another reporter interviewed the US soldiers. Captain Ronny Johnson said he had grown increasingly alarmed as the Land Rover approached. He radioed a forward platoon in Bradley Fighting Vehicles to alert it to the potential threat. "Fire a warning shot," he ordered as the vehicle kept coming. Then, with increasing urgency, he told the platoon to shoot a machine-gun round into its radiator. "Stop [expletive] around!" Johnson yelled into the company radio when he still saw no action being taken. Finally, he shouted at the top of his voice, "Stop him, Red 1, stop him!" That order was immediately followed by the loud reports of 25mm cannon fire from one or more of the platoon's Bradleys. About half a dozen rounds were heard in all. "Cease fire!" Johnson yelled over the radio. Then, as he peered into his binoculars from the intersection on Highway 9, he roared at the platoon leader, "You just [expletive] killed a family because you didn't fire a warning shot soon enough!" Sergeant Mario Manzano said: "It was the most horrible thing I've ever seen, and I hope I never see it again." He added that the wounded mother just sat in the vehicle holding the mangled bodies of her two children. "She didn't want to get out of the car," he said.[35] The soldiers were nervy and trigger-happy because two days earlier a suicide-bomber had driven into a checkpoint, killing four marines when his bomb detonated.

But the Pentagon's official statement chose denial rather than extenuating circumstances. It said the vehicle was only fired on after the driver ignored shouted orders and warning shots, which Captain Johnson contradicted (any shouts would have been in English anyway). It said the shooting killed only seven people and was "under investigation." The Central Command statement added: "In light of recent terrorist attacks by the Iraqi regime, the soldiers exercised considerable restraint to avoid the unnecessary loss of life." Added Navy Commander Barbara Klus, a senior nurse, "Some poor Marine is going to go home and have nightmares about this (shooting), because the Iraqi leaders don't care about their own people."[36] This seems tenuous logic. Questions of morality should in any case focus less on the frightened front-line soldiers who were clearly shocked by their own actions than on the desk-killers who send them in to kill and then lie and deny all moral responsibility. But such actions have consequences. Another reporter focused on the anguish of a gunner on an Abrams tank that carried the legend "Bush and Co." on its barrel. He had learned days afterwards that he and the other tank gunners had blasted to death two innocent Iraqi civilians driving a Toyota Camry, brothers who ran a family tannery that sold half-finished leathers to luxury fashion houses in Italy. The gunner was suitably shaken and contrite. But the report casually reveals that "hundreds of Iraqi civilians" had been "inadvertently" killed in this way, and that this had generated "a wave of bitterness eroding some of the gratitude that has swept Iraq for the American forces."[37] Indeed, it did.

The journalists themselves suffered when a US tank fired on the Palestine Hotel, killing two of them. The tank commander insisted that fedayeen had been firing on them from the hotel and that they had a spotter directing their fire on its roof. Reporters were unanimous that this was not true, and that journalists were the people with the binoculars on the roof. But the commander stuck to his story. He regretted the loss of life but maintained that his soldiers had the right to self-defense. On the same day US tanks took out the Al-Jazeera building, just as it had in Afghanistan, this time killing one of its reporters.

It is important that journalists keep giving us such terrible accounts of war. Al-Jazeera and other Arab channels did just this, repeatedly, specializing in pictures of injured or grieving survivors, especially small children, amid ruined houses and neighborhoods. This fueled the outrage expressed across the Arab and Muslim world. But Al-Jazeera reported the truth—being expelled at one point from Baghdad by the regime for their pains. Al-Jazeera did a much better job than did the American television networks whose military experts portrayed war as a game of sanitized chess with graphics, more virtual than real—and no victims. The closest American viewers got to the dead and maimed were distant images, accompanied by voiceovers saying, "The Iraqis claim . . . but the Pentagon says . . ." War kills people, and in urban and guerrilla circumstances it kills and maims civilians, horribly. That is why we should make war only in truly desperate circumstances, or when it achieves compensating benefits. Iraq did not qualify on the first count. Did it on the second?

THE PACIFICATION: A POLITICAL FAILURE?

The killing tally might be justified if the US found evidence of major Iraqi WMD or terrorist activity. Over a month after the war ended, it had found *none*. But it might also be justified if the US could bring to Iraq peace, prosperity and democracy—after all, the invasion was called "Operation Iraqi Freedom." The US administration had called repeatedly for "regime change." We all knew that the desired change was *from* Saddam, but what was it *to*?

This was unclear since plans kept changing. The administration first encouraged exiled Iraqi opposition groups, then seemed to discard them. Exiles were then offered roles as interpreters and guides for the US army, becoming policemen afterwards. Only 74 turned up for training, rather than the 3,000 they had prepared for. With a grant of $90 million to spend, officials were calling it the "million-dollar-a-man army."[38] After the south of the country was occupied, 500 Iraqi exiles were flown in to form the nucleus of a so-called "free Iraqi army." The exiles were few and had no resources already on the ground. But by now, the exiles seemed suddenly back in favor again with the Bush administration.

For a time Germany and Japan after 1945 were held up as the models, complete with Tommy Franks as General Macarthur, a military shogun running Iraq. Bush officials confided that the Iraqis were too fractious to run their own country until the US had instructed them in the ways of rule. Bush's senior advisor on the Middle East, oilman Zalmay Khalilzad, explained that "political reconstruction . . . will involve thorough reform of the government, de-Ba'athizing Iraq, removing elements used by Saddam to enforce his tyranny. Officials guilty of crimes against humanity will be prosecuted." He said confidently, "We would have the commitment of resources necessary, and we would have the will to stay for as long as necessary to do the job." This was a fully fledged "nation-building" program, rejected in Afghanistan, but embraced in this more strategic and oil-rich country. The US and its troops would stay on in force for several years, until the Iraqis could rule themselves.

The plan brought immediate scorn from scholars of Japan like Chalmers Johnson, John Dower and Ian Buruma, who emphasized the enormous difference between Japan and Germany versus Iraq. Japan and Germany had long been united, with homogeneous cultures and prior experience of democratic institutions. They were also very war-weary, and in Japan the Emperor had remained in place (so had everyone except a few war criminals), lending legitimacy to Macarthur.[39] But the scholars didn't have to worry about the false analogy. The news came that the Macarthur Plan was "no longer a viable answer." Instead a "nation-building extremely lite," lighter than in Afghanistan, seemed to be embraced. A leader would emerge from within Iraq itself, heading a "federal democracy that would allow the various regions and tribes some degree of autonomy."

That would be wonderful news, though it had never yet been achieved in all Iraq's history. Iraq had been united by force—by the Ottoman and British Empires, the Hashemite monarchy, the Ba'athist Party and finally Saddam. The administration said there was no point in planning for this, since "events on the ground" would play the biggest role in determining the new leadership. "Either an individual or group of leaders inside Iraq would emerge with sizable support and look like the natural leaders, the natural next wave," said one official. Another emphasized, "No Hamid Karzai is going to be anointed beforehand." At the same time, however, another plan surfaced. A White House official said, "We'd be quite happy to see Iraq under U.N. mandate. That should be quite feasible if the war is fought under clear authorization of the Security Council." Since the Council did not authorize the war, this plan fell by the wayside.

In February 2003, in testimony to the Senate Foreign Relations Committee, US officials Douglas Feith and Marc Grossman reverted to a two-year version of the Macarthur Plan, with all military and civilian administrators reporting to General Tommy Franks. They said they did not know how the US would manage the Iraqi oil industry, who would cover the costs of repairing damaged oil installations, or how they would install a democratic government. "How this transition will take place is perhaps opaque at the moment. Hopefully there will be people who come up and want to be part of the government," Grossman said.

"There are enormous uncertainties," added Feith. "The most you can do in planning is develop concepts. ... That's our problem. We have been thinking this through as precisely as we can, given the uncertainties."

Some senators expressed incredulity at this, and regretted they had already given full approval to military action. "There is no informed consent. The American people have no notion of what we are about to undertake. They believe it will be swift and successful and largely bloodless," said Senator Biden, the senior Democrat. The officials repeated assurances that oil revenues under the military occupation would pay the costs of the Iraqi people's needs and would be the property of all Iraqis. But Feith added: "The administration has not yet decided on the organizational mechanisms by which this sector should be operated." Grossman said the Iraqi opposition in exile would not control decisions for all Iraqis. Instead "the United States government will make its decisions based on what is in the national interest of the United States"—which did not reassure the Muslim world. Nor did Feith's insertion of anti-Palestinian comments into his statement. Pentagon officials continued to admit they had no clear idea of what would happen after an invasion. "We still do not know how US forces will be received," one said. "Will it be cheers, jeers or shots? And the fact is, we won't know until we get there."[40]

Perhaps none of this incoherence matters much, for the Bush administration's *real* Plan A differed from all these. All the rhetoric of regime change and the beating of the war-drums during 2002 and early 2003 was intended to achieve one simple end: to precipitate an internal coup in Iraq, with the new regime willing to do business with the US and relinquish WMDs. This was expected to be discontented Sunni military officers with no intention of establishing a "federal democracy." Iraqi generals and colonels were emailed and promised safety and dollars. CIA men with suitcases were readied again. "Hopefully, they will come up," as Grossman had wishfully put it, *was* the policy. But, said a senior CIA official, "The negotiations went nowhere. All of them have proved futile."[41] There was no coup.

White House Press Secretary Ari Fleischer fell back on an even simpler solution: "The cost of one bullet, if the Iraqi people take it on themselves, is substantially less than that. Regime change is the policy, in whatever form it takes." One bullet for Saddam would be the ideal. Forget democracy, just avoid dead Americans and hopefully get rid of any remaining WMDs and pump the oil.[42] Everything would be fine if by great good luck Plan A as coup or bullet worked.

But Plan A didn't work, so a Plan B was needed. But there wasn't one. In his 2003 State of the Union speech Bush elaborated for 20 minutes on the consequences of not invading Iraq. He said not a word about the consequences of invading Iraq—not a word about the new Iraqi regime, not a word about the consequences for other countries, and not a word about possible consequences for the US. This was imperialism on the fly, obsessed by military power alone. *The US went into this invasion with no credible plan for political reconstruction.* Once again it was all military power, and no political.

After the invasion was underway, postwar plans became clearer in principle, though their practice was still being disputed among the allies and within the US administration. Britain was prepared to see its troops remain in Iraq for a while but wanted UN coordination of any postwar interim regime. Australian Prime Minister Howard said his troops would depart home immediately victory was assured, but also wanted UN approval. The US announced that it alone would lead the immediate postwar regime (with or without UN approval), though the UN could play a "humanitarian and advisory," i.e. a subsidiary, role. This was the next unilateral/multilateral battle to be fought, though since the Americans said they owned this "piece of real estate" it seemed clear who would win the debate. Blair caved in, Howard was irrelevant.

This American government was expected to last somewhere over six months (said Wolfowitz). It would then gradually give way to an "interim government," mainly staffed by the Iraqis themselves. Would the exiles dominate it? The Pentagon said yes, State no. But US officials envisaged calling a national constitutional congress assembling Iraqis from all regions, tribes and ethnic groups who would then choose the members of the government. This was in imitation of the *loya jirga* assembly called in Afghanistan, though this constitutional form had already existed there. No such institution existed in Iraq. Sometime further down the road elections would be held, resulting in a fully constitutional government of Iraq.[43] Wolfowitz kept saying he had faith in the Arabs, especially Iraqis. They could build democracy themselves, he said—like the Romanians had. Of course, the Romanians did not have an occupying army to worry about.

The transition to the interim government would be engineered by Americans. But which Americans? The man first given the chief civilian role in Iraq, heading the Pentagon's Office of Reconstruction and Humanitarian Assistance, was former Lieutenant General Jay Garner. He had experience of quite successful Kurdish relief and nation-building efforts in their autonomous zones in the north of Iraq. He was a defense missile contractor and a personal friend of Rumsfeld. Incredibly, he also had a pro-Israeli, anti-Palestinian record in the Middle East through his ties with a conservative Zionist security organization (in which Dick Cheney and Richard Perle were also involved). This was simply amazing for a man whose job would be to conciliate Arabs! Under him were three American regional governor generals, in the persons of two retired generals and a retired ambassador. Only one of them spoke any Arabic. Despite also being called "Viceroy," Garner would be no Macarthur. The staffing of the 23 Baghdad ministries was firmly in the hands of Deputy Defense Secretary Paul Wolfowitz, which Garner resented. Do we call Wolfowitz the *roy*, the king, or does that title belong to Rumsfeld? All the initial ministers would be Americans.

The State Department sought to challenge this Pentagon-run government. It did not like Wolfowitz's exile nominees, and especially not Chalabi, who it described as "the Pentagon's man," close to Cheney, Wolfowitz and Perle but without support in Iraq. Chalabi had last seen Iraq in 1958, when he was 13 years old. He was also a wanted man, with a conviction in Jordan for serious business fraud. One official at State confided, "It looks like we're going to do exactly what we promised we wouldn't—take small groups of exiles with limited influence in Iraq and bring them in as the bulk of a transitional government." State also wanted a somewhat bigger role for the UN, so as not to alienate the allies and neighbors and get them all implicated in the reconstruction project. Nor did State like the Pentagon's rumored plan to privatize the oil industry. Powell had repeatedly assured the world that the Iraqi people would control their own oil. Privatization would threaten that, since Iraqi assets would be bought up by foreign oil companies and rich Iraqis (like the Chalabi clan) who would invest their profits in offshore banks (as had happened in the privatization of the Russian oil industry).[44] The Iraqis might see little of their oil—but, went the refrain, "How did our oil get under their sand?"

Since in the last two years the Pentagon had repeatedly triumphed over State and it now physically controlled Iraq, it would obviously triumph again. Wolfowitz also sensed a way to square a financial circle, for the administration's budget plans for reconstruction did not seem to add up. Reconstruction estimates for Iraq ran at about $20 billion per year for five years, i.e. $100 billion. Then add on Iraq's current external debt of between $60 and $130 billion and reparation claims against it from neighboring states of $200 billion. This was a total of around $400 billion! Bush had earmarked from his $75 billion war budget only $3.5 billion for relief efforts and war damage repairs in Iraq, and only for the period up to September 2003. The administration promised that US tax payers would not pay much of Iraq's reconstruction costs. It was almost inconceivable that this debt-ridden, budget-slashing administration would come up with more than a few billion per year. Rumsfeld, Wolfowitz and John Snow, the new Treasury Secretary, all said they expect the international community and the Iraqi government to provide most of the money. Yet the international community would be much more grudging if Iraq were run by the Pentagon than the UN. This issue seemed set for a rerun of the same unilateral/multilateral arguments that the US had been failing to win over the last two years. It was also difficult to see how Iraq could raise its own billions. Wolfowitz claimed Iraq could generate $50–100 billion oil revenues over the next two to three years, i.e. $25–50 per year. That seemed much too high, oil might yield revenues of $15–20 billion a year over that period. But the Iraqi government has operating bills of about $11 billion per year (it essentially had no other source of immediate revenue), and then there was the foreign debt and reparations. To pump more Iraqi oil would involve additional reconstruction costs. And if more were pumped, its price would fall. Iraq would not see a short-term oil bonanza.

So the only way to make sense of Wolfowitz's sums is that he intended to privatize or pawn Iraqi oil assets. Only the foreign oil companies could afford to buy, though they might use some Iraqi front companies. This would bring a quick flow of dollars to the Iraqi government to finance reconstruction. But it would then have sold off the only major national asset, probably to Anglo-American corporations. Alternatively, future oil revenues might be pawned to pay for reconstruction now.[45] Now it really would be our oil under their sand.

The international community might stump up more dollars, and the Bush administration could go against its normal policy (described in Chapter 2) and lead a reduction and restructuring of the Iraqi debt, and pressure the neighbors to scale down their reparations demands. But even so, the sums required were so large that only three alternative outcomes seemed likely: (1) sell off or pawn Iraqi oil assets; (2) levy higher taxes on Americans; (3) let Iraq decay, except for its oil-fields. Number (2) would impress the world, but seemed politically unlikely. Numbers (1) and (3) would confirm the world's worst beliefs about the invasion. Obviously, in reality, things would not be so stark. Elements of all three were likely to generate a muddling through, a very gradual, halting recovery which would be unevenly spread through the population, with the future of the oil industry the main economic flash-point.

But money was a less immediate problem than order. If the US didn't get a coup within Iraq before or during the invasion, it would have to rule at first through military force. Though it knew this in principle, it had done no actual, realistic planning for it on the ground. Pentagon arguments about force size had been entirely over what was necessary to win the war. But I have emphasized that would-be imperialists dealing with more backward enemies (i.e. not with Germany and Japan in 1945) have always needed many more soldiers to pacify a country than to invade it and defeat it on the battlefield. Battles require force concentration in only a few locations, pacification requires force dispersion throughout the conquered territory. If imperialists lack local armed allies and regime defections, they need more troops. If there is no "surrender" from a government-in-being, then they need even more—immediately.

The Bush administration, with its usual overconfidence, had come to the opposite conclusion, envisioning a two-year occupation by only 75,000 soldiers, less than the invasion force. In contrast Kenneth Pollack, the former CIA expert on the region, had taken Bosnia as the model, and then factored in an Iraqi population of five times the size. By this admittedly crude method, he reached a required occupation force total of over 200,000 for the first two years, reducing down below 100,000 by five years. At the Pentagon, General Shinseki seemed to put it even higher, saying the occupation forces would be "several hundred thousand." Unnamed sources promptly tried to discredit him as the embodiment of outmoded heavy infantry doctrine.[46] The Americans and British had between them only just over 100,000 troops inside Iraq in early April, and almost all of them were still hunting down stubborn pockets of resistance, concerned with their own "force protection."

Since none of what the Pentagon had expected came to pass, they were in the worst-case scenario, needing over twice their actual force levels. The occupation forces were over-stretched, deploying soldiers trained for mass killing, not pacification or policing. When Saddam's regime collapsed at the beginning of April, so did all public authority. At this point the Americans and British probably needed 300,000 trained "peacekeepers"—though the label would not be entirely appropriate to describe the violent methods they would often have to use. By mid-May they had 145,000. In Baghdad they had 30,000, for a city of 4.5 million.

The first problem proved to be neither inter-ethnic violence nor massive nationalist guerrilla resistance, but looting. From April 7 a rolling wave of looting and violent vandalism spread across the major Iraqi towns, from Basra to Baghdad to Kirkuk to Mosul, and apparently in smaller towns too. Regime palaces and official buildings were the most favored targets, but this rather shockingly included hospitals, which were looted of their supplies and equipment. The US was unable to deal with the continuing civilian casualties caused by the guns of Saddamites, looters and Americans, by cluster bombs still exploding, and by the diseases spreading through disruption to water and electricity supplies. NGO and UN relief offices were also looted for their food-stuffs, water-purification aids and medicines. Also distressing was the looting of 100,000 items from the Iraqi National Museum in Baghdad. The Museum was an Iraqi national treasure, a source of national pride. Its artifacts attested to five thousand years of civilization in the country, beginning with Sumer itself, "the cradle of civilization." It seemed ironic that relics from the Empire of Sargon of Akkad, whom in an earlier work I had called "the first personality of history" (conquering Sumer in about 2310 BC), would now be looted thanks to the incompetence of his American imitators four thousand years later. Two days later the National Library was looted, though mostly burned. Looting spread also to residential neighborhoods.[47]

The motives seemed very basic. Deprived people, suddenly freed from repression (indeed from all restraint), were acquiring cars, computers, furniture, furnishings, copper pipes, electrical wiring—whatever seemed shiny or useful. Most were cheerful and non-violent looters, though they did a lot of vandalism. But some were clearly establishing wholesale businesses with looted goods filling trucks—"post-Saddam privatization" we might call it, anticipating IMF programs for Iraq. But they were often armed and dangerous. The Museum staff described the looters as drawn from all classes, including educated people who knew the value of what they were stealing. Looters usually had a sense of entitlement, justifying their actions as "taking back from Saddam what he had stolen from us," testimony to the human ability to find moral reasons for whatever crimes we commit.

The looting continued erratically for over a month, taking away much of the country's infrastructure. Ironically, many Iraqis were calling for more American force. When it did not come, they looted weapons to defend themselves. "America promised us liberation and democracy," said a Baghdad computer programmer, but, "this is not liberation. This is not democracy. This is a jungle. We now live in a jungle."

Rumsfeld preferred to describe the looting as an "untidiness." "Stuff happens," he said. "Freedom's untidy. And free people are free to make mistakes and commit crimes and do bad things." But it was his mistake which had turned "freedom" into anarchy. It had added another string to the bow of anti-imperialist rhetoric in Iraq. It especially alienated those who otherwise might be least likely to cause trouble, with property that they hoped to increase through a period of peace.

US troops were finally directed to attempt some policing and provision of basic services. US soldiers had far too much fire-power and far too little training to be effective policemen. On April 30, faced with a demonstration in Fallujah, they blasted away at the crowd, killing 13 unarmed Iraqis. Next day, they killed three more. This was no task for the Third Armored Division. And with no more men available and fighting continuing, all they could do was ask for volunteers from people who had staffed essential services under Saddam. They divided the volunteers into groups of water engineers, electrical workers, policemen, etc. and attempted to discard regime loyalists. As the British had already discovered in Basra, this provoked shouted denunciations and counter-denunciations. The tribal leader the British had appointed as "mayor" of Basra had promptly been denounced by rival leaders, and so had some of the policemen volunteering there.

How could non-Arabic-speaking troops decide who was trustworthy Ba'athist functionaries were most likely to speak English. How could one of the leading volunteers, the former chief of police for Baghdad, not be implicated in the previous regime's crimes? But could the Americans manage without him? It was a captain in the marines, with no Arabic, who had to decide. Jay Garner and his hundred-plus staff were mostly still planning in their Kuwait seaside villas. American political power was in reality only talk about democracy and plans for future administrations, but it was still not on the ground in Iraq.

The patrols also faced further fighting. Iraqi resistance evolved into more sporadic hit-and-run guerrilla raids. In the last two weeks of May, ten American soldiers were killed mainly in Sunni areas of the country. The population is highly armed, as the looting revealed. The absence of risings or defecting officers and the ambivalence of the popular reaction boded ill for the political aftermath. The pro-American Iraqi exiles represented almost no one and had no organizations on the ground. There was also the possibility of ethnic/religious conflict being sparked among Iraqis. Reporters in the northern city of Mosul noted the hostility with which its mostly Arab inhabitants greeted the Kurdish fighters liberating their city. Reporters also noted the complex reactions of Shiites.

The US misrepresented the Saddam regime when it characterized it as *only* a repressive Sunni, Tikrit-based dictatorship ruling through force and fear. As scholars of Iraq noted, Saddam had increasingly ruled through "tribalism," though the word only makes strict ethnographic sense when applied to rural areas, since urban populations no longer seriously identified themselves as belonging to tribes.[48] Underlying Saddam's "tribalism" was actually the most common type of political structure found across the world today—whether regimes are formally democratic or dictatorial. This is a patron–client system, where the central regime rules through local notables who can dispense government patronage to their own local networks of clients. In the case of Iraq, Saddam added bloody repression of excluded patron–client networks, while the most favored clients had to join the Ba'athist Party, which thus encompassed notables across the whole Arab population, Sunni or Shiite.

The loyalty of many of these would be skin-deep, especially among Shiites. They might be open to counter-offers, once they saw that Saddam's power was destroyed. US hopes for a client government rested mainly on people who wanted a job with an income, and there would be plenty of these. But it would be absurd to expect that this would be a democratic regime. It would still be controlled by the notables, most of them the same families as under Saddam. Once Saddam's regime was gone, some of his genuine opponents would also emerge from the woodwork, and most Iraqis welcomed both the end of Saddam and the invasion. Most people under any regime are apolitical, wanting only to get on with their lives in peace. There would be many local clients.

But US policies had not been geared to increase their numbers. Though it had expected Shiite risings, its own policies had consistently thrown Sunnis and Shiites together as "the enemy." As emphasized in Chapter 6, US counter-terrorism policy made no distinctions between Sunni and Shia, while Shia Iran sat alongside Sunni Iraq in the Axis of Evil. The US threatened Iran during the invasion and warned the Iraqi Shiite liberation army, the Al-Badr brigade stationed in Iran, to stay out of Iraq. "We want them to stay out of the fighting altogether," said an official, "we don't want to expose US troops to any additional danger." Military priorities, especially "force protection," ranked far higher than concern for the political aftermath. As a consequence some Shiite leaders opposed the Americans as well as Saddam. There would have to be political struggle among Shiites who hated Saddam before the Americans could get secure clients. Nor could US bombing distinguish between religious sects. Reporters found many Shiites standing amid the wreckage or watching television in cafés in other Arab countries who angrily made the point. Saddam had for years been downplaying Iraqi nationalism in favor of a common Islamic and Arab solidarity among all groups. The main resistance to the Americans might come from Islamic-tinged Arab nationalism.

It was especially difficult to predict the behavior of Shiites. Their connections with Iran to the East and Lebanon and Hezbollah to the West would weaken their Iraqi nationalism but strengthen their hostility to the US. Their hatred of Saddam might lead them toward the Americans. They might want reprisals against Saddam's favored Sunnis, or demand more autonomy than the Americans would desire. All this made for factional disputes within them, as was immediately manifest in a tragic incident in the main mosque in the holy city of Najaf. Two rival clerics were attempting to conciliate their differences when a group of armed assailants, hostile to one of them, killed them both. This was chaos.

The Kurds were no immediate problem, since most of them welcomed the American invasion. But they began to ethnically cleanse hundreds of Arabs almost immediately. This was understandable since many of them had been cleansed out of their houses and land by Saddam. Tit-for-tat. Kurdish nationalists would obviously also try to secure the oil of Kirkuk as a bridgehead for an independent Kurdistan. So in the north and south alike, even if things initially turned out as the Americans wanted, their ability to hold Iraq together might require considerable force. Invasion had been an extraordinarily high-risk strategy, undertaken without any real political strategy on the ground.

Sandra Mackey, an expert on Iraq, cautioned before the invasion that success would require deep understanding and sympathy for "the real Iraq" and an ability to grasp why Saddam Hussein had been able to rule for so long. She ended her book with this caution: "the United States can no longer afford to be seduced by its own military power or by a naive faith that foreign worlds always can be simplified and mastered."[49] Unfortunately, those two qualities sum up exactly the new imperialism. Its militarism was highly effective, but it thought of little else. Its freedom and democracy was talk, abstract and rhetorical. Its real political plans were rudimentary.

Since Iraq will not soon be a democracy, it makes no sense to talk about "majorities." Some organized minorities favor a client regime, some oppose it, with the masses torn between the desire to return to normalcy and opposition to foreign military occupation. The course of the invasion made clear that the Ba'athist Party and its fedayeen were sufficiently organized to form an urban resistance movement afterwards. Their weakness would be their association with a deeply unpopular regime. But patron–client networks now deprived of power might give them more local support, and they will try to appropriate the popular rhetoric of Arabic and Islamic resistance against imperialism. They had sympathy in neighboring Arab countries, as became clear during the invasion. Thousands of young Arab volunteers tried to reach Iraq to join the struggle, and hundreds arrived. Most Iraqis might not welcome them, but they were yet another element in the witches' brew that became Iraq.

Will this all blow over, as the US hopes? It seems unlikely, given inter-ethnic/religious violence, civil chaos, and the emergence of a potential national liberation movement against the occupation. The United States seems ill-equipped to deal with the armed factions, some of them shooting against Americans. The US must respond with force, and may be more generally seen as the colonial occupier and resisted in low-intensity but debilitating guerrilla warfare. General Garner soon took the rap, being replaced by Paul Brenner, a neo-conservative from the State Department. His problems remain the same. He recognized this by dropping plans to form a transitional government starting in July. This could be delayed for a year, officials said. Iraqis protested unavailingly at this further denial of self-government, but the lack of public order made it inevitable.[50] Is this better than Saddam? Not yet.

All this will tie down many US troops for years, with blowback among the neighbors and on the supply of terrorists. The neighboring regimes will remain two-faced and fairly repressive. They will not risk elections that would bring anti-American governments to power. Freedom and democracy will remain distant dreams. Everybody warned the US about the effects on terrorism. The Italian Interior Minister, Giuseppe Pisanu, said terrorism in Italy "would be even more worrying if there were a war in Iraq." Authorities in Spain and Britain gave similar warnings. More dead Muslims meant more international terrorists, they all said. Two weeks into the invasion President Mubarak of Egypt declared: "When it is over, if it is over, this war will have horrible consequences. Instead of having one bin Laden, we will have 100." There were soon two major terrorist incidents. On May 12 suicide bombers killed 34 people in Riyadh, Saudi Arabia, including eight Americans. It is believed that the organizer, escaped from Tora Bora, recruited 18 others, almost all Saudis with no known terrorist or criminal records. On May 16 bombers killed 31 persons in Casablanca, Morocco. The organizer had possible links to al Qaeda but recruited 13 others, with no known records, almost all under 25 years old. They were residents of a Casablanca slum district who had been radicalized at a local mosque over the previous eighteen months. These were *new* terrorists, the blow back from Afghanistan and Iraq.[51] The occupation might also change the nature of terrorism. Islamism and Arab and Iraqi nationalism—hitherto enemies of each other—might become more united in opposition to the oppressor; as might Sunni and Shia. During the American bombardment the Islamist movements in Palestine announced they were sending volunteers to Iraq, not to defend Saddam, but (as an Islamic Jihad leader put it) because "the cause of Iraq is an Arab and Muslim cause and we are a part of the Arab and Muslim nation." Added a Cairo volunteer: "this is a war for oil and Zionism. We want to help Iraqis, not Saddam. I know I might die. I don't want to kill people but I will if I have to, to protect people like those children with their heads missing."[52] Attacking the American occupiers would not be technically "terrorism," since the targets would be military ones. Even bin Laden and al-Qaeda could recover popularity in the Arab world if they turned back from civilian to military targets.

This would still be no Vietnam, for the resistance could never win conventional warfare against the US. But in Chapter 5 I noted that the last thing US policy should ever do is create another Muslim international brigade like the one the Soviets created in Afghanistan. All international terrorists so far came from that brigade. If the US got bogged down in Iraq, then Muslims might arrive as volunteers and Iraq would feed back into their own various national liberation struggles, just like Afghanistan did in the 1980s and 1990s. Urban guerrilla warfare, into which other Arabs could slip, could be an enduring cancer, eating away the entrails of American imperialism, steadily consuming hundreds of American lives and billions of dollars.

Without the UN, the legitimacy of the occupation regime will be minimal. If I were Bush I would ask the UN to run Iraq, spend the dollars and take the heat. The disadvantage would be that if UN or NGO personnel get killed, their organizations pull out. The US faces two problemmatic transitions, from war-fighting to armed pacification, and from there to peacekeeping. The UN would be effective in the second transition, but the first one requires US soldiers. Yet there are not enough soldiers and the US have not planned for either transition. The new imperialists are heavy on military and light on political power. The US has the military power to (imperfectly) conquer Iraq, but it lacks the political power to securely rebuild it. It also lacks the ideological power to counter the regional blowback. It uses its economic power to bribe the autocratic regimes of the region, but this makes the prospects for democracy in the region recede further. It aids the oppression of the Palestinians, and once again it was bombing and killing Muslims. This is a new militarism, not a new imperialism.

Not Americans but Iraqis will suffer the worst consequences. War is so wild a form of justice, so terrible a risk, that it must not be entered into from some grand world schema unconnected to the lives of the people it destroys. That is the worst indictment of US policy toward Iraq.

CONCLUSION: COMBATTING OR LIVING WITH WEAPONS OF MASS DESTRUCTION

I have analyzed two contrasting cases. When confronting the North Korean case, the US was being forced back to the second policy option, deterrence. The US cannot compel North Korea to disarm without an extremely serious, possibly nuclear war. It has to accept a leveling of the playing-field. In future it has to rely on mutual deterrence between itself and a poor, southern but nuclear state, North Korea. Japan might then have an incentive to acquire its own WMDs, especially if it detects a weakening of US resolve to defend it. However, this does not seem like a disaster, for these states plus nuclear Russia and China seem rational states, likely to behave as Waltz says nuclear states will. Most are also committed to diplomacy with one another, and proliferation would probably spread this too. The unification of Korea under Southern leadership might then be a further progressive step, since international amity in the region would probably increase. A general nuclear disarmament in East Asia might then be a little closer.

Iraq was different. Here invasion seemed to reveal that multilateral containment had already worked. There was no WMD arsenal. But the invasion also ensured that the region remained insecure, as does Iraq itself. As long as this remains true, some states will have an incentive to acquire WMDs. The first and best option is international amity. In this region that prospect is further receding, thanks to US policy.

What will Iran do to prevent suffering the same fate as Iraq? It is, after all, the third member of Bush's axis of evil, apparently next in line for American aggression. Will it roll over and submit, or will it attempt a quick dash for nuclear weapons, like North Korea? In early 2003 came signs of sprinting. Having already announced the construction of two nuclear plants, supposedly to generate electricity, the government said it would begin processing spent nuclear fuel rods and mining uranium. As Richard Boucher, the US State Department spokesman said, this seemed to "clearly indicate Iran's intention to build the infrastructure for a nuclear weapons capability." Bush the Younger had given Iran the most powerful incentive of all: fear of military invasion. Mohammad Khatami, the democratically elected reformist Iranian President, warned America not to "test its luck once more" by "confronting this nation." At the same time the regime tried to assure the UN that it had no intention of breaching its norms.[53] Iran is now half democratic. But not the form of the regime but perception of geopolitical threat will determine whether it acquires weapons of mass destruction. American aggression is increasing that perception of threat for Iran—and for the "axis reserves," Syria and Libya. The US is a major obstacle to any possibility of international amity in the region.

The US policy of preemptive regime change undermines any flexible, carrot-and-stick policy toward states like Kim Jong Il's North Korea and Saddam's Iraq. Aggressive rhetoric is also damaging for states which show rogue-like tendencies but which are deeply divided and so potentially more malleable, like Iran. It is most damaging applied to states which are either harmless to the world, like Cuba, or posing very little threat, like Syria. No other state besides North Korea is close enough to a credible nuclear, biological or chemical weapon that it cannot in principle be induced away from that goal, provided the international community remains united and willing to systematically alternate the carrot and the stick. Saddam did not refute that logic (though he did test it severely), since neither proviso was ever met. Current US foreign policy does not effectively combat the threat of proliferation, since its aggression gives poor Southern states an incentive to acquire WMDs which level the playing-field between themselves and the US.

But the new imperialists reject such pragmatism. This is a struggle against good and evil, they say. Since we have the power to overthrow evil with our military power without causing too many casualties (they hesitate a little about North Korea), we have the moral right to do so.

However, in the case of Iraq I have shown they are probably wrong. They are unlikely to bring peace, freedom and democracy to Iraq, let alone to the Middle East as a whole. We must return to the imperfections of pragmatic multilateralism, since the world itself is imperfect, not black and white.

NOTES

1. In their joint memoir, *A World Transformed*, New York: Alfred Knopf, 1998.
2. The dollar/euro conflict is emphasized by William Clark, "The Real Reason for the Upcoming War with Iraq," *www.mediamonitors.net*.
3. "Strategic Energy Policy Challenges for the 21st Century," *Report of an Independent Task Force*, available at *www.rice.edu/projects/baker/Pubs/workingpapers/cfrbipp_energy/energytf.htm*.
4. *Al-Ahram Weekly*, November 28–December 4, 2002, issue no. 614.
5. Bob Woodward, *Bush at War*, New York: Simon & Schuster, 2002, pp. 48–9, 60–1.
6. John Donnelly and Anthony Shadid, "Iraq War Hawks Have Plans to Reshape the Entire Mideast," *Boston Globe*, September 10, 2002.
7. Osama el-Ghazali Harb, "As Another World Emerges," *Al-Ahram Weekly*, February 20–26, 2003, issue no. 626.
8. *Los Angeles Times*, September 9 and 27, 2002; *New York Times*, October 10, 2002; Jospeh Cirincione et al., *Deadly Arsenals*, New York: Lannegie Endowment for International Peace, 2002; Peter Bergen, *Holy War Inc.*, New York: The Free Press, 2001, p. 23; Pollack, *The Threatening Storm: The Case for Invading Iraq*, New York: Random House, 2002, pp. 153–8.
9. *Los Angeles Times*, November 4, 2002; Dana Priest, "CIA Fails to Find Iraqi Link to Terror," *Washington Post*, September 11, 2002.
10. *Los Angeles Times*, January 29 and February 6, 2003.
11. Leaked to the BBC, *news.bbc.co.uk*, February 5, 2003.
12. Full transcript at *smh.com.au*, February 12, 2003.
13. The use of poison gas in Iraq was not new. The British RAF had repeatedly sprayed mustard gas on Iraqi and Kurdish rebels in the 1920s, and the Ba'ath regime used it on Kurds in the 1960s. Saddam's usage caused no alarm in the West at the time. He received his chemical materials from American, German and British suppliers

while their governments turned a blind eye. Among the blinded American officials was Donald Rumsfeld who paid two visits to Baghdad to secure Saddam's alliance against Iran. The US was backing Iraq against Iran and Kurdish rebels, and did not care how Saddam fought his war. Not until 1990 was the US concerned over any of Saddam's WMDs. See Andrew and Patrick Cockburn, *Out of the Ashes: The Resurrection of Saddam Hussein*, New York: Harper-Collins, 1999, pp. 86–94.

14. The reports are at *www.pm.gov.uk/output/Page6117.asp* and *www.cia.gov/cia/publications/iraq_wmd/Iraq_Oct_2002.htm*. For the inspectors' reports and Powell's evidence see *Los Angeles Times*, January 21 and February 6 and 13, 2003. For the unhappiness of the intelligence services, and Powell and Straw, see various reports in the *Guardian*, the *Observer* and the *New York Times*, May 30–June 3, 2003.

15. Cirincione et al., *Deadly Arsenals*, ch. 16; Anthony Cordesman, "If We Fight Iraq: Iraq and its Weapons of Mass Destruction," Center for Strategic and International Studies, Washington, June 28, 2002, available at *www.csis.org/burke/mb/fightiraq_wmd.pdf*; and The International Institute of Strategic Studies, "Iraq's Weapons of Mass Destruction: A Net Assessment," London, September 9, 2002, available at *www.iiss.org/*.

16. *Los Angeles Times*, September 20, 2002 and January 29, 2003.

17. Charles Duelfer, "Weapons of Mass Destruction Programs in Iraq," testimony before the Subcommittee on Emerging Threats and Capabilities, Armed Services Committee of the US Senate, February 27, 2002.

18. Kenneth Pollack emphasizes Saddam's recklessness, *Threatening Storm*, pp. 252–70. But see Phyllis Bennis, *Calling the Shots*, pp. 28–37, and John Mearsheimer and Stephen Walt, "An Unnecessary War," *Foreign Affairs*, December 2002.

19. *El Pais,* Madrid, April 9, 2003; news.bbc.co.uk, April 22, 2003.

20. "Iraq Is a Tryout for the Doctrine of Anything Goes in Order to Preserve the Superiority of America's Greatness," *Al-Hayat*, February 14, 2003, at *www.alhayet.com*; a similar argument came from Anwar Abd al-Malik in *Al-Ahram*, February 18, 2003 (both in Arabic).

21. "Can the US Go it Alone against Saddam?" *Guardian*, August 31, 2002; Tony Perry, "US Arms Pipeline Flows to Gulf Arabs," *Los Angeles Times*, November 15, 2002; "To Kuwaitis, War in Iraq

Sounds Fine—as Long as Hussein Goes" and "Turkey Mulls Letting US Use its Bases," *Los Angeles Times*, January 14, 2003; Gareth Jenkins, "Turkey's Bait," *Al-Ahram Weekly,* December 12–18, 2002, issue no. 616.

22. Dr Muhammad Bassam Yusuf, "America, Democracy and Exhortations from the Devil," *Al-Sha'ab*, December 12, 2002, at *www.alarbnews.com/alshaab* (in Arabic).

23. *Al-Ahram Weekly*, December 19–25, 2002, issue no. 617.

24. The "no-fly zones" originated as a hasty response by the US, Britain and France to Iraqi repression of Kurdish and Shiite rebellions in the aftermath of the Gulf War. When France withdrew, the US and the UK flew alone. In the Security Council China, Russia and others condemned the no-fly zones as a violation of Iraqi sovereignty, since the UN never specifically authorized them. They are technically correct. Though the relevant UN resolution condemned Iraqi actions, it did not authorize any specific action. This means that when the Iraqis fire on the British and American planes, they are not violating any international law.

25. Pollack, *Threatening Storm*, pp. 53, 58–9; Bennis, *Calling the Shots*, p. 170; Sarah Graham-Brown, *Sanctioning Saddam: The Politics of Intervention in Iraq*, London: I.B. Tauris, 1999, pp. 59–60.

26. *Threatening Storm*, pp. 222–7. Pollack adds the pursuit of war crimes charges against Iraqis, which might hinder Iraqi compliance, which is the main point of the exercise.

27. Pollack, *Threatening Storm*, p. 106; Therese Delpech, "Time for Clarification in Transatlantic Relations," in Michael Barletta, ed., *WMD Threats 2001: Critical Choices for the Bush Administration*, Monterey Institute, Center for Nonproliferation Studies, Occasional Paper no. 6, 2001; "Smart Sanctions: Restructuring UN Policy in Iraq," *www.fourthfreedom.org*.

28. I have drawn in this discussion from Robert Litwak, *Rogue States and U.S. Foreign Policy*, ch. 4 (the Egyptian quote is from there); Pollack, *Threatening Storm*, ch. 3; and Andrew and Patrick Cockburn, *Out of the Ashes*, ch. 12. There are three contrasting insiders' accounts of UNSCOM in "Ambassador Rolf Ekeus: Leaving Behind the UNSCOM Legacy in Iraq," *Arms Control Today*, vol. 27, June/July 1997; "Interview with Rolf Ekeus: Manipulation of UNSCOM by US," *www.casi.org.uk/discuss/2002/msg01070.html*; in Scott Ritter: *Endgame: Solving The Iraqi Crisis Once and for All*, New York: Simon & Schuster, 2002; and in Richard Butler, *The*

Greatest Threat: Iraq, Weapons of Mass Destruction and the Growing Crisis in Global Security, New York: Public Affairs, 2000.

29. Suggests Marwan Bishara, in *Al-Ahram Weekly*, December 12–18, 2002.

30. Galal Nassar, "The Real Threat?" *Al-Ahram Weekly*, December 5–11, 2002, issue no. 615; "Arab Allies To U.S.: No War Please," *CBSNews.com*, August 27, 2002.

31. Interview in the *Financial Times*, September 17, 2002.

32. Pepe Escobar, "Cluster Bombs Liberate Iraqi Children," *Asia Times*, April 4, 2003.

33. Cahal Milmo, "The Proof: Marketplace Deaths Were Caused by a US Missile," *Independent,* April 2, 2003. For the eyewitness survivors' accounts, see *Los Angeles Times*, March 29, 2003.

34. Meg Laughlin, "11 in Iraqi Family Died Trying to Flee to Safety," *Philadelphia Inquirer*, April 2, 2003; *Aljazeera.net* April 1, 2003.

35. William Branigin, "A Gruesome Scene on Highway 9," *Washington Post*, April 1, 2003.

36. Sharon Schmickle, "Shooting Incident Arouses Double-edged Sympathy," *Knownews.com*, March 28, 2003

37. John F. Burns, "G.I. Who Pulled the Trigger Shares Anguish of 2 Deaths," *New York Times*, April 12, 2003.

38. *Los Angeles Times*, March 29, 2003.

39. *Guardian*, October 15 and November 20, 2002; *Los Angeles Times*, October 17, 2002.

40. Jonathan Wright, "The U.S. Plans for Two-Year Occupation of Iraq," *Washington Post*, February 11, 2003.

41. *Los Angeles Times*, March 29, 2003.

42. *Los Angeles Times*, October 1, 2 and 17, and December 8, 2002; *Guardian*, October 12, 2002; *TaiwanNews.com*, October 18, 2002.

43. Maura Reynolds and Robin Wright, "Pentagon Postwar Plan Takes a Hit," *Los Angeles Times*, April 5, 2003.

44. Agence France-Press, February 10, 2003; Brian Whitaker and Luke Harding, "US Draws Up Secret Plan to Impose New Regime on Iraq," *Guardian*, April 1, 2003; *newsday.com* March 26, 2003; *businessweek.com*, March 31, 2003.

45. Mark Tran, "Bush War Budget Does Not Add Up," *Guardian*, March 25, 2003; Jonathan Steele, "Read the Small Print: the US Wants to Privatise Iraq's oil," *Guardian*, March 31, 2003; Warren Vieth, "Iraq Debts Could Add Up to Trouble," *Los Angeles Times*, April 4, 2003; Robin Wright, "White House Divided over

Reconstruction," *Los Angeles Times*, April 2, 2003; David Teather, "Future oil sales may be pawned to banks," *Guardian*, May 19 and May 31, 2003.

46. *Los Angeles Times*, February 26, 2003.

47. For the spread of looting, see *Los Angeles Times*, April 7–13, 2003, and *New York Times*, April 14, 2003. For its results, see Phil Reeves, "Chaos in the street, cholera in the city and killings in broad daylight," *Independent*, May 9, 2003; Peter Finn, "In Moroccan slum, zealotry took root," *Washington Post*, June 3, 2003; *www.albawaba.com*, May 14, 2003. For Sargon, see my *The Sources of Social Power*, Cambridge: Cambridge University Press, 1986, vol. 1, pp. 133–50.

48. Sandra Mackey, *The Reckoning: Iraq and the Legacy of Saddam Hussein*, New York: Norton, 2002, ch. 9.

49. *The Reckoning*, p. 396.

50. Patrick Tyler, "In reversal, plan for Iraq self-rule has been put off," *New York Times*, May 17, 2003.

51. Marlise Simons, "Europeans Warn of Terror Attacks in Event of War in Iraq", *New York Times*, January 29, 2003; Ian Black and Chris McGreal, "Conflict Will Create 100 bin Ladens, Warns Egyptian president," *Guardian*, April 1, 2003.

52. Black and McGreal, "Conflict Will Create 100 Bin Ladens."

53. *Los Angeles Times*, February 14, 2003.

NINE

THE NEW MILITARISM

We saw in action that the new imperialism turned into simple militarism. True, its immense offensive strike-power also rests on a sizeable economic base, though this now looks a little fragile. But its actions have steadily lost ideological legitimacy abroad, and in both Afghanistan and Iraq the US lacked and wilfully ignored the political power that might bring peace and order after invasions. Threats, bombings and invasions now dominate its foreign policy—threats are made almost daily, bombings seasonally, and an invasion every two years. A neo-conservative chicken-hawk coup had first seized the White House and the Department of Defense. Then they bent a more cautious General Staff and an unwilling State Department to their will. Congress, TV and radio were mobilized by manipulation of the 9-11 atrocity into patriotic self-censorship. The chicken-hawks have avoided critical scrutiny, and so most Americans will probably continue supporting them until the chickens come home to roost. Real civilian control of the military—a requirement of democracy—is declining.

The new militarism has the customary strengths and weaknesses of militarism—power but not authority, ruthless arrogance leading to overconfidence, eventually leading to hubris and disaster. Whereas in the recent past American power was hegemonic—routinely accepted and often considered legitimate abroad—now it is imposed at the barrel of a gun. This undermines hegemony and the claim to be a benevolent Empire. Incoherence among its military, economic, political and ideological powers forces it to retreat to its strongest resource, offensive military devastation. This is being deployed not in conflict with major powers—China, Russia, Europe—but with small, poor states of the

South. The US defines two main zones of threat, in North-East Asia and the Middle East.

In North-East Asia American plans remained on hold until after Iraq. The new militarists might try the same medicine on North Korea, the strongest of these poor countries, though only by virtue of what lies within firing-range of its artillery batteries. US military action could produce massive Korean casualties on both sides of the border and the possible use of nuclear weapons. No end could justify these means. Better would be some version of the Clinton carrots-and-sticks deal. Even buying North Korea away from nuclear weapons would be cheaper than war, in dollars as well as lives. South Korea and China, and perhaps Japan too, fear a crumbling North Korea. Hopefully, they can talk the US out of militarism and into carrots and sticks. Deterrence between secure nuclear states may not guarantee peace absolutely, but it is more likely to avoid disaster than confrontations between an aggressive superpower and a threatened failing regime driving toward nuclear weapons.

But the main campaign of the new militarists lies across the central zone of Islam, stretching from Libya to Afghanistan. Their goal is to make the region more friendly, orderly and democratic by force, by killing "rogue" Muslims and intimidating sympathizers. Since the region only contains fairly weak Muslim states, they believe military power can bring greater good to the region. They remain oblivious to warnings that the spectacle of Christians and Jews killing and intimidating Arabs and Muslims might not be the best way to persuade other Muslims to cooperate.

Warnings came from people who should know. King Abdullah of Jordan, the most supportive Arab ally, said a war on Iraq "would open up a Pandora's box across the Middle East," which " would destabilise American strategic interest in the Middle East" and undermine the coalition in the war on terrorism. Crown Prince Abdullah, the real ruler of Saudi Arabia (his father is terminally ill), also an American ally, said:

> In all frankness, I have great concern about America's credibility and I care about how America is perceived. In the current environment we find it very difficult to defend America, and so we keep our silence. ... We see children being shot at, buildings being destroyed, trees uprooted, people encircled, territories closed and women killed, unborn children delivered at check-points. The reasons that lead people to become suicide bombers, these are the reasons they do so.

President Mubarak of Egypt, another ally, shortly after 9-11 warned President Bush that "any attack involving a Middle East country would produce grave results, that would seriously complicate the situation throughout the Middle East." He added, "the Israeli–Palestinian conflict is causing 80 percent of terrorism in the world today." President Bashar al-Assad of Syria (not an ally) began by saying, "The war in Afghanistan will inevitably attract recruits to bin Laden's cause." A year and a half later he added, "The U.S. led war against Iraq will create a fertile soil for terrorism in the region."[1]

The new militarists continue to ignore the advice. They are considering the same medicine for Syria and Iran. Consistent with the rhetoric of "rogue states" and the "Axis of Evil," Rumsfeld, Powell and Bush issued a crescendo of threats during the Iraq invasion. Rumsfeld said that the US would "hold Iran responsible" for any anti-Saddam Shiite fighters moving from Iran into Iraq. Claiming that Syria was supplying night-vision goggles to Iraq, he said the US regarded "such trafficking as hostile acts and would hold the Syrian government accountable." Powell, speaking to an applauding Jewish audience, said Iran "must stop its pursuit of weapons of mass destruction" and Iran and Syria "must stop support of terrorism against Israel." Syria, he added, "bears a responsibility for its choices and consequences." Syria denied the night goggles. US intelligence sources differed as to whether there was any credible evidence of this.

Then the threats focused on Syria, which was predictable, since Syria is the weaker of these two countries. Bush insisted Syria must change course—it must not allow fleeing Iraqis into Syria, it must cease sponsoring terrorism and it must give up the chemical weapons he knew it possessed. Administration officials added that recent smuggling between Syria and Iraq had amounted to "astronomical levels," in violation of UN resolutions. One concluded, "All eyes are on Syria and its next steps are critical." Another said, "Here's your chance to prove they're rogues. And if you don't act, then you're not just permissive, you're guilty too. ... This is zero hour." Members of Congress promptly endorsed the threats by introducing the so-called "Syrian Accountability Act," which would impose sweeping sanctions until Syria ceased all such activity.[2]

There was no new information here. Neither Syria nor Iran sponsor *international* terrorism, directed against the US. Everyone knows they support Palestinian and Lebanese *national* terrorists involved in a struggle against Israel, which all Arab countries see as an oppressor. Both countries are widely suspected of attempting to develop chemical weapons. But so are about 15 other countries, including Israel. The smuggling was the natural response of desperately poor people to sanctions which cut off their links to their main trading partners, Iraqis. There has been massive smuggling over Iraq's borders from Turkey, Syria and Jordan, but their governments have not usually been involved. Part of the openly declared policy of the UN and the US over the two previous years had been to develop a "smart sanctions" policy which could buy out the poor neighbors from smuggling. But the new militarists had abruptly shifted policy. Now local opposition to Israel, proliferation issues, and any opposition to American militarism would be dealt with with threats of force, and then with force. While the US threatens countries so menacingly, they might feel entitled to try to acquire WMDs for the same reason that Israel had already acquired them—there really are military powers near by who threaten their survival. In their case, it is the United States. Part of the solution is obvious: stop threatening them.

If the US did move on either country, it might have only Israel as an ally. British Foreign Secretary, Jack Straw, loyal ally in Iraq, responded to these speeches by insisting Britain would have "nothing to do" with threats from Washington against Iran and Syria. He even announced a relaxation of export controls on dual-use civilian and military equipment for Iran. "Iran is a completely different country and situation from Iraq," he said. "Iran is an emerging democracy and there would be no case whatsoever for taking any kind of action."[3] The European Union said it was moving toward free trade with Iran, to help normalize relations. This was denounced by the State Department as an "unwise" move. Europe is preparing to oppose the US over Iran. Would even the new militarists invade either country on such pretexts, with only Israel for an ally? Yes, if they thought they could do it successfully.

More likely immediately, however, is "containment"—threats, economic pressure, sanctions, the occasional bombing raid. This is better than invasion, but still counter-productive. Syria and especially Iran, and the movements they support, have deeper roots than Saddam Hussein did in Iraq. Reform is a popular cause in Iran. It is helped along not by pressures and threats, but, as Straw also said, by normalizing relations. Fear of American (and Soviet) imperialism is what brought the ayatollahs to power in the first place. Fear of America remains their main card today. That fear should be removed. Carrots might be offered Iran not to develop nuclear weapons. Syria should be also treated gently, so that it can become a normal state. It is so poor that rather limited development aid would work wonders. It would be much cheaper than the new militarism. But of course it is pragmatic and morally imperfect. This does not appeal to the neo-conservative chicken-hawks. They believe instead that they can rid the world of rogues and weapons of mass destruction—by showering them with weapons of mass destruction! It does not seem to me like good against evil.

In one respect the new militarists are sensibly taking Osama's advice. They are removing US troops from Saudi Arabia, stationing them instead in Iraq. Wolfowitz declared this during the invasion and later said that this had been a "huge" reason for the invasion in the first place.[4] The off-shore strategy of relying on tiny, bought states for bases is surely much cheaper. But cheaper still would be for the US to put equal pressure on Israel and the Palestinians. They are finally learning the futility of armed struggle. They will take the final steps for compromise if they have their heads knocked together. Only the US can do this. What is the point of all that US aid if it cannot be used to pressure them to conciliate? That—and not force—would also normalize Hezbollah and Hamas into political parties, and help Syria normalize as a state. The US eventually published the long-delayed "road map" for settlement in Palestine, agreed jointly with Europe and Russia. But without US threats against Sharon's rightist government, how could that be enforced? The prospects for that seem remote, given the deep ties of the chicken-hawks with Israeli extremists, Powell's humiliation last time he went to Jerusalem, the identification of Hezbollah and Hamas as enemies of the United States etc., etc. None of this should be any more difficult for a Republican administration in the US to achieve than a Democratic one. Republicans have more of the military-industrial-oil lobby to overcome, Democrats have more of the Jewish lobby. These are not left/right issues, but issues of American national interest—and also the peace of the world. Most Arabs now see US foreign policy in their region as being run by Sharon. I do not believe that, but it is difficult to counter their argument when I can find no rational argument for US policy.

Let us consider three contrasting Arab views of their plan. An unsympathetic view came from General Sa'ad al-Din Al-Shadhili, former Chief of Staff of the Egyptian armed forces:

> The first [goal] is to gain control of oil and Arab wealth. The second is to prevent Islamic organizations from attaining power. The third is to keep the

Arab countries divided. The last is to assist Israel in becoming a superpower in the region.[5]

He believed the US intended to use the threat, and if necessary, the use of force to cow Iran and Syria into submission, then Saudi Arabia, then the Arab liberation movements. He correctly noted that this was also Sharon's openly stated agenda. The general doubted this would work. It would produce either massive Arab resistance or—if the Arabs remained divided—regional chaos, encouraging more terrorism and state terrorism, disrupting the flow of oil, and preventing any end to the Palestinian crisis. He was a pessimist.

Lebanese writer Saleem Nassar was more sympathetic. Once Iraq was stabilized, he said, the Americans expected

> a chain of events to unfold on the level of the entire region. Specifically, they are betting on the victory of the reform trend in Iran, which will guarantee that Iran grows closer to Washington, provides new climates which allow the lifting of the sanctions and boycott, and insures the flow of oil and gas. They also anticipate that Iran will stop its support for Hizbollah and for rejectionist groups in the West Bank and Gaza. [This] ... would strip the Ba'athist regime in Syria of its legitimacy. ... This make it easier for Hizbollah to give up its weapons, to request that Palestinian organizations stop their activities, and for Lebanon to reclaim its independence and political stability. Since America's rule over Iraqi oil will reduce its dependency on Saudi oil, the result will give the Kingdom a less influential role in American foreign policy, along lines that Israel proposed.[6]

But Nassar also believed this to be overconfident, since American actions would also embolden Israeli extremists and generate risings in the Arab streets, forcing the region's governments not to cooperate with American plans. His vision is of regional instability but not disaster.

Islamists see a holy light at the end of the tunnel. The exiled Syrian Islamist Dr Muhammad Bassam Yusuf told America, "You are the tyrants of the age, the only group that has no right to boast about democracy, freedom, liberation and development, because your logic is the logic of the oppressive Pharaoh." He then reached a rather utopian conclusion: "The Pharaoh was yesterday's tyrant whom God destroyed and eradicated, and you will be eradicated just as they were, and only justice and truth will remain."[7] He quoted supportive koranic verses resonating strongly among his Muslim audience. I cannot share his faith. I doubt God will strike down the Americans, and US military power can kill much of the human opposition in the region.

But can the US achieve more positive results? The new militarists believe the plan for domination is not about oil or Israel but to bring the region toward peace, order and democracy. Then the few "rogue" deviants can be isolated and defeated by force. The democracy part of the vision seems absurd, as a leaked State Department document of March 2003 recognized. Bush the Younger had stirringly proclaimed "a new regime in Iraq would serve as a dramatic and inspiring example of freedom for other nations in the region." Here he was expressing the so-called "domino theory of democracy" popular among the new militarists. Autocratic regimes would topple one by one as a response to the postwar Iraqi example and continued American pressure. The State Department document said this was "not credible." It warned the US to beware of a more menacing domino effect of democracy. Elections, it said, could "in the short run" lead to the rise of Islamic-controlled governments hostile to the US.[8]

The elections held in Muslim countries over the period of invasion preparations confirmed this warning. Pakistan, Bahrain, Morocco and Turkey all held elections in October–November 2002. Islamist parties made substantial gains in all four. In Pakistan their parliamentary seats rose from 3 to 78, in Morocco they rose from 14 to 42. In Bahrain's first local elections for over 30 years, Islamists won over 60 percent of the seats. Local commentators attributed these results partly to blowback from the war against terrorism. In Turkey the causes of the triumph of the moderate Islamic coalition were more complex, though neither the secularism nor the IMF-imposed neo-liberalism of the previous government had brought it popularity. This democratically elected Islamist parliament rejected its government's proposal of joining in the Iraq invasion.

The Israeli elections of January 2003 produced the mirror-image effect, with Sharon and other rightist parties sweeping to victory amid war frenzy. Elections were not held in Jordan in August 2002 because the king canceled them. Islamists would have swept the polls, energized by events in neighboring Iraq and Palestine. Then in the Iranian local elections of February 2003, the freest ever held in the country, Islamists swept reformists aside, exploiting reformist divisions and a low poll. Observers said that US pressure had undermined the pro-Western stance of the reformist and contributed to their splits.[9] All the evidence is that the vast majority of Arabs, indeed of Muslims as a whole, have only been enraged by the Iraq invasion. So America's Arab clients are now even less interested in holding elections for anti-American candidates would win them. Elections would now bring Islamist and perhaps pan-Arab democracy, not pro-American liberal democracy. And among America's uneasy allies, it brings not elections but repression. That is the reality of what the new militarist will bring to the region.

Can the new militarism even bring order? In Iraq they were so obsessed with military victory that they overlooked political preparations. Continuing repression by the US, Israel and the client Muslim states will likely bring disorder. The US counts on its military strike-power, plus its client regimes and the divisions (discussed in Chapter 5) between nationalists, pan-Arabists and Islamists. The new militarism perversely strengthens these opponents. No one's options are good. Americans are attacked and betrayed by unreliable client states. The states feel trapped between the actions of the US and Israel, and the people with whom they sympathize but must suppress. Their authority weakens. The streets, mobilized by a mixture of nationalists, pan-Arabists and Islamists, are repressed by their states and lack the power to throw the Americans out of the region. Problems are intensified by the Likud right, now in power in Israel, seemingly with a lock-hold over the White House, killing Palestinians on a daily basis. This looks a bleak future for Arabs. During the Iraq invasion, Western reporters wrote of the utter despair engulfing moderate Arab intellectuals, trapped between these forces, with no positive policies to offer.[10]

The new militarism will also increase terrorism. US intelligence reports suggest that many new cells have recently been formed across the Middle East and North Africa. They do not directly say that this is blowback, but it is. The new militarism will also strengthen the connections between Islamists, pan-Arabists and nationalists, and specifically between international (Al-Qaeda type) terrorists and the purely national freedom fighters/terrorists like Hamas or Hezbollah, creating more enemies for the United States. In Iraq it will actually convert terrorists into legitimate guerrillas attacking military targets. It will also intensify the state terrorism necessary for a military regime to counter them.

Since America remains well protected by its oceans, Americans abroad will have to bear the brunt. In the run-up to war most American victims in the region were civilians. A nursing aide, a USAid diplomat, three Baptist missionaries and a software executive were killed in Iraq's neighboring countries. The assassins are thought to have been new terrorist recruits ("amateurs"). One of the victims was perhaps a legitimate military target, though not in uniform. He was the software executive installing computer programs in Kuwait for US generals to plot their Iraq battlefield strategy from a computer keyboard. His boss, the vice-president of the euphemistically named "Tapestry Solutions" corporation, said, "We are stunned by this senseless act of violence."[11] Senseless? They actually hit a military target for a change. Sixty-five civilians in Riyadh and Casablanca were killed immediately after the war. But, given the senseless occupation of Iraq, American soldiers there will now bear the brunt of the attack. Given the senseless strategy of Bush's war on terrorism, I await the first Hamas or Hezbollah attacks on Americans abroad for 20 years. The US must remember the first law of holes: if you are in a hole, stop digging. When you are in a hole caused by killing Muslims, stop killing Muslims.

In the long run, the killing will drain American imperial resources, especially the will of the American electorate to maintain it. The US is going against the tide of history. At the beginning of the twenty-first century, sovereign nation states cannot be successfully ruled or dominated by foreign militarism. The new militarism brings more resistance, more violence, more devastation. Tacitus would be right about the Americans in the Middle East. They make a desert and call it peace.

The new militarists have also provoked global blowback among countries far more significant to US interests than Iraq. Traditional and new allies are unhappy; France, Germany and Russia have found a new capacity to coordinate opposition. Over Iraq, the US got only UN Resolution 1441 in November 2002, which supporters of both invasion and continued inspections then claimed legitimated their positions. Kofi Annan said it did not authorize an invasion. Pressured by Blair and Powell, Bush tried for a second resolution in February 2003 authorizing invasion. He failed miserably. Not only did France and probably also Russia and China signal willingness to veto it, but extensive bribing and pressuring of smaller states on the Security Council failed to win their votes. Only the US, Britain, Spain and Bulgaria, four out of its 15 members, publicly declared they would vote for it. The British and Americans hastily withdrew their resolution. The Bush administration took comfort from the support offered by Britain, Spain and Italy, plus what Rumsfeld called the "new Europe" of the East. Later Powell claimed that 47 states (still only a quarter of the UN members) supported the invasion. But only Britain and Australia actually committed any troops to the war. Spain and Italy mouthed merely rhetorical support. So did the Eastern Europeans, except that Poland provided 56 soldiers and Hungary allowed Iraqi exiles to train on its territory.[12] Poland quickly got its reward, 48 f-16 fighters, almost one per special forces soldier! As the Polish Foreign Minister crowed: "Its the contract of the century." In the 1991 Gulf War 29 countries had provided troops.

The new militarists seemed overconfident of what they call "the new Europe." Predictably, this derived from their purely military perspective—these countries are new or aspiring members of the NATO military alliance. They value membership in NATO, and so are responsive to US pressure behind the scenes. But they are also aspirant members of the European Union. As we saw in Chapter 2, their economies are much more dependent on Western Europe than on the US. Germany alone is a bigger investor and trading partner in Eastern Europe than is the US. In order to prosper, the new Europe will be drawn into the old Europe.

Old Europe offered comfort to the new imperialists in its disunity. This prevented the world's biggest economy from taking any collective stance for or against American imperialism. The supply and price of the oil so essential for the European—and the East Asian—economy would be determined for better or worse by the US alone. If its Middle Eastern imperialism succeeded benevolently, then Europe and East Asia would thank the US for cheaper oil. If it succeeded, but not benevolently, and the US grabbed the oil for itself, they would grumble. They will grumble when the US changes Iraqi oil sales from euros to dollars. If American imperialism fails, and ensuing regional disorder disrupts oil supplies, they will curse the US. But whatever the outcome, the Europeans will remain powerless to intervene themselves.

Almost 200 years after Austrian Chancellor Metternich first said it, Europe remains "a geographical expression." Much more recently, a Belgian Foreign Minister coined the famous put-down "Europe is an economic giant, a political dwarf and a military worm."[13] His words remain true today. Europe can try to rise up to "balance" the United States on economic matters, as it is already doing over Iran. But it has no powers of military intervention. American power is not yet in decline. Americans, insulated within their self-censorship, do not even know how isolated they are in their militarism. It is not powerful Europeans, but puny Arabs and Muslims who will expose the soft underbelly of American military. Unfortunately for them, they will do so through further suffering.

Eventually, decades in the future, Europe will become more of an actor, and (if they are still around) this would cause serious problems for American militarists. European public opinion was already united in its opposition to the Iraq war. An EOS Gallup Europe poll conducted in

January 2003 in 30 European nations found large majorities opposed to US action against Iraq and to their own countries' participation in such action if it lacked UN approval. Eighty-two percent of the citizens of the EU full member countries said a military intervention in Iraq without UN approval was unjustified. But so did 74 percent of citizens in the 13 candidate member countries, including the "new European" countries. Europeans, new or old, found the new imperialism in action repellent. Since most of them lack the self-muzzling media enjoyed by Americans, they perceived global reality very differently. While most Americans seemed to think that an invasion of Iraq would liberate the Iraqi people, contribute to peace and reduce terrorism, most Europeans not only disagreed. They also thought it bizarre that bombing the hell out of a small, weak, impoverished Muslim country might be thought to have any merit at all. Americans should understand that our President is almost universally seen across Europe as the epitome of the swaggering, boasting, adolescent bully of little brain, though brandishing enormous bombs, both smart and dumb. All this greatly constrains what support European leaders might give to the new militarists. European repugnance will endure—as new imperialists like Robert Kagan themselves emphasize. It will influence electoral outcomes and bring closer political geopolitical unity in Europe.

The blowback from the new militarism could quickly blow Tony Blair, Bush the Younger's only real ally, out of office. What can one say of a British Prime Minister who commits the lives of 40,000 of his country's soldiers to the command of foreign generals serving the interests of a foreign Empire. Sidelined by the US generals in Basra, with no significant role in the reconstruction regime, at least the British forces had the good sense to hang around Basra's fringes and not kill too many Iraqis. Blair, unlike Bush, did not regard Sharon as his "friend," yet the invasion would benefit Sharon's extremism, not conciliation in Palestine. Blair kept assuring Parliament that the US would be immediately publishing its "road map" for Palestine. Bush eventually did so on May Day 2003. The Palestinians accepted it, Sharon equivocated. I remain deeply sceptical of Bush's willingness to force him to the bargaining table. Bush let Blair have his say over the role of the UN in post-Saddam Iraq, but then ignored him. Blair seemed oblivious of how easy it is for terrorists to penetrate into the UK. America is 5,000 miles from the Middle East. Unlike Britain, it lacks organized Muslim communities and Londistan's firebrand clerics.

Where was the British national interest in this folly? I have been repeatedly asked by Americans to explain British participation in the invasion. I can only explain it as a tragic mistake. Blair hoped to get UN approval, and by the time this proved impossible, he was in too deep to withdraw. It was a world-historical mistake because even Bush would have thought twice about invading alone, without British support. I feel some sympathy for a man who believed he could influence Bush into moderating his stance, but failed and got trapped inside the military tent. But he should have taken heed from the sad demise of his ally Colin Powell, humiliated in Jerusalem in April 2002, now reduced to being Rumsfeld's echo. True, Britain still suffers from post-imperial military delusions, and Blair, like Bush, has a Christian Soldier desire to bring good to the world by force. But these are not sufficient explanations for Blair's actions. Note that Blair's policy on Europe differs from his role over Iraq. He wants to unite Europe and join the euro currency zone. This will happen, sooner or later, whatever transpires in Iraq. Britain will be a part of the eventual European actor.

Not only Europeans opposed a war in Iraq. Large majorities in polls conducted in late 2002 and early 2003 in Turkey, Pakistan, Thailand, Hong Kong, Japan, Australia, Argentina, Brazil, Chile, Uruguay and Canada all opposed the war. I could not find polls in *any* country outside the US which deviated. A major survey conducted in 21 countries in May 2003 revealed a further decline in attitudes to the US. Most countries were opposed to what they saw as American unilateralism and to the war on Iraq, support for the war on terrorism declined, "the bottom has fallen out of support for America in most the Muslim world" (i.e. outside as well as inside the Middle East), and Bush was ranked below most other world leaders (in the Muslim world he was usually ranked below bin Laden!). The global blowback in attitudes has been substantial.[14] True unilateralism—going it quite alone—was not the real desire of the new militarists. It was forced upon them by the lack of any significant global support. If East Asia also became alienated by the much greater danger the new militarism might bring to its own region, very serious consequences might result.

In its foreign adventures, the US had grown accustomed to getting its way by extensively bribing neighboring and strategically located countries. It preferred smaller countries, since these came cheaper. The support of Turkey would have cost a staggering $30 billion. Enemies come cheaper than such allies! But the policy completely failed in early 2003. It might succeed on other occasions. But countries with the economic clout of France, Germany, Britain, Italy, Spain, Russia,

China, Japan and India cannot be bought—not because they are principled, but because the bribe would have to be too large. If such countries do take a stance against the US, the US has few inducements to dissuade them. But the new militarists do not seem to care about any of this. They *can* act unilaterally, and no one can stop that.

Only in the medium term does the world, especially its richer parts, have a real weapon to use against the US. The dollar is the world reserve's currency by consent. Like the UN, there is American leadership, but underneath there is multilateralism. Of course, capital flight is decided more by markets than governments. But if European and East Asian investors lose confidence in the health and stability of a permanent American war economy, they will hedge their investments. Then if the euro or the yen were made more attractive by public policy, the capital flight would escalate, slashing American economic power. Once that happened, the US would be reduced back to its own resources, and Americans would baulk at paying for the entire military machine themselves. Even without major capital flight, the euro will strengthen as Britain, the Norwegian oil economy, and Eastern Europe join it. American economic hegemony would give way to a dual reserve currency. The dollar and the UN have been central to American hegemony in the world, that is to routinized, usually legitimate leadership. Hegemony involves multilateral commitment to the rules of the game, and such commitment brought major advantages to the United States. Abandon it, and the sun will shortly thereafter set on the American Empire, quicker than it did on the British, far quicker than it did on the Romans.

The world does not want American militarism, and it may not even need an American hegemon. Until very recently it never had a hegemon. Britain was not hegemonic in the nineteenth century, despite what some "world-systems" and IR theorists say. Britain had the biggest navy and the most advanced economy. It tried to lead a free-trade regime, though other countries chose whether or not to follow. Britain had the reserve currency, though maintaining it after about 1880 required the cooperation of other powers. It had virtually no power over continental Europe, Russia, China, the Far East or the US. Elsewhere its Empire was about the same size as the other Empires combined. Before then, all the world's Empires shared borders with rivals with whom they had to come to terms. Rome learned to respect the power of Persia/Parthia to the east and the barbarians to the north (desert lay to the south and oceans to the west). Nor has the US even brought order to the world. The last decade, in which the US has been the hegemonic power, contained more wars, civil wars and terrorism than previously. How could so many theorists buy the Hobbesian notion that the countries of the world needed one sovereign power to bind them all? Americans must themselves decide whether they wish to resume hegemony and then stick by its rules. But if they go for Empire and fail, they lose hegemony too. The world would not much care. It could live with the multilateral consequences.

We have caught glimpses in this book of what would be a better, more rule-governed world. Anti-proliferation policy and parts of the war against terrorism were most effective when combining American leadership with multilateral agencies. The US provided the military muscle, the UN or broad regional alliances the economic support, political coordination and ideological legitimacy—all necessary power resources for effective action. There was tension between them, and overall policy was neither perfectly nor smoothly accomplished. The US refused to submit to international laws, while the UN tended to be divided and ineffective. It still is. The Iraqi aftermath is likely to be messy—the US willing (provided the financial cost is low) but unable to effect reconstruction on its own, the UN backing off as soon its aid workers get killed. The world has not yet reached a very effective multilateral compromise. It would have to be one in which both the US and UN stuck by the rules they had collectively made. We had barely started along the path of developing those rules when the new militarists blocked it. It is difficult to be optimistic when they are so ruthlessly embarked on their disastrous course. Even getting back to where we all were during the Clinton years would now be a great achievement. But if we have learned anything, it should be to move toward a better future through combining American leadership and acceptance of international law and norms regulating world conflict.

Indeed, anti-proliferation policy—which is what Iraq, North Korea, Iran and Syria are supposed to be about—worked better when it abandoned the entire rhetoric of "rogue states"and combined material carrots with credible sticks. The carrots gave would-be proliferators an alternative way out, a perception of how their own actions might reduce the threats confronting them. In the absence of carrots, their reaction was to move covertly to acquire WMDs as their only deterrent against the aggression of others—especially of the United States. A policy of treating regimes simply as rogues only makes them more rogue-like. So the new militarists were tempted into invading them and changing regimes, producing blowback which only worsened disorder.

There is no simple solution to the world's problems. Some causes of terrorism and state terrorism lie in deep-rooted problems which the US and the UN lack the power to eliminate. Yet patient application of economic development programs and ethnic/religious conflict conciliation could gradually, painstakingly yield some results. At present US development programs remain the stingiest of all the Northern countries, though they could all do more. To encourage economic development across the South is not mere idealism, since the Northern economies would also ultimately benefit. Yet the war on Iraq produced divisions preventing co-ordinated action. These clearly stymied any action at the G8 summit meeting in early June, 2003. The war on terrorism, with its bias in favor of state terrorism, has also seriously deflected the US away from its intermittently useful record in ethnic/religious conciliation. Nowhere is this more flagrant than in American policy toward Israel/Palestine, the running sore of US foreign policy.

But outside the scattered "black holes" of ethnic/religious conflict, many of them amid failing states and economies, the world is not actually very dangerous. It should not be dangerous at all for Americans—so prosperous, so comfortable and so well-protected in the sea-girded continent we dominate. Dangers loom *because* of American militarism—seeking to drive into the ground the few failing communist remnants in the world, seeking extra-territorial control over oil supplies, stationing American troops where they have no business, invading foreign countries uninvited and supporting state terrorists. No significant danger would occur if the US stopped doing all these things. Quite the contrary.

The new militarists argue that all their enemies could be crushed by American power. They are wrong. American powers are uneven and unsuited for Empire, especially a benevolent one. The American Empire is not yet over-stretched, but its stretch is incoherent. This giant's military might sits uneasily with economic and geopolitical resources that originate in multilateral arrangement. It is too stingy to invest properly to consolidate Empire, as we saw in Afghanistan and Iraq. Its militarism also greatly outstrips its political capacity to rule any conquered country and contradicts the ideology of freedom and democracy that the US (and the world) holds dear. The giant is forced back to militarism alone, and this is not enough for Empire. The new militarism becomes part of the problem, not the solution. The world is not black and white, good and evil. It is imperfect and various shades of gray. Whatever our ideological goals, virtuous and otherwise, we also need pragmatism to cope with the real, imperfect, messy world.

Luckily, the United States is a democracy, with the political solution close at hand in November 2004. Throw the new militarists out of office. Otherwise the world will reduce Americans' powers still further.

NOTES

1. Various reports in *New York Times* and *Los Angeles Times*, February 22–29; *Times* (London), December 14, 2002; *english.pravda.ru/hot spots/2002/07/30/33406.html*; *www.CNN.com* March 13, 2002.

2. *Los Angeles Times*, March 29 and 31 and April 14, 2003; Knut Royce, "Evidence against Syria Is Questioned," *Newsday*, April 3, 2003.

3. *Guardian*, April 3, 2003.

4. *Los Angeles Times*, April 13, 2003. Department of Defense News Transcripts of interview with Paul Wolfowitz, May 9, 2003.

5. In *Al-Sha'b*, December 27, 2002, available in Arabic at *www.alarab news.com*.

6. "'Bush Doctrine' aims to change all the regimes of the region," in the secular newspaper *Al-Hayat*, February 15, 2003, available in Arabic at *www.alhayet.com*.

7. "America, democracy and exhortations from the devil," *Al-Sha'b*, December 12, 2002, at *www.alarabnews.com/alshaab*.

8. Greg Miller, "Democracy Domino Theory 'not credible,'" *Los Angeles Times*, March 14, 2003.

9. Galal Nassar, "The Real Threat?" *Al-Ahram Weekly*, December 5–11, 2002, issue no. 615; *Eurasianet.org*, April 5 2003.

10. See, for example, Susan Sachs, "Egyptian Intellectual Speaks of the Arab World's Despair," *New York Times*, April 8, 2003.

11. *Los Angeles Times*, January 22, 2003.

12. *Washington Post*, April 18, 2003. Though Poland nominally paid $3.5 billion for the f-16s, it received in return deals and loans worth over $12 billion. The Arab "allies" contributed small contingents of troops for the defense of Kuwait. They were not risking invading Iraq. Kuwaiti firefighters did venture over the border.

13. What Mark Eyskens actually said was: "Europe is an economic giant, a political dwarf, and, even worse, a worm until it concerns itself with elaborating a defense capability." I have adapted and extended his metaphor to describe the American Empire.

14. In one Polish poll 52 percent supported the US war, but this was reversed weeks later when 75 percent of Poles opposed it—see *slate.msn.com/id/2078876/* February 20, 2003. The Pew Global Attitudes Project, *Views of the Changing World*, Washington, DC: The Pew Research Center for the people and the press, June, 2003.

INDEX